SHEPHERDS
ABIDING
IN THE FIELD

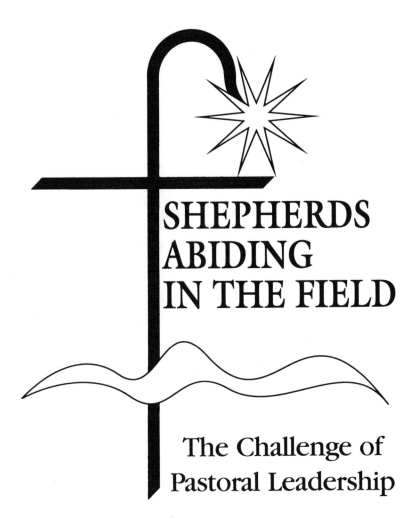

SHEPHERDS ABIDING IN THE FIELD

The Challenge of Pastoral Leadership

Edited by Leonard M. Young

Congregational Services Division
Reorganized Church of Jesus Christ of Latter Day Saints

Herald Publishing House
Independence, Missouri

Congregational Services Division
Reorganized Church of Jesus Christ of Latter Day Saints

Copyright © 1997
Herald Publishing House
Independence, Missouri

Printed in the United States of America
Herald House Item # 12-059032
ISBN 0-8309-0765-3

Library of Congress Cataloging in Publication Data
Shepherds abiding in the field : the challenge of pastoral leadership
    / edited by Leonard M. Young.
        p. cm.
    "Congregational Services Division, Reorganized Church of Jesus Christ of Lat-
ter Day Saints."
    Includes bibliographical references.
    ISBN 0-8309-0765-3 (alk. paper)
    1. Pastoral theology.   I. Young, Leonard M., 1950-   .   II. Reorganized Church
of Jesus Christ of Latter Day Saints. Congregational Services Division.
BV4011.S475   1997
253–dc21   97-7399
                                                                                          CIP

97 98 99 00 01   5 4 3 2 1

Table of Contents

Introduction

Leonard M. Young

And there were in the same country, shepherds abiding in the field, keeping watch over their flocks by night. And lo, an angel of the Lord appeared unto them, and the glory of the Lord shone round about them; and they were sore afraid. But the angel said unto them, Fear not, for behold, I bring you good tidings of great joy, which shall be to all people. For unto you is born this day, in the city of David, a Savior, who is Christ the Lord.....And suddenly there was with the angel, a multitude of the heavenly host, praising God and saying, Glory to God in the highest; and on earth, peace; goodwill to men. And it came to pass, when the angels were gone away from them into heaven, the shepherds said one to another, Let us now go, even unto Bethlehem, and see this thing which is come to pass, which the Lord has made known unto us.—Luke 2:8-15

Just imagine! You are at work. You are busy doing the ordinary things that you do every day in your place of employment, and suddenly, you receive the most startling news of your life. You had thought that life was tough, that you were alone in your troubles. And then, without warning, the presence of God breaks through into your little place of confinement. You hear that even though you thought no one cared about you, even though you saw little hope for the future, even though you thought God was up high and far away, in that moment, God became like you, joined with you, and would thereafter be at one with you and all of creation.

These must have been the feelings of those shepherds who were "abiding in the field." But as we look back on that significant event, it is easy for us to think that their reactions were different from those we experience today. In the present we feel we have already received God's message of reconciliation and love in Jesus Christ. And even with that knowledge we often feel alone, unfulfilled, unsuccessful, and without any hope.

The message of the angels to those shepherds is the same message we need to hear today: "For unto you is born this day, in the city of David, a Savior, who is Christ the Lord" (Luke 2:11).

The reaction we have to such a message may be similar to that of those shepherds. We may become "sore afraid." But what are we afraid of? Are we afraid of the news itself? Are we afraid of the implications of that news for our lives? Are we afraid of the transformation that may take place within us and within our society if we take seriously the message of hope and joy resident in the proclamation of the Savior?

In congregational leadership today there are many obstacles to receiving the "glad tidings of great joy" that the scripture says accompanies the proclamation of the gospel message. We struggle with inadequate numbers of volunteers, inadequate budgets, lack of training, and a host of other issues. Our reaction is much like that of the shepherds: we are "sore afraid." It appears, however, that the only antidote to this kind of hesitancy is the elixir of joy. Joy is the antidote to fear. When we feel the joy the angels proclaimed we become transformed from our natural fear to a state of expectancy, hope, and possibility. In these moments we find that the lone angel is replaced by a "multitude of the heavenly host." Everywhere we look we can find reinforcement for the call to discipleship if we hear the message with joy.

Today congregational leaders are shepherds in the same sense as those who heard the joyous tidings out in their field that night. But when we talk of leaders and pastors as shepherds, there are many negative images that accompany the positive ones. Some years ago I remember Jack Conway talking about an experience he had had in a prayer service in which he was moved to counsel those in attendance. He had heard them testifying to their need for a shepherd to show them what to do because they were not capable of finding their way. They were emphasizing their incompetence and their need to be directed. Jack felt moved to affirm to them that they had many gifts and skills that could be utilized in the work of spreading the gospel and that they should not envision themselves as "dumb sheep."

For too long many disciples have seen the role of shepherd as giving direction and the role of the sheep as expecting direction. In the world of animal husbandry, shepherds may give most of the care to the sheep, but in the world of ministry a shepherd is best able to offer ministry when he or she understands well the sheep's needs and then helps them move in the right direction.

Congregational leadership today is the art of two-way ministry rather than the more traditional one-way ministry. Leaders who take people along on the journey are much more effective than those who simply go it alone. In fact, many leaders have testified over the years that they have experienced personal transformation when they have allowed themselves to be the recipients of ministry as well as the givers.

Leadership Is a Plural Noun

Someone once said, "Anyone who thinks he is leading when no one is following is only taking a walk." By definition, leadership is a group activity; there is no singular form of the word "leadership." Leadership is plural because it implies that someone is involved in assisting someone else to move in a certain direction. In my congregational experience the most successful congregational leaders have been those who understood the simple idea that you cannot be a leader by yourself.

Few if any leaders are blessed by God with every gift necessary to be a good leader. Some of us are good organizers, but struggle with being spontaneous. Some of us are creative, but lack the structure to help others grasp and appreciate our creative ideas. And some of us are caring and compassionate, but lack the skills to give direction to congregational life. No one has all the tools necessary to bring ministry in every situation of life. God has called the church to live in community precisely because of the fact that by ourselves we have only our own resources to draw upon, but as a team of servant ministers we are fully gifted as the body of Christ.

Congregational leadership used to be unique among all other forms of leadership because it emphasized the feeling, doing, and being dimensions of life. In recent years the science of leadership has become much more holistic. It is not uncommon today for leadership theorists to talk about leading the whole person and emphasize building a team based on principles, values, actions, goals, and actual accomplishments. In the past leadership was more focused on managing people through coercion, manipulation, and persuasion. Today leadership is seen as the process of helping people see their place in the group's vision and discover what they have to contribute to the fulfillment of the group's mission. Leadership is no longer something done by "the one at the top." Leadership is relational team building.

"Pastor" Defined

"A pastor is a shepherd who leads a team of disciples toward the kingdom." On the surface this may sound like a simple definition of a complex task, but I suggest that pastoring has three primary components which are all caught up in this one sentence.

1. *A pastor is a shepherd.* In the modern world there are fewer and fewer people who understand the role of a shepherd. When shepherding was a common occupation, it was easier to imagine what a shepherd of people was supposed to do. The first thing learned when tending sheep is that a good shepherd knows the sheep. A shepherd who spends many hours with the sheep on the hillside soon becomes aware of the personality of each one. A shepherd may have to care for one animal more than another because that one needs more attention or gets lost more easily. Shepherds who don't know their sheep eventually end up losing one or more of them.

Shepherds care for their sheep. They do not ignore the needs of their sheep but try to keep them healthy and see to their growth and safety. In the same way leaders are concerned about the growth and health of those with whom they offer ministry. A leader's concern for the congregation is similar in many ways to the concerns of one family member for another. Shepherding is the process of caring for the family and helping each member grow.

Shepherds keep the flock together. They keep in close contact with the sheep so they do not wander off and get separated from the flock. Congregational shepherding also has a component of "keeping the flock together." Celebration in the body of Christ involves gathering the congregation for worship, education, and fellowship. Leaders are concerned about those who do not join in the gathering and take steps to see that those sheep are not separated from the flock. Spiritual and emotional separation are just as important as physical separation. In fact, spiritual and emotional separation usually precede physical separation. Congregational shepherding involves helping the congregation to be united in heart as well as in physical proximity.

Shepherding a congregation involves knowing, caring, and gathering. These actions are necessary to build a caring community. The shepherding role of the leader is closely linked to the celebration dimension of congregational life. As leaders build relationships with members, they learn to celebrate uniqueness and individual giftedness. If a leader does not know the flock, it is difficult to see them as anything but a group. The ability to appreciate people as individuals with different needs, hopes, and gifts is essential to offering personal ministry. Caring is also closely related to celebration. To care for someone is to celebrate their worth. Leaders who offer caring as a shepherd are celebrators of life as a gift from God. Gathering the flock enables the spirit of celebration as all rejoice in their association with the community. The leader who facilitates the gathered nature of the community of faith is the "host for the party." The host welcomes those who come and rejoices that they have decided to share with the group. Congregational shepherding builds the caring community through the process of celebration.

2. *A pastor leads a team of disciples.* As stated before, the central focus of leadership is pointing the direction, casting the vision, and taking the first steps toward the newly envisioned future. The role of leaders is to expand the congregation's vision of the future and motivate people to create the future together with God.

It may be helpful to think of the leadership in terms of scientific field theory. Margaret Wheatley, in her book *Leadership and the New Science,*[1] proposes a new way to understand vision. She sees vision not in linear terms but as a force field. Imagine how difficult it would have been to grasp the concept of radio before it was demonstrated in 1901. After all, disembodied voices traveling through air without wires would have seemed quite far fetched. Yet today we know that radio waves are all around us. They fill up what appears to us to be empty space. When you turn on your radio receiver, however, this invisible field of radio waves comes to life and we hear music and speech.

Wheatley suggests that in the same way radio waves surround us without our awareness, an organization's vision can be viewed as a field. Visionary ideas can be motivational and inspiring if they are grasped by those in the congregation. In the same way that we turn on a radio to hear music, if vision is a field, then the role of the leader is to turn as many people on to the vision as possible. Leaders try to push the vision into every corner of the congregational environment. And when the vision becomes an innate part of the congregation's culture, disciples are called to mission by their perception of the vision.

Leadership based on vision rather than management based on policies, procedures, and structures is scary to those of us who have been raised in top-down environments of control. Vision-based leadership

11

allows the internal motivation of the disciples to be the governor of actions and behaviors rather than the organizational rules. Such leadership is open to the diversity of gifts resident in congregational members and is willing to allow people to approach the task of ministry in different ways as long as discipleship is informed by the congregational field of vision.

The leader who embraces the need for vision will not seek to control through giving directions but will seek to empower by allowing others to turn on their radios, listen to the music, start singing the song, and ultimately catch the vision. This type of leadership is focused on the ends and not only on the means. Visionary leaders see where God is calling the congregation but steadfastly refuse to insist that theirs is the only way to get there. This perspective calls for teamwork in turning vision into reality. When leaders recognize that there are different perspectives about the best way to accomplish visionary things, they will integrate their strengths with those of other disciples to broaden the vision field and increase the chances that the vision will come to pass.

Teamwork is based on the concept of mutually compatible actions. However, to be part of a team does not mean to move in lock step with everyone else. Field theory presupposes that many of us will go off in different directions in search of the path the kingdom vision calls us to walk. Those who embrace this view of leadership will recognize that not only is their congregation unique among all the congregations of the church, but that each disciple is unique among all other disciples. Such leaders will rejoice in that vision of ministry.

The task of congregational leadership means uncovering the vision God has for the congregation and then helping a team of committed disciples open their eyes to see their place in the envisioned community.

3. *The pastor moves toward the kingdom.* The children's story of Ferdinand the bull illustrates why some people find the concept of visionary leadership difficult to embrace. Ferdinand sat day after day on the hillside and dreamed about a better life, but he never did anything about it. Vision without action is mere dreaming. To put dreams into action is the process of mission. Moving toward the kingdom is the mission of the church. Mission involves transforming communities and individuals. As our communities are transformed, the kingdom becomes more and more visible. As our lives and the lives of others are transformed, Christ becomes progressively more visible in the lives of every person.

Congregational leadership includes the strenuous step-by-step actions of kingdom building. Congregational life should be focused on caring for those within the family of the church. It should also have an equal concern for those who are not part of the fellowship. Outreach to others is what distinguishes the church from the world's other organizations. The mission of the church focuses on personal and world transformation. Leaders who see the vision of the kingdom will take steps to engage their congregations in witnessing, compassionate service, and community development.

The first step in involving others in mission is doing it yourself. Missional activities must be modeled as well as preached. The missionary-focused leader who discerns human hurts, hopes, and needs right at the church door must takes steps to be personally involved in transformational ministry. Modeling is the beginning of effective missional leadership: people do what they see. This is a primary principle of motivation. If the leader does not "walk the walk" the followers will just "talk the talk." Leadership credibility is developed and maintained when the leader's preaching and actions are congruent.

The second step in moving toward the kingdom is to highlight those who are actively involved in mission. That which is valued is promoted and nurtured in congregations. If leaders value mission as essential to congregational life, it will be important for them to make heroes out of the missionaries. I am not suggesting that we go on a glory trip, but I am suggesting that the sharing of testimonies and the recounting of missional successes is important to ongoing motivation for witness and service.

The third step is to develop ministries of mission that involve everyone. There are many ways that individuals with different gifts can be involved in the congregation's mission. Not everyone is a salesperson or a community organizer. However, each of us has the potential to make some contribution to mission.

Over the years I have noticed at least four different mission gifts that appear to be found in congregations. Some people are like the disciple **Andrew** who eagerly went out and actively won souls for Christ. Andrew was a catalyst who met people easily and readily challenged them to become disciples. Some are like **Timothy**, the companion of the apostle Paul, who grew disciples one to one—Timothy was a mentor who took people under his wing and helped them to grow into disciples. Some people are like **Barnabas**, another companion of Paul, who cared people into the fellowship of the church. Barnabas was an encourager who built relationships, loved others, and gradually enfolded them into the church. Some people are like **Abraham**, who prayed for Lot as he faced Sodom and Gomorrah. Abraham was a minister of intercession who continually offered prayers for others that they might be touched by the divine presence.

The fourth step in mission is to set goals that will encourage people and foster their growth. If you don't have a goal to aim at, shooting becomes interesting. I once saw a Peanuts cartoon in which Charlie Brown was shooting arrows at a wooden fence in his backyard. After he shot each arrow he would go over to the fence and paint a bull's eye around the arrow. Lucy came out of the house and said, "Charlie Brown, you're doing that wrong." Charlie responded, "I know that, but this way you never miss." Without missional goals, actions of service and witness have no purpose. By aiming at nothing you may hit what you shoot at, but what have you really accomplished? Actions without goals are random and unfocused. Mission is the process of focusing the service and witness of the congregation on specific human hurts, hopes, and needs.

The fifth step in moving people toward the challenge of kingdom building is to take away their fear of failure. Many people are afraid to reach out to others because they don't have a lot of confidence in their ability to make a difference. They worry that they may fall flat on their face. It is important to affirm that any effort expended on behalf of another person out of a spirit of love is missional. Leaders can take away the fear of failure by "going with" disciples as they witness and being willing to take the blame for failures and give away the praise for successes. Abraham Lincoln once sent a telegram to General George Meade who was reluctant to pursue the Confederate armies after the battle of Gettysburg. The telegram said: "Pursue the enemy, I think the South can be defeated. If you are successful destroy this telegram. If you fail, publish it." Lincoln took away Meade's fear of failure and he was then motivated to action.

Moving toward the kingdom requires well-planned, decisive action. The leader who is mission oriented will seek ways to uncover the emerging kingdom, point people in the direction of its fulfillment, and step out in action. A few years ago, former Apostle William T. Higdon summarized the process of congregational leadership when he said, "Our job as leaders is to uncover where the Holy Spirit is creating sparks and then throw gasoline on them."

This Book

The authors of this book have been asked to write about the key challenges facing congregational ministers as we approach the twenty-first century. Our hope is that as you read this book you will feel a new call to leadership, witness, and service. This book is written for all those shepherds who are faithfully abiding in the field of life's ministry challenges and opportunities.

Notes

1. Margaret Wheatley, *Leadership and the New Science: Learning about Organization from an Orderly Universe* (San Francisco: Berrett-Koehler, 1992), 53–57.

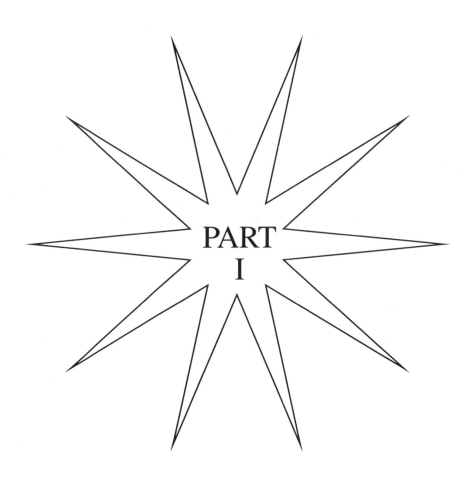

PART
I

The
Vision
of
Pastoral
Leadership

SHEPHERDS
ABIDING
IN THE FIELD

Chapter 1

Having Been Commissioned: The Ceaseless Call

Danny A. Belrose

...Lift up your eyes
Upon this day breaking for you.
Give birth again
To the dream.

Women, children, men,
Take it into the palms of your hands,
Mold it into the shape of your most private need.
Sculpt it into the image of your most public self.
Lift up your hearts
Each new hour holds new chances for a new beginning.
Do not be wedded forever
To fear, yoked eternally
To brutishness.

The horizon leans forward,
Offering you space
To place new steps of change

Here, on the pulse of this fine day
You may have courage
To look up and out and upon me,
The Rock, the River, the Tree, your Country
No less to Midas than the mendicant.
No less to you now than the mastodon then.
Here on the pulse of this new day
You may have the grace to look up and out
And into your sister's eyes,
And into your brother's face,
Your country,

And say simply
Very simply
With hope—
Good morning.
> —Maya Angelou
> from "On the Pulse of Morning"

When Maya Angelou read "On the Pulse of Morning" at Bill Clinton's first presidential inauguration, I heard *the call*. The call transports me from fantasy to reality, from value to principle, from the transitory to the authentic. It is a "ceaseless call"—an ongoing *commissioning* which is not frozen in time by the sweep of a red pen circling a date on a kitchen calendar. It is the ever-present beckoning of the divine will constantly seeking my response—a response that is dulled by my otherwise fierce allegiance to the mundane and transitory. Elizabeth Barrett Browning said it best:

Earth is crammed with heaven
And every bush aflame with God
Only those who see take off their shoes
The rest, sit around and pick black berries.[1]

For me there are rare and blessed moments when the eternal breaks in on the temporal, and the temporal is prepared to receive it and my soul responds, *"YES! This is primary! This is what really matters!"* In such moments life's priorities are dramatically realigned. I am Spirit-reminded that life has meaning and I am intricately invested in it. Such is the call. It awakens a deeper sense of being.

This ceaseless call emanates from deep within my soul. Yet, at the same time, it is transcendent. It comes from without. It breaks in and reconnects me with all of life. It comes unannounced and in many disguises—nature, art, music, poetry, a look, a blaze of color, a whisper, a touch, a feeling. Perhaps it is the language of my soul, reminding me *who* I am and *whose* I am. Perhaps it is the pulse of each fine new day that beats unheard and unnoticed until by some gift of grace it is momentarily birthed in my consciousness.

But what has this to do with a call to ministry? Certainly, everyone can lay claim to sobering, even emotive experiences that urge one to take the gift of life more seriously. What does it mean to be commissioned of Jesus Christ? What is the unique role of priesthood? How does one respond to the call and challenge of pastoral leadership—to be, as the title of this book suggests, a "Shepherd Abiding in the Field?" In this chapter I will examine some core expectations inherent in the call to pastoral leadership.

Calls from Within and Without

He was young, idealistic, and enthusiastic. Strangers, circumstance had thrown us together in a long distance car ride to a district conference at which his call to the Aaronic priesthood would be considered. His excitement about the call was in steady competition with a keen sense of humility. "I am not worthy of this high and holy calling," quickly established itself as an ongoing litany in our conversation. It was refreshing and enlivening to experience both the passion and the deep intent he brought to this important moment in his life. I remembered my own experience of being called to priesthood and the uneasy mixture of excitement and anxiety that surrounded it. Yet, the litany of "unworthiness" (though understood), became bothersome.

"This is certainly an important time in your life. I am excited for you. I am sure you will give a good ministry, but, this is not the highest and holiest calling."

"What do you mean?", he said.

"You are a member of the church, aren't you?"

"Yes," he nodded.

"You have been baptized?"

"Yes, sure!"

"Well, that's it. When you were baptized, you gave all that you could give. You gave God your life and said, 'Here, take it. You can do more with it than I can.' You can't give any more than that. The highest and holiest calling is to be a disciple of the Lord Jesus. There are no promotions or graduation ceremonies beyond being a faithful follower."

Brad was middle-aged, bright, and successful. He was a convert to the church and had entered into congregational life with conviction. Presented with a priesthood call, he was perplexed and confessed to me that he didn't know what to do with it. "I'm already doing most of the things this office requires, what will priesthood do for me?" His question was neither self-serving nor disrespectful.

"Perhaps, you are asking the wrong question." I replied. "Maybe you should ask, 'What can I do for priesthood?'[2] Priesthood is not something you put on like a new suit of clothes. The question is, 'Do you sense a call?' And if you do, it is not what the call does for you. It is what you do with the call. Ask yourself, 'What am I being asked to bring to this opportunity and what is my best response? What is expected of me? What am I called to give, not what will I receive? But, more important, do you hear this call from within as well as from without?'"

Calls come from within as well as without. Our tradition primarily associates calling with priesthood and our emphasis is on hearing such calls from without. In other words, priesthood calls are initiated and processed by third parties. By the time a call is presented to a potential candidate several individuals have been consulted to the exclusion of the one being called. One's personal conviction of his or her call (the call within), though considered valid and important, is secondary to the process and not primary.

Our all-but-exclusive association of calling with priesthood has fostered a perception that being called is a fixed event. One is called and ordained on a particular date. End of story. This event mind-set or paradigm is so pervasive that many of God's "chosen people" remain God's "frozen people." That is, many who sense an inner conviction of God's call to service remain immobilized because they are awaiting a burning bush event. They have been put on hold waiting for a call that, ironically, has already come—a call that is simply waiting to be acted upon. Too many of us are waiting for certitude. The great Christian preacher Leslie Weatherhead put it this way:

> I have met men and women who have expressed desire to serve, say on the mission field, or in the ministry, or in some other sphere of service, and they have told me that they are only waiting for "a call." The question I always want to ask them is this: "What do you expect to happen? Do you expect God to come to you in a vision, or in a dream, or to call you by name, or to come near to you in some uncanny way? What if your own desire to serve Him is His Voice? Granted that the desire to serve is freed from self-interest, may that very desire not be a call? From whence has the desire come?"[3]

The call to Christian service (ordained or unordained) is a ceaseless call—a call within that comes unbeckoned and unexpected in myriad ways to remind us of the salvation acts we constantly forget. Such calls may be experienced in the singing of a hymn, a verse of scripture, the beauty of a sunset, the clasp of a hand, the hope in a child's face. The virtue kindled in us in these moments is not of our own making. In Weatherhead's terms our acknowledgment and desire to respond is itself the call. By whatever means or venue, this ceaseless call breaks in on us and we are apprehended by grace. But what has this to say specifically about priesthood?

Calling and Priesthood

Priesthood, with its multiple offices and portfolios of responsibility, is a rich blessing to the church. In recent years, with the advent of a more inclusive worship style wherein the gifts of all are celebrated (ordained and unordained), some have questioned the need for priesthood. What is its purpose and function? For me, four things stand out:

1. *Priesthood are called to administer the sacraments.*

2. *Priesthood are called to function in presidency.* Fundamental to priesthood is its responsibility to give spiritual leadership to the corporate body of the church at all jurisdictional levels.

3. *Priesthood are responsible to call the membership to faithfulness.* It can be argued that this is everyone's stewardship responsibility. However, basic to the pastoral charge of priesthood leadership is the commission to care for the needs of the church community. Priesthood are called to instill hope and trust, to offer guidance, support, and encouragement to the church. This is servant-leadership, a ministry of *being with* the members as opposed to *being above* the members.

4. *Priesthood symbolize the numinous.* This role is primarily lived out in administering the sacraments but goes beyond this particular function. The church is not a social club or community service agency. It is a divine creation—a community of Christ extending the ministries of Christ. We are *about something* infinitely greater than the sum of our parts or membership. Left to our own devices, we quickly would become self-reliant. As mentioned previously, we must constantly be reminded of the salvation acts we know, yet consistently forget. That is why we worship—to be reminded of God's mighty acts in the past, the present, and promised future. We need to be reminded of the Divine. Otherwise, we

find smaller gods and base allegiances. Priesthood, then, has an important symbolic function. It reminds us that we are claimed, loved and sustained by a mystery beyond our containment and comprehension. In other words, priesthood is a symbol that God is involved. To paraphrase Paul Tillich the symbol of priesthood

> participates in that to which it points...opens up levels of reality which otherwise remain closed for us... unlocks dimensions and elements of our soul which correspond to the dimensions and elements of reality.[4]

It is clear, however, that this symbolic relationship is focused in the idea of priesthood itself and what it represents and not in the persona of given individual priesthood members.

All Are Called

A misappropriation of this symbolic representation, however, has the potential to lead to an unhealthy emphasis on priesthood which may devalue calling and service beyond its ranks. We are prone to rank and categorize service and ministry. Hierarchical relationships seem almost inescapable despite our best intentions. On one hand, we declare that ministry does not require the unction of hands and prayer to be ministry.

> All are called according to the gifts of God unto them; and to the intent that all may labor together, let him that laboreth in the ministry and him that toileth in the affairs of the men of business and of work labor together with God for the accomplishment of the work intrusted to all.[5]

It is common to hear the phrase, "the highest calling in the church is member." Yet while we acknowledge that calls to priesthood are but focused expressions of specialized service within the broader call to discipleship, our tendency has been to place priesthood service at a premium.

I confess a personal uneasiness about language or terms that stratify and separate rather than unify. I find little comfort in the phrase "office of member" which, in my opinion, smacks of an attempt to mollify the unordained. It appears to reinforce a mindset that ordained ministry is the normative expression of Christian service. Rather than leveling the playing field, the term "office of member" implies one cannot really be appreciated unless one is seen as holding a title—even the nondescript title, "office." After all, priesthood has *its* strata of offices; should not membership be recognized as an office? Then again, a less critical view might see this as an appropriate expression of "the priesthood of all believers."

Be that as it may, the phrase "being called" has been so inextricably wed to priesthood that it has been robbed of its bite beyond the ranks of the ordained. Seldom do we hear laity say they are called to a particular task or service. Such a call is sensed within; it is not processed externally by others. It has no ritual to authorize or celebrate it. There is seldom any external or corporate recognition of its validity. Ironically, fundamental to priesthood is its responsibility to awaken people to God's invitation to life—to help others hear God's ceaseless call in their lives. We need to find healthy ways to honor calls to service (ordained and unordained).

The Call Begins in the Passive Voice

The call to Christian service begins in the passive not the active voice. One of our major problems is that we do not begin at the beginning where we are supposed to begin—we begin at "the end." We try to put the cart before the horse. Sometimes our Christian service is as futile as trying to eat tomorrow's leftovers today.

What am I saying? Simply this, Christianity is not primarily a demand. It is a gift! It does not say first, "Do this!" or "Go there!" Its first words are not "Do" or "Go" but "Come" and "Receive!" You see, for Christians, life and power begin in the passive voice—in what has been done for us rather than in what we can do! It is not that we love, but that we are loved. Our frequent tendency is to push right into the active voice of doing without experiencing the sheer wonder of God: "Behold, what manner of love the Father hath bestowed upon us" (I John 3:1).

What happens in the active voice (our service or doing) depends first on what happens in the passive voice. The ceaseless call is a never-ending apprehension of God's grace. It reminds us that "God has given us the gift of life and the gift of Christ." Whenever we are claimed by such grace we can do no other than to respond in praise and thanksgiving with a desire to be our best and do our best! And what is our best? What are we called to be? To begin with, we are called to be accepting. But this may not mean what we think it means.

Called to Be Accepting

Acceptance does not mean "anything goes." In an interview with Bill Moyers, historian Barbara Tuchman lamented that our society is experiencing a "loss of moral sense, of knowing the difference between right and wrong, and of being governed by it." "Somehow," she says, "people don't take wrongdoing seriously. Perhaps there's just too much of it. We're not surprised anymore. We're just used to it."[6]

Tragically, we are reticent to make "common-sense" righteous judgments. Many have bought into a distorted perception of "Christian acceptance" characterized by social conformity. Reginald Bibby, sociologist and preeminent analyst of religious practice in Canada, believes the Christian church has sold out to culture:

> The issue of religion's sellout to culture has been virtually dropped in the 1990s, largely because the reality has now been pretty much taken for granted.... At the personal level, there has been a widespread "secularization of consciousness"—a change in the way people interpret their worlds.... Religion neither tends to interpret life nor inform behaviour.... Religion's role is specialized, its influence marginalized, its organizations routinized.[7]

Even when friends destroy themselves through poor choices or addictive habits, we hesitate to intervene. Fearing alienation, we look the other way. We bite our tongues and refuse to make righteous judgments. After all, isn't our Christian calling to love them, to be with them, to accept them where they are? Really? Frankly, our love affair with this paradigm of Christian acceptance is damnable. It is denial of reality, a selling out to sin and a distortion of what real love demands of us. We are called to be accepting, but we are not called to accept the status quo. True love cares about the beloved. Douglas John Hall says it well:

> Love doesn't just accept everything. If it's love, it cares about the real condition of the beloved; and if the beloved is in fact a distortion of the person that he or she could be, then the only role that true love can assume is one of truth and the intention to change. "Jesus loves me" does not mean that Jesus likes me, and makes no great demands upon me. Jesus loves me—therefore I had better be prepared for some embarrassing moments of truth, and some hard work![8]

The Jesus who is not ready to accept me just as I am is not ready either to accept the world, our world, just as it is. This love, far from accepting the status quo, wills to alter it (the world/ you and I) drastically—and especially among those whose economic and physical well-being makes them prone to believe they are already the accepted and approved of God![9]

The church's mission is to be a counterculture—to be a redemptive agent of transformation. It is called to be "accepting" (that is, there are none beyond the circle of its ministries), but it is not called to condone. The call to be truly accepting of others requires the courage to risk the demands of love and compassion.

Called to Be Compassionate

Jesus' acceptance of others in no way dulled his passion to be an agent of social change. He clearly advocated an alternative social vision centered in compassion. His statement in Luke 6:36: "Be compassionate as God is compassionate"[10] was radically counter to the purity system which dominated and stratified the Hebrew culture of his day.

> The ideology of the dominant elites of his day was expressed in the alternative *imitatio dei*: "Be holy (pure) as God is holy (pure)." Purity was the core value of the social world of first century Palestine, and (as in many societies and religious communities before and since) it created a purity system. Purity was thus political, shaping the structures of society, and generating sharp social boundaries between pure and impure, whole and non-whole, rich and poor, male and female, Jew and Gentile.[11]

What then does it mean to be compassionate? Marcus Borg points out that in the Bible, compassion is both a feeling and a way of being that flows out of that feeling. A woman feels compassion for the child of her womb (I Kings 3:26); a man feels compassion for his brother, who comes from the same womb (Genesis 43:30). Borg tells us that "womb-likeness" is behind the expression "the tender mercies of God." As "like a womb," God is the one who gives birth to us, who loves us, feels for us, and who provides life-giving, nourishing care that is embracing and encompassing.

Compassion, which is "life-giving," is not one dimensional. In a real sense, it has two sides. It not only responds to, but advocates for, those in need. Compassionate ministry does not emerge from a position of superiority and is thus not equivalent to mercy.

> Compassion is very different from "mercy." In English, to be merciful implies a superior in relationship to an inferior, as well as a situation of wrong doing; one is merciful to someone to whom one has the right (or power) to act otherwise. Compassion suggests something else. To paraphrase Wil-

liam Blake, mercy wears a human face, and compassion wears a human heart.[12]

The Two Sides of Compassion

There are two sides to compassion. Compassion, from the Latin *compassio* (*com* "with" + *pati* "to suffer"), is a feeling of distress and pity for the suffering or misfortune of another. We most often equate compassion with expressions of tenderness and empathy. This is compassion's soft side. But compassion has a harder side that is frequently overlooked. Passion (*pati*) also means any strongly felt emotion. Compassion in this sense means passionately speaking or acting out against conditions that may cause suffering. The call to be compassionate requires the courage to stand firmly against systems that disenfranchise or marginalize others. Jesus driving the moneychangers out of the temple was an act of righteous indignation and compassion! A compassionate minister is not simply called to hold others' hands, but to call people, when necessary, to accountability. She or he speaks out passionately and unreservedly against inequity as an advocate for peace and justice. In Wayne Ham's words, "Passion must be wedded to power." This is our hope for Zion:

> A global community where those things that have divided us will merge. A community where compassion will be wedded to power for the blessing of the world. A community where both men and women will be gentle; where both women and men will be strong. A community where all will be rich in the Spirit and will share equitably the blessings of abundant life. A time and place where we will care for the young. A time and place where we will care for the old. A time and place where all God's creatures will be cherished and we will know how to live in harmony with God's creation.[13]

Called to "Re-present" Hope

"Know[ing] how to live in harmony with God's creation" presses us up against the reality of suffering. Suffering is a common denominator to life. No one falls outside its circle. Pain, hunger, death, loss, loneliness, struggle, rejection, fear, anxiety—the list is endless and no respecter of persons. Thus, pastoral leaders are "wounded healers" (fellow sufferers) called to present hope to those for whom hope is but an elusive dream and to "re-present" hope to those whose hopes have waned.

The key here is knowing *how* to live "in harmony." Harmony does not mean the absence of conflicting or negative elements. Harmony is a creative combination of contradictions. The Zionic dream is *not* the hope for some paradisiacal land of Oz "where troubles melt like lemon drops far above the chimney tops!"[14] The Zionic hope is life lived fully in harmony with God's purposes where *suffering that should be*, is, and where *suffering that should not be*, is not!

Douglas John Hall says that suffering is inherent to the created order. There is suffering necessary to human development (integrative suffering) and suffering that detracts from life (disintegrative suffering).[15]

Hall's thesis is that integrative or developmental suffering is beneficial; that is, it "should be" in order for us to become. For example, loneliness (a form of suffering) enables one to know the joy of love and companionship, in the same way that anxiety (another form of suffering) authorizes comfort, relief, or joy! Lehi puts it this way,

> For there must be an opposition in all things. If not so,... righteousness could not be brought to pass; neither wickedness; neither holiness nor misery; neither good nor bad. Wherefore, all things must be a compound in one." II Nephi: 1:81–83)

Certainly pastoral leaders must minister hope to the bruised and brokenhearted—the lonely and hurting—but they are also called to confront head on any suffering that need not and "should not be." I am referring to suffering that stems from personal and corporate evils such as pride, envy, greed, self-gratification, and aggrandizement. These are born of distorted human freedom. Christian ministers must make clear the message of hope found in the responsible stewardship of life.

> It is within the purview of the human creature, as biblical faith envisages this unique being, to keep the negative in the service of the positive, to keep death in the service of life, to keep the struggle oriented towards integration and away from disintegration....The disintegrative element is present, and it is never far from the surface of creaturely existence.... [T]he steward is called to tend the process, to enhance the principle within it, to reduce the pull of death with which the life principle is necessarily bound up, to accentuate the integrative and thus diminish the power of the disintegrative dimension.[16]

This responsibile hope-giving stewardship is positive response to the ministry of the Lord Jesus. The gospel does not find its power in positive thinking, quick self-help programs, or what we have labled "core values." The good news of Christianity is rooted in the principal belief that Jesus lived, was crucified, rose from the dead, and is coming again. Whatever theological interpretation we place on Jesus' death, resurrection, and second advent, these beliefs are foundational to our faith and central to our hope. There are no substitutes. We are called to represent and to *re*present the living hope found in Jesus. It is a call beyond the comfortable pew and the stained-glass sanctuary.

Called to Go Beyond

> Which one of you, having a hundred sheep and losing one of them, does not leave the ninety-nine in the wilderness and go after the one that is lost until he finds it? When he has found it, he lays it on his shoulders and rejoices. And when he comes home, he calls together his friends and neighbors, saying to them, "Rejoice with me, for I have found my sheep that was lost." — Luke 15:3-6 NIV

We are prone to forget our "lostness": *"I once was lost, but now I'm found, was blind, but now I see."* We cavalierly sing the familiar hymn oblivious to its powerful reminder that we too were among the lost in some way, at some time. For everyone who has been lost and found, Someone has come. The ceaseless call of Christian ministry commissions us to seek the lost, to go beyond the sanctuary. Indeed, we are called to take sanctuary and safety to those who have no sanctuary. This requires the courage to leave the ninety-nine and to go after the one who is lost until he or she is found.

We need to recover our missionary passion! The Great Commission was not the Great *Suggestion*. John 3:16 does not read "For God so loved the *church* that he gave his only Son." If we are to be shepherds abiding in the field we must ask ourselves, Shepherds of what field? Where am I being called to serve? Are there new fields for me to explore? fields beyond my comfort zone? fields beyond the comfort of the sanctuary? Is this where I will find meaningful ministry and give meaningful ministry?

Called to be Contextual

Context gives meaning. For example, words in a given conversation, in and of themselves, do not have meaning. Words find their meaning in the context of a particular sentence, at a particular time and place, and within a unique set of circumstances conditioned by the relationship and history of the personalities involved. Similarly, the contextual minister is one whose ministry is enlivened by prudent choices and actions that fit the circumstance and particular need. In other words, to be contextual one is challenged to provide the right ministry at the right place, at the right time, for the right reasons, to the right people, rather than the wrong ministry at the wrong place, at the wrong time for the wrong reasons to the wrong people. "Is there anyone among you who, if your child asks for bread, will give a stone? Or if the child asks for a fish, will give a snake?" (Matthew 7: 9-10 NRSV).

Contextual ministers do not live out their lives answering questions that are no longer being asked. They resist being "answer persons" and strive to engage life's questions contextually as a fellow explorer. They neither deny life's inequities and unevenness nor ignore them. They embrace and proclaim a healthy eschatology—a promised hope that evil will not in the end prevail. The contextual minister continually holds up his or her motives, understandings, and theology to the bright light of honest evaluation: What do I believe and why do I believe it? Do I give others an honest hearing? Am I really open to new understandings or am I closed? Am I living in the past or the present? Is my faith fixed and static? Can I articulate my faith? How do I live out my faith as a servant-leader?

> Faith and doctrine must become, ever anew, conscious of the questions, attitudes, values, fears, aspirations, and the like, which dominate the milieu to which the gospel is to be addressed. Theological truth is not static. It must always be discovered afresh.... The gospel, far from being the steadfast, unchanging, rather obvious "proclamation" that it is frequently assumed to be, is in fact always in need of restatement; for its principal object is to address, engage, convict, and make new;... It will be gospel (good news) only if and insofar as it confronts the quite specific problematique (if you like, the bad news).[17]

Contextual ministry, then, is not merely contemporary; it is measured by its meaningfulness. It is a fresh hearing of the good news confronting the bad news in all its emerging disguises. Metaphorically speaking, one is hard pressed to minister to a world in which one does not live. In a sense all ministers are resident aliens challenged with the responsibility of doing their best to understand the context in which people live. Contextuality demands our highest competencies.

Called to Be Competent

Three Temple School courses and an ordination prayer do not add up to competency. We have been admonished to magnify our callings. The onus of ministry is not simply for one to give his or her best; it is the continual striving to discover one's best. The role or job description of each priesthood office can be seen as intimidating. It is natural to ask, "How can I hope to do all that?" The answer is, "You can't!" Focus on what you can do, not on what you can't do! The task is to appropriate your specific gifts and talents to the overarching portfolio of responsibility designated to a particular office. This is an ongoing duty that demands a willingness to experiment in new arenas of ministry—to discover latent competencies and to develop them.

You cannot measure your effectiveness or competency without self-discovery. And self-exploration means asking tough questions about your emotions, basic abilities, passions, and hopes. What is it without fail that excites you in your ministry? Which ministerial activities make you depressed? If you could accomplish only one task in life, what would it be? Who are the three or four people you most respect and why? What groups of people do you feel most naturally drawn to in ministry?

Few of us excel at everything we attempt. Discovering what you do best gives you power to say no to ministries that are best performed by others and power to say Yes! to those ministries to which you are specifically called. Competent ministers seek to know themselves, their environment, and their God. Competency will not rest on yesterday's laurels. It demands a willingness to be self-correcting and a devotion to disciplined study, training, and prayer. Such competency is not rooted in inflated self-reliance. We are never equal to the demands of ministry. But we are commissioned, and being commissioned means we are empowered by the One who sends us.

Having Been Commissioned

Ministry is not a solo act. It is never independent; it is dependent and interdependent. We are yoked together with our congregations as they raise hands to support and acknowledge our calling, and we are yoked with the Lord Jesus. We are *co*-missioned! The ceaseless call (experienced in those "aha" moments of God's amazing grace) reminds us that we are commissioned to "preach the gospel to the poor, ... heal the brokenhearted, ... preach deliverance to the captives, and the recovering of sight to the blind; to set at liberty them that are bruised; to preach the acceptable year of the Lord" (Luke 4:18-19). Who is equal to such a task? Only one—the One who summons us, commissions us as coworkers, and calls us friends. The assurance of such friendship and grace is the glue that holds us to the task of ministry even in times of doubt.

> I believe without miracles I have prayed for.... I believe because certain uncertain things have happened, dim half-miracles, sermons and silences and what not. Perhaps it is my believing itself that is the miracle of my life; that I, who might so easily not have been, am; who might so easily at any moment, even now, could give the whole thing up, nonetheless by God's grace do not give it up and am not given up by it.[18]

Called, Claimed, and Persuaded

The ceaseless call has laid a claim on my life. It claims me and reclaims me. It calls me from minimums to maximums, from tradition to truth. It calls to me through scripture, reason, experience, and heritage. Though my response to God's ceaseless call is at times flawed, imperfect, wanting—it will not let me go.

I am claimed by the teachings of Jesus. I am claimed by the basic moral and ethical values of the Christian message. I am claimed by the enrichment of Christian fellowship. I am claimed by Christianity's central message of love that calls for sacrifice, not as a virtue but as a willing price to make a positive difference in the quality and stewardship of life—a stewardship beyond anthropocentrism, which appropriates a salvation that embraces environment and ecology. I am claimed by the Christian mandate to transform inequitable social structures that stratify human beings, thereby privileging some while denying others their ultimate worth. I am claimed by the crying need to see the gospel as a sacrificial agent of leaven penetrating and trans-

31

forming all arenas of life. I am claimed by the Restoration's vision of community where the bruised and brokenhearted are blessed and where people are not marginalized because of gender, race, sexual orientation, or philosophy.

When I experience God's ceaseless call, I know there is ultimate union, a connectedness to life. I know that there exists an intelligence, a source that causes all to be. I know there are external principles independent of culture or personal subjectivity. I know that I am a soul and that each soul has ultimate worth. I believe God calls to us on the pulse of each new morning—and some mornings we hear it clearly. That is why I am involved in Christian ministry. Ultimately, it is a sense of call that escapes articulation. I can neither explain it nor adequately describe it, but I do hear it. It calls to me each morning.

> Lift up your eyes
> Upon this day breaking for you.
> Give birth again
> To the dream....
>
> Here on the pulse of this new day
> You may have the grace to look up and out
> And into your sister's eyes,
> And into your brother's face,
> Your country,
> And say simply
> Very simply
> With hope—
> Good morning.

Notes

1. Origin unknown.
2. This conversation reveals our tendency to view priesthood philosophically in terms of "realism" (i.e., priesthood has an existence independent of the person) as opposed to "nominalism" (i.e., priesthood is in essence a "name" or descriptor rather than something universally self-existent).
3. Leslie D. Weatherhead, *The Transforming Friendship* (London: Epworth Press, 1976), 103.
4. Paul Tillich, *Dynamics of Faith* (New York: Harper & Row, 1957), 41–43, as quoted in *The Essential Tillich: An Anthology of the Writings of Paul Tillich*, edited by F. Forrester Church (New York: Macmillan, 1987), 42.
5. Doctrine and Covenants 119:8b.
6. Barbara Tuchman as quoted in Bill Moyers, *A World of Ideas* (New York: Doubleday, 1989), 5–6.
7. Reginald W. Bibby quoting Finke and Stark, 1992:275, in *Unknown Gods* (Toronto, Ontario, Canada: Stoddard Publishing Ltd., 1993), 112–113.
8. Douglas John Hall, "We Would See Jesus," *The Living Pulpit* (January–March 1994).
9. Ibid.
10. Scholars suggest that the use of the word "perfect" in Matthew's version is due to Matthew's redaction.
11. Marcus J. Borg, "We Would See Jesus," *The Living Pulpit* (January–March 1994).
12. Ibid.
13. Quote by Wayne Ham from a class conducted in Calgary, Alberta.
14. From "Somewhere Over the Rainbow" in the *Wizard of Oz*.
15. Hall describes integrative and disintegrative suffering in chapter 2, "Creation: Suffering and Becoming" in his work, *God and Human Suffering: An Exercise in the Theology of the Cross* (Minneapolis, Minnesota: Augsburg, 1986).
16. Ibid., 68–69.
17. Ibid., 22–23.
18. Frederick Buechner, source unknown.

SHEPHERDS
ABIDING
IN THE FIELD

Chapter 2

The Kind of Church We Are: Re-imagining the Zionic Symbol

Kenneth L. McLaughlin

As the Reorganized Church of Jesus Christ of Latter Day Saints prepares for the next century, it is imperative to ask—and attempt to answer—questions of foundational importance to the denomination: Who are we? What kind of church are we? What do we stand for? What are our distinctives? Do we have a legitimate reason to exist? Are we really any different from other Christian faith communities?

Frankly, these are not new questions. Every generation of believers has asked questions of identity. It is hoped every generation to come will do the same. But we may be at an unusually important time for such questions to be pondered. The last thirty-five years for the RLDS Church has been an exciting and also difficult period of international growth and global understanding. With this has come the increasingly apparent need to revisit many of the underlying identity claims made through the years by our movement. Moreover, the church in developed nations finds itself in a world that simply did not exist a generation ago. We have moved from one epoch of history—the modern era—into the next: currently called the postmodern world. Few people have been challenged in one short life span to deal with such a rapid movement of technology, information, social structures, and the arts. It has not been easy.

Contrary to what some folks have indicated to me, I do not believe any person or group of church leaders in recent years has intentionally sought to shake the foundations of our denominational identity. I do not believe someone simply sat around one day and said, "Hey, let's change the church. It's getting kind of boring, and we don't have anything better to do." Rather, as the church sought to be faithful to its call to go into all the world and also remain relevant in its contemporary context, the church found absolute necessity in once again asking the age-old questions of identity—perhaps this time with more intensity and even a bit more anxiety than any time since 1830.

When giving ministry in the field, I am often asked church-identity questions. Many times I have sensed concern—perhaps even fear—in the voices of those posing such questions. With others, I suspect the questions are asked with preconceived answers already in place. Still others appear alarmed that the answers of past generations may no longer be adequate for today. Regardless of the rationale for asking, I believe it is time for us to continue taking a serious look at the question of denominational identity. Such a look will take time, energy, and must occur primarily in our congregations, with the assistance and input of church leaders and scholars. Our "conversation" on church identity will be lengthy, at times difficult, and will likely take a course different from the one we might currently predict. Our conversation will never fully end. But one thing is certain. Such a task will be well worth our best efforts.

Let me start this chapter by making one thing very clear. I firmly and fully believe that the RLDS Church is a *completely authentic expression* within the body of Christ and that we stand with other Christians united in sharing and living out the good news of God's love expressed in Jesus Christ. While most of the message of the gospel is a common message shared with the hundreds of millions of other Christians in the world, the RLDS Church has a meaningful, unique contribution to make in the individual lives of human beings and in the life of our global society. If I did not believe this, I could not give my life energies so gladly to the Christian cause as expressed in the life of the RLDS Church.

The One True Church

For most of its 167 years of existence, our faith community had a viable identity that appeared to serve the church well. We were the "one true church on earth," and all others were somehow flawed in a way that made them unworthy of joining. Practically all that we did and said was permeated by such a belief. Our sacramental practices—especially baptism and Communion—reflected this model of identity. Our missionary efforts used this premise in a foundational way, particularly when attempting to persuade already-baptized Christians to deny the efficacy of their original baptism and join our movement through another baptismal ritual. In addition, our view of the authority of the Christian clergy was completely informed by the premises underlying the model. The one true church model was woven into the very fabric of our church life. It gave us the satisfaction of knowing why we existed, the comfort of having more light and truth than all others, and the solemn obligation to not only share the good news of Jesus but also the good news of the exclusive correctness of our movement.

This model was so thoroughly ingrained into RLDS thought that I believe it was difficult for many good folks to ever seriously challenge it, even when their hearts and minds told them it was time to do so. Personally, I recall that my first feeble attempts to do so were dealt with politely and sincerely by congregational leaders, but usually went something like this: *"Well, Ken, of course there are good people in other churches and certainly they do good works as best they know how, but...."*

Perhaps you have had the same experience. But over and over again, I found all the reasons given for supporting such a model to be unpersuasive. They simply did not hold up when tested against biblical principle and daily life observation and experience. The model was not sustainable even through prayerful deliberation and historical understanding. Although I could not articulate my thoughts and feelings, I was quite certain that the one true church model—though viable and valuable for my forebears in the church—was not only inadequate but inaccurate.

It is my belief that over the last thirty-five years, many—perhaps most—members of the RLDS community have come to mutually recognize the inadequacy and inaccuracy of this model. I have observed in recent years that members have a newly found ease in discussing the one true church model. Again and again I have heard people respecting the strength of such an identity, but faithfully proclaiming the need for a more mature, biblically accurate identity that is consistent with God's intent for the church today.

I would like to think we are retiring the one true church paradigm "with honors." That is to say, I believe we are moving away from

37

this model without mocking it or undermining its important role in our early years as a movement. Our transition from close to open Communion is certainly one strong indication that we are well along in the process of retiring the one true church model without finding the need to deprecate it.

So now what?

If, then, we are retiring the one true church model, which was central to the core of our identity, what do we do now? With what is it replaced? Must there even be a central symbol or model that captures the essence of who we are denominationally? Let's take a look at these questions.

I have had several baffling conversations recently concerning what I call the "all or nothing" approach to the one true church model. Let me explain. I recall a conversation with a faithful RLDS member who said: "Ken, unless we are the one true church, then we are a fake, we are nothing. I might as well belong to the Methodist Church down the street." The conversation went on, and nothing I said seemed responsive to this gentleman's perception.

I have since pondered this conversation many times, and was surprised when several others approached me over the next few months with similar views. If I were to have the good fortune to relive these conversations, I would try to express my thoughts something like this:

Dear friends, there is nothing fake, phony, or artificial about the RLDS faith community. Our heritage of faith began long before the birth of Jesus of Nazareth, being shaped and formed in the soul of Judaism, as well as in other early religious concepts, perceptions, and practices that few of us have ever had an opportunity to study. Our heritage is found in generations of believers, as the Christian life was faithfully and courageously lived out by our church foremothers and fathers in countless unrecorded acts of love, mercy, and grace. Our heritage is found in the swirl of events in rural New York State in the early 1800s and in a young man with religious genius who found himself forming a movement based on principles of community, ongoing conversation with the Divine, and responsiveness to the current context of life.

The RLDS Church is very real—both in its strengths and in its shortcomings. It is a movement with sufficient self-assurance that it can now examine its own history with increasing objectivity, yet with no less passion and respect than in previous generations. Our community of faith has reached a level of maturity that gives itself permission to examine and call into question every aspect of its existence, upholding and cherishing those core values and principles that are worthy of universal application. We can then release—with respect—those traditions, interpretations, and practices that are limited by time, understanding, and circumstance.

One sure way for the church to become artificial or phony is to cling blindly or naively to past practices and interpretations that are incongruent with our best understanding of scripture, experience, tradition, and study. Moreover, to do so flies in the face of the RLDS tradition of openness to more insight into the divine will.

The RLDS Church is a fully authentic, empowered, and authorized community of people dedicated to God through their faith in the life, teaching, death, and resurrection of Jesus Christ. However, its authenticity comes not at the expense of other communities of faith. Rather, it shares authenticity and empowerment with them.

It's like this. There are four people in my immediate family. Each one is a fully authentic, empowered, and authorized member of that family. But even so, each of us is also different, unique, and wholly distinguishable from the others. Not one of us is the one true member of the family no matter how much we might wish it to be so.

Thus I urge you to consider, dear friends, that although we are not the "one true church," we are also not bogus or fake. We are indeed a worthy, viable, and honorable participant in the family of faith communities.

So what do we do now? Do we need to replace the one true church model with another one? Is there a central symbol or image that can help us understand our identity and role? For me, the answer to the last two questions is a clear, resounding, "Yes!"

No organization or institution can remain healthy and productive unless it has some sense of who it is and its purpose for existence. That is, all organizations and institutions—including ours—needs a strong sense of identity. Although there is a real danger in clinging too long and too hard to one identity model or image, it is my firm belief that such a model or symbol is vital. I do not believe it is healthy for us now in the RLDS Church to journey much further without seeking consensus on a central identity model, symbol, or image. We simply cannot afford the price of vagueness, confusion, or indecision on this question.

The day will most likely come that whatever model or symbol of identity we use today will be inadequate or inappropriate in the future. We have no way of predicting how long such a model might serve the church well. It thus becomes our responsibility to recognize the continual need for evaluation and assessment. It also means we must have the faith and courage to replace, modify, or reinterpret whatever model or symbol we use.

What kind of church are we?

As the church made preparation for building the Temple in Independence, inspired counsel helped us understand the Temple's role in the pursuit of peace. Temple ministries were designed with the peace emphasis in mind, and daily worship experiences dedicated to the theme of global peace continue to this day. Peace colloquies and awards brought to our attention the technologies of peacemaking and those people in the world who have had unusual impact in this regard. Mediation and reconciliation training has occurred at an increasing rate in denominational and congregational settings. World Conferences have deliberated and approved legislation aimed precisely at issues of peace and justice. I cannot recall a time in the life of our community of faith when the pursuit of peace has been so prevalent.

Is our identity as a "peace church"?

I think not. Don't get me wrong. I am most pleased with all the ministries of peace taking place within our movement. The Temple has been a real blessing in this regard. But I do not believe our central core or identity is as a traditional peace church. We are not, and are not becoming, like the Quakers or Mennonites. That is not who we are, though we surely have many lessons to learn from all of the fine peace churches in the world.

I am not persuaded that we have the commitment of time, resources, or energy to become a traditional peace church. Moreover, I am not convinced that is what we are called to be. Even with the Independence Temple dedicated to the pursuit of peace, our identity is a bit different from this, although issues of peace and justice must lie at the core of any Christian identity.

If not a peace church, then what?

So what are we? Are we left with creating a "new" identity from thin air? I don't think so at all. In fact, I don't think we have to look too long or hard to find such an identifying symbol. By looking at the core teachings and images used by Jesus, and by examining the primary symbols and concepts that have pervaded the RLDS movement since its beginning, I come to a basic conclusion: ***The Reorganized Church of Jesus Christ of Latter Day Saints is a community-building church.***

This is who we are and who we have always been. We are a church committed in practice, outlook, and ideal to the establishment of God's beloved community on earth: Zion.

For the past few years, the image or symbol of Zion has been mentioned from time to time in our literature. It can be found in our hymnody and preaching. But frankly, there has been little talk from church leaders about Zion. Some, in fact, have intentionally discouraged the use of the term and the promotion of its use as the central identifying image of the church.

I think I understand, at least in part, why there has been such a reluctance to use Zionic images in the last few years. Past interpretations of this vision of the kingdom on earth are simply no longer adequate or even productive in our current life circumstance. Zion once stood for ideas of gathering, of the elect, of refuge from the world, and of exclusivism. Zion was tied to a specific place—Independence, Missouri—rather than to all of God's planetary creation. Zion historically was translated into specific economic and living arrangements involving land ownership, banking, and leadership.

On the one hand, I must admit that many of the historical notions of Zion appear not only naive and unworkable to me, but also societally dangerous and contrary to the promotion of abundant life. On the other hand, I greatly admire our RLDS predecessors for their courage and absolute commitment to making tangible the New Testament vision of God's reign of justice here on earth. I join them in taking quite literally the teachings of Jesus that firmly plant our call to ministry in the here and now, and not in some ethereal future. I join them in taking quite seriously their belief that the gospel is to be lived out holistically in all of life's arenas. That is, I join them in their commitment to living out the holy call in political, economic, and environmental ways.

Surely we have arrived in our growing understanding of the Zionic symbol enough to realize that Zion must stand for inclusion and for the global well-being of all God's children on each continent. Surely we understand sufficiently that the call to kingdom building is a call to people of all faiths, races, and lifestyles. Surely we have begun to grasp the reality that *no one* is really saved unless *all of us* are saved together.

I submit that Zion has been and continues to be woven into the fabric of who we are and what we are called to be and become. Zion—in our hearts not only for the thousands of years of our Judeo-Christian heritage but also since the beginning of the Restoration movement—is an appropriate and timely symbol of who we are.

Zion—the global community where all are held in mutual regard and all enjoy the tangible blessings of the earth—is our reason to come together as a denomination. We are here to build community.

My entire life experience, whether in my nation of birth or abroad, persuades me that people everywhere and in every imaginable life circumstance are in need of community. They are in need of being together and staying together for the common good. People cannot fully exist in isolation. And the world cannot fully reflect God's infinite love for the world until the beloved community spans every island and continent.

Re-imagining

The word "imagination" is far too often relegated to something that children have but finally relinquish as the reality of life sets in. Imagination is also something we adults may value in artists and entertainers but don't give much attention to in other areas of life. I can only think of a handful of times where I was truly encouraged to develop my imagination as a divine gift. In some groups people with vivid imaginations are written off as less valuable and perhaps even less stable.

In the last few years I have come to realize how crucial it is for people of faith to have lots of imagination, and to spend considerable time cultivating and using their imaginations. Part of my new realization comes from appreciating the work of New Testament scholar Walter Bruggemann, and from the work my wife, Sue, has done in this regard. But this realization also comes as my own theological understanding of God has grown. I have come to understand that God does not create our future in isolation. Nor is there a single, predetermined course for either me or the world that I share with you. Indeed, God works with us in partnership to create that future. My personal faith statement is that the future is truly open, something that can be shaped and formed (yet not dictated) by us.

For whatever reasons, many of which are mystery, God has elected to give us individually and as communities, enormous powers both to create and to destroy. We have capacities the dimension of which we fail to understand. And we are both blessed and cursed by the use of those powers by ourselves and others, for the use of human power is always accompanied by consequences for us and others.

When we begin to comprehend and actually believe in our ability to create the future in partnership with God, then we realize how important it is to imagine that future. Daydreams no longer are seen as silly, but rather as *necessary* agents in the visioning and creating processes.

Joseph Smith Jr. apparently understood this quite well. His mind overflowed with imaginative understanding and insight. He realized the power to cocreate the world with God. At times his imaginings were of profound, prophetic impact. Like all human beings, he also had imaginings that would best have been left not acted upon.

If the symbol of Zion is to be used as the central symbol of our identity as a community-building church, then one of our tasks as leaders becomes clear. We are called to re-imagine, together, the Zionic symbol. And even as this re-imagining occurs, we are also called to facilitate congregational ministries consistent with our identity.

Components in Re-imagining

I do not pretend to have expertise in the field of re-imagining. I know of no checklists or procedural guidelines that ought to be followed. I have not attended any classes or workshops on such a subject. However, there are some obvious components to the process, as well as others that could be added to the following list:

1. An open mind, willing to suspend one's urge to immediately evaluate or judge the merits of a new idea, particularly if such judgment is based primarily on tradition or past practice;

2. background study and reading of literature pertaining to the Zionic enterprise;

3. personal reflection, including time for prayer and silence;

4. lively dialogue with those who stimulate your thinking;

43

5. regular association with people involved in community-enriching activities and ministries;

6. conversation with people who, by virtue of formal training, understand issues pertaining to Christian community;

7. self-awareness that permits honest confession of personal bias, especially as influenced by life experience;

8. willingness to explore the unknown;

9. willingness to step out of one's personal comfort zone;

10. commitment to creating a congregational climate of honesty, mutual regard, and good humor;

11. capacity to listen to and appreciate diverse opinions;

12. maturity to evaluate and give deference to views that are closely aligned with core values of the Christian faith; and

13. courage to distance oneself from the conventional wisdom and popular culture of the day.

This is no simple list. Yet these are the kinds of attributes that free us to cocreate the future together with God. Congregations are challenged to exhibit such qualities if they are to serve faithfully the call to establish the cause of Zion.

The Congregation's Zionic Call to Action

Leaders will often be the ones asked to facilitate the re-imagining of the Zionic symbol. They should rightly look to the World Church for assistance in the task, yet realizing that in the days ahead congregations will take an increasing role in shaping the destiny and success of our movement. How is it, then, that a congregation can live out the church's identity as a community-building church? Let me suggest that within the framework of the Communities of Joy emphasis, the following might be good places to start.

Vision

Congregations need to have a vision of what they can do and be in cocreating the future. This vision can be birthed and nurtured by leaders who lovingly guide, stimulate, and call the congregation to task. This requires leaders who have sufficient theological grasp and pastoral grace to lead the congregation confidently in understanding who they are and what they can become. Part of the essential vision for every congregtion should be a consideration of how the call to "seek to bring forth and establish the cause of Zion" can be lived out among their fellowship given the unique talents, gifts, and skills resident in the congregation.

44

Mission

Each year, congregational leaders need to help establish and implement one or more concrete, attainable missional ministries needed in the broader community in which the congregation resides. However, such a ministry should contain some dimension that distinguishes it from the kind of service project that any secular organization could perform. That is, a missional ministry is one that is performed so that the spirit of humanity and the Spirit of God intentionally intersect. It is timely for us to articulate clearly why it is that we do what we do.

Celebration

Congregations are more than service and social clubs. They are called to be worshiping communities that meet often and care for each other throughout life's journey. The cause of Zion is a cause for celebration as we witness the love of God touching the hearts of those who are close to us and as we share the spirit of celebration with the communities in which our congregations are found.

It's Who We Are

I am excited to be a part of the RLDS community at this point in its life. I say this fully aware of the precarious position in which many of our congregations find themselves. I join you in mutual commitment to membership in a community building church that still has hope and confidence in the future. I am honored to be associated with men and women who understand and take seriously the call of Jesus to be actively engaged in the creation of the beloved community: the kingdom of God—Zion. After all, it's who we are.

SHEPHERDS
ABIDING
IN THE FIELD

Chapter 3

Beyond "One True Church": Developing a Relational Ministry for a Secular World

W. Grant McMurray

During a recent trip to Washington, D.C., I had a few minutes to spare between meetings and ventured out onto the Mall in front of the United States Capitol. I knew that on that particular weekend there was to be a remarkable display of the Names Project AIDS Memorial Quilt, and I was anxious to view it. I was not prepared for the impact it would have on me.

The project has been developed over a period of several years and is designed to memorialize the lives of many of those who have died of AIDS. A gigantic quilt has been constructed of individual blocks, each one measuring three feet by six feet, approximately the size of a grave. On each of the blocks, friends and families of AIDS victims have prepared a memorial statement about one or more individuals in their acquaintance. These blocks are linked together to form an enormous mosaic of remembrances and poignant farewells.

The exhibit in Washington, D.C., spread the quilt across the full length of the Mall, ranging from the Capitol to the Washington Monument, an area measuring approximately one mile. There were 40,000 individual quilt blocks, commemorating 70,000 different individuals. The sight is difficult to imagine, but standing on the steps of the U.S. Capitol and looking out over the Mall was an absolutely extraordinary experience. That vast expanse of land was covered with cloth.

I ventured out onto the Mall and walked down the pathways that had been prepared for the masses of visitors that weekend. I was surprised by the powerful emotional reaction I experienced as I walked among these tributes to people I did not know. They were poignant remembrances of fathers and husbands and sons and daughters and lovers and friends. Some were artistic and elegant. Others were crude and simple markings on a piece of muslin. I found tears forming in my eyes as I was overcome by the powerful message of the quilt.

Each quilt block was given a row and column number that allowed it to be uniquely identified. Alongside the exhibit there were booths where one could find a book indexing the names of all the people represented by a quilt block. There you could look up a name and then go find the location of that block. I walked over and looked up the names of a few people in my acquaintance whom I knew had died of AIDS. I found no listing for anyone I personally knew.

Then, just out of curiosity, I looked up my own name—McMurray. I wanted to know if there was anyone in the exhibit who carried my name. There was one who spelled the last name in the same way I spell mine. His name was John D. McMurray. I did not know him.

Another aspect of this exhibit was the reading of the names. Various people, many of them movie actors or writers or politicians or other celebrities, had signed up to read aloud some of the 70,000 names. This reading went on perpetually throughout the day, the names droning on over the loudspeaker, commemorating the individual lives represented by this display.

I walked back toward the Capitol side of the Mall and passed in front of the speaker's stand, where the names were being read. I was preparing to leave the area and move on to a meeting I had scheduled. As I walked past the stand, someone was reading aloud from the list of names. Just as I passed in front of the speaker, I heard him read the name "John D. McMurray."

I froze in my tracks. The words pierced my mind like an arrow. Two things passed through my consciousness. First, I thought about the incredible mathematical improbability that I would look up one name in 70,000, then hear that very name randomly pronounced at the moment I walked in front of the reader. The odds of that happening are too staggering to contemplate.

But even more powerful was the fact that I had heard *my* name called. I knew it wasn't truly *my* name; in fact, it was the name of someone I did not know. But on another level it was my name; it was the name "McMurray." To hear it read aloud in the context of such an exhibit was overwhelming. For the first time, the emotional impact of the quilt took on a new and personal dimension. Now it was not just the presence of strangers, but *my* name was there as well. Now everything was different. Now it was me and I had to look at it in an altogether new way.

The Call to Ministry in a Secular Society

As I thought about that experience, I realized it was a wonderful metaphor for ministry. When we serve as ministers, whether ordained or unordained, we personalize the gospel. That is to say that our understanding of Christ emerges from the journey of our lives, for that is where we encounter him. We realize there is something universal about the human experience, and therefore our individual life is a gift pertinent to our ministry. When we comprehend that principle, we move from a ministry based on doctrinal propositions to one founded on relationships. Our life becomes its framework. Our name has been called.

A call to ministry gives us the voice to tell the story of the gospel, not because it belongs to you or to me but because it belongs to each of us, and because we sense within our own experience the universal yearnings of all humankind. It is that point in life when one realizes that somehow our own life has intersected with the gospel in such a way that we are compelled to share what we have discovered in a very personal way.

We live in a complex world and what it means to be a minister has been radically altered. People today think differently about religious institutions; they have different needs, and their understanding of ministry has taken on new forms. Things are changing and we who would be ministers must be sensitive to those changes and able to respond to them.

Many students of the Western cultural scene have analyzed the religious situation and noted widespread unfamiliarity with traditional Christian symbols and stories. Alan Walker writes:

> ...Christian knowledge and awareness are now the echo of an echo of an echo—too faint to be heard. This means, for example, a feeling of awkwardness, even embarrassment, at entering a sacred building. There is ignorance in the ways of Christian worship. Therefore, such people no longer desire to enter churches. It means an almost complete ignorance of Christian stories, biblical references, the traditional language of the pulpit.[1]

Secularism characterizes much of the modern world and poses a profound challenge for churches in their ministry. In a significant book, *How to Reach Secular People*,[2] George G. Hunter III identifies various characteristics of people to whom the churches need to appeal. He says that people are seeking life *before* death, that they are more concerned about meaning and purpose in the here and now than in speculations about salvation in the next world.

They are also driven more by doubt than by guilt. I remember when I was a young boy our family felt an obligation to be present whenever the doors of the church were open. Not to do so created a sense of guilt within us. We need only look at attendance patterns in our congregations today to see that that ethic no longer guides very many of us. Instead, driven less by guilt and more by doubts, people are comfortable with raising questions, with pushing limits, with challenging traditional practices.

By the same token, there is a negative image of the church out there in our society. Part of that has come from certain high-profile ministers whose lifestyles or partisan political involvement have led to media criticism. More than that, however, is the awareness that churches often appear to talk about things that aren't that relevant to the everyday lives of people. Furthermore, religion sometimes was seen as filling in the gaps between what science could tell us and what was observable in our world. God often became, as the theologian Dietrich Bonhoeffer once said, "the God of the gaps." As scientific understandings expanded, God became smaller and smaller to those who understood religion in that inadequate way.

Our world also has many people who are alienated and untrusting and have low self-esteem. There is a sense of separation from the institutions that we used to depend on—government, schools, economic systems. I saw a bumper sticker not too long ago that read, "Don't vote for anybody, it only encourages them." Such cynicism is widespread and affects the way churches are viewed as well.

Likewise, many people experience the breakdown of home and family. Children often find they do not grow up in a climate of love, nurture, and support. Trust is rooted in childhood, and if it is missing from those formative years it is very, very hard to recover as an adult. We see, as a result, people who do not have a strong sense of self. They depend solely on others for affirmation, respond readily to peer pressures and materialism, and see relationships primarily in terms of power.

Sadly, many people also live in a world they experience as out of control. Some of that is seen in personal ways as they look around their own neighborhoods and see widespread evidence of drug abuse, addictions of various kinds, teen suicides, AIDS, and all manner of dependencies and maladies.

Some even look at the world and feel that history itself is also out of control. There is a sense of fatalism abounding in many places, a feeling that "no one is in charge," and that our society moves into the future without a strong sense of direction or a compelling set of values. When communism collapsed in the Soviet Union and elsewhere, most Westerners saw that as a positive development. But it happened so unexpectedly and with such transforming results that it left many uneasy about the stability of the world in which we live.

The RLDS Church has not been immune to any of these factors in the larger society, and we have added our own unique set of problems. In fact, our preoccupation in recent years with internal matters of polity and procedure has kept us from getting focused on ministering to the very world we have just been describing. It is time now for us to turn our attention to the form and function of ministry and to ask how we can match our personal and institutional callings to the needs of the people we seek to serve in the name of Jesus Christ.

Five Things We Need

As I have thought about the daunting call to ministry in the complex world in which we live, there are at least five things that we ministers need to give attention to if we are to serve effectively and responsively in our time. We can each strive to discover them within our own personal ministry as well as work together to create them as part of the institutional ministry of the church.

1. *A coherent way of looking at the world and at life.* It is a fact that many people in the world today find the churches irrelevant to the questions they face in everyday life. They often see religion answering questions that are no longer being asked and ignoring things that are crucial to living in contemporary society. The Catholic Church officially announced a while back that Galileo was right—the sun does not revolve around the earth (as an ancient but still extant church position had stated). The proclamation met with scornful response because it came hundreds of years after scientific consensus had formed around Galileo's theory. It became an illustration of the apparent irrelevance of many church positions in the modern age.

The point is not to disparage the Catholic Church, however, for most of us in the churches have been lazy in our thinking and resistant to change in our theology, scriptural understandings, historical interpretations, and social positions. Joseph Sittler has written, "The principal work of the ordained ministry is reflection: cultivation of one's penetration into the depth of the Word so that the witness shall be poignant and strong."[3] This requires that we be faithful students, willing to risk creative thought so that the gospel passes through our minds on its way to our hearts.

Orval Faubus was a segregationist governor of Arkansas, famous for his role in the 1957 race riots in his state. Of him, someone once said, "Perhaps the most charitable thing that could be said of the Arkansas governor was that he had misunderstood the past, miscalculated the present, and ignored the future." It is critically important that the church not be victimized by the same malady as Faubus. Instead we must embrace the past with understanding, give due consideration to the needs of the present, and look expectantly and prophetically to the future.

Religion shapes the way we see the world, causing us to look at it with "theological eyes." There is nothing insidious about "theology," even though the word seems threatening to some. Theology is merely disciplined reflection on the nature of God, humanity, the life and ministry of Jesus Christ, and the purpose and mission of the church. If we are to speak with any degree of authority to the world, we must have a coherent way of understanding and explaining it in the Christian context.

The Restoration movement was founded on the principle of restoring again and again the sacred proclamations of the faith. This has far less to do with recreating an ancient body of truth than it does with creating anew in every age the profound truths at the heart of the gospel. To do so with integrity requires reflection on scriptures and traditions that they may be made intelligible to that secular world to which we are called in ministry.

2. *A sense of corporate story.* Alan Jones, an Anglican minister and scholar, in a wonderful book on ministry, *Sacrifice and Delight*, has said:

> One of the reasons we face daunting psychological and social problems is that people have little or no sense of history—of their own personal history as well as of a historical perspective stretching over hundreds of years. People

are free, free from history, and therefore free to be alone, cut off, free to drift. And they are not really free at all.[4]

What Jones is referring to here is the enormous need of people and institutions to have a sense of identity that is framed by the story of their individual and collective lives.

The older I get the more anxious I am for my two sons to understand where I came from. By that I mean what it is that characterizes my life, my decisions, my commitments, and how that is rooted in the things I came to understand as a child and shaped anew as I grew. I don't do that because I want them to be "just like me." Far from it. What I want them to know is how I got to be this way. They can then be free to make their own choices based on the experiences of their lives along with whatever learnings they choose to extrapolate from mine and from their mother and other significant influences in their lives.

We have reflected at length in the church on our struggle with identity. Part of that comes from our historic efforts to distinguish ourselves from the Mormons and to construct an identity that is uniquely our own. Part of it comes from the new self-understanding that has emerged as the church encounters other cultures and is forced to examine what is truly universal about the gospel message. And part of it comes from the continual effort to match the gospel principles to the world to which the church is called in ministry.

What is important here is that we find ways to embrace the powerful meanings of the past while not feeling restricted to only those understandings. The profundity of scripture comes in part from its ability to speak to every age in new and refreshing ways. Likewise, our history offers up continually new ways of seeing the world through the journey of a people who have struggled with the same fundamental issues that we do, but in an entirely different context. Our task is not replication of the past but a faithful rendering of those principles in contemporary terms.

To tell our story is to bear our testimony, both individually and collectively. It is to say, "This is where I've been, what I've seen and heard, and what I've come to understand. This is why I am the way I am." By sharing in the telling of such stories, we build a rich constellation of experiences that enhance our understanding of one another and help us find the foundation on which we continue to build.

3. *Transformation in how we look at ministry.* There is perhaps no topic more compelling to me at this stage in my life than a ful exploration of what we mean by ministry. Our priesthood system provides us with an opportunity to expand that concept in remarkable and life-changing ways. However, it also has the potential to bog us down in trivialities and archaic images if we allow it to do so. It is critically important that we dialogue with one another about what it means to be a minister in the Reorganized Church of Jesus Christ of Latter Day Saints.

As I assumed the awesome responsibilities of my office and calling in April 1996, I tried to speak honestly to the church about my feelings and struggles. I tried to be candid about my imperfections and to acknowledge my dependency on God and on the support of family, friends, and colleagues. I tried to say as candidly as I could that I was burdened by the expectations of the office and could not possibly fulfill those on my own.

While a few people felt I was shunning the task I had accepted (to be a prophetic voice to the church), most seemed to understand that my effort was only to respond authentically to the ministerial call. As I had hoped, most related that to their own call and saw the correlation.

If we are honest with ourselves, we surely struggle with the expectations that are placed on us by those who would have us be all-wise, all-knowing, spiritually sensitive, unreservedly committed, thoroughly organized, and eloquent and courageous in our witness. We look at our lives and find them wanting. I do, and my effort was only to acknowledge that in a public way and to thereby give everyone else "permission" to do so as well.

Sometimes I think we are plagued with role models of those we would like to emulate. We often think if only we could be as powerful a preacher as this person. Or as effective a teacher as that person. Or as sensitive a pastoral minister as another person. Or have the gift of prayer, or music, or scholarship, or whatever it is that we may desire for ourselves.

Probably, if we had the opportunity to really burrow inside the hearts and minds of those we would like to replicate, we would find uncertainties and confusion and regrets. We would find distinctly human people, struggling to respond to their call. In other words, we would find someone just like us.

And so, the task of each of us as ministers is primarily this. Find your own voice! Discover your personal and distinct calling, based on your own giftedness. You are called to be uniquely you, not anyone else. To be anything less is to diminish your ministry and deplete its power.

That is not to say that we cannot grow, develop new skills, or identify qualities we would like to have and then learn them. To the contrary, we are urged to magnify our callings and to utilize our talents rather than just protect them. But what is important is that we build on the gifts God has given to us and find ways to use those gifts in the cause of the kingdom.

The fundamental framework of our ministry comes from the one thing on which every one of us is the world's leading expert—our own life. This is where we have found our way to the heart of the Christian faith and it is the place where whatever truths we have embraced have become known to us. It is where we find the stories that permit us to identify with the lived-out experiences of others, and thereby provide common ground on which to minister. To be honest and authentic in terms of sharing our fears and struggles, as well as joys and triumphs, is the key to a ministry that will touch the lives of others.

4. *Learning how to stand for peace and justice.* Before the design of the Temple was announced, the vacation church school material invited children to draw a picture of what they thought a Temple dedicated to the pursuit of peace would look like. I remember seeing one child's drawing. It was a building with a tall spire, at the top of which was a cap hinged so that it could open like a lid. In the picture, the top was opened up and blasting out of the spire was a missile with the words "Peacemaker" written in big letters along its side. I thought it unlikely that this design would catch on.

Another child wrote a letter to President Wallace B. Smith, expressing support for the Temple project. She said that she was enclosing five cents to assist with the project and that, in addition, she was going to "stop hitting my brother." I smiled to myself and thought that she had caught the spirit of the place.

These humorous stories remind us, however, of the important task of learning how to be a people committed to peace and justice. On the one hand this does not appear to be a difficult expectation. Surely we all affirm those principles without much question. Who can be against peace and justice? But the much more telling point is what it means for those of us who are ministers. In other words, how is our ministry different than it was before this emphasis was given to the church through prophetic direction? What do we do differently than before?

The peace emphasis provides us with a wide band in which to offer our unique ministries. Some of us may find that working on inner peace or reconciling relationships is the most effective place of service. Others may want to get involved in community, national, or even global peace efforts. As a church we need to find ways to dialogue about the focus of our commitments to peace and justice. But it is abundantly clear that this transformational calling to peace and justice ministries has a profoundly personal dimension to it. It permits us to respond in accordance with our own best skills and insights.

In the process, we have an opportunity to see our mission in far more ambitious terms than we have before. It is time for this hardy band of people we call the church to stand up and be counted in the name of the Lord Jesus. It is time for us to engage in an outreaching ministry that can make a difference in the world we serve in his name.

5. *Building communities of compassion and outreach and healing.* Finally, our church's call to ministry urges us to create what we sometimes describe as "communities of joy." These are places where the essential spirit of the gospel is fostered between men and women of all ages sharing in a community that worships and studies and works together. Being a community is hard work. It means that those of us with leadership responsibilities must tend the flock and be sure that a significant portion of our energy is devoted to making those communities successful.

We all urgently need a place to stand. When my sons were in high school I noticed how important it was for them to have a group to belong to. They both participated in the National Forensics League, and there they found a community of friends who shared common interests, who enjoyed life in similar ways, and who were devoted to a mutual task. This place to stand was an important contributor to the success they enjoyed in high school. They didn't wander aimlessly. They had a place to be.

Life is like that. We all need such a place. That place has to be safe. It needs to be where we can share past guilt, present fears, future hopes. It needs to be where we can laugh and cry and feel needed. Our congregations must nurture a climate of trust that allows us to share our life journey without fear of embarrassment or threat or trivialization. To the extent we are able to provide such places, our people will be blessed. To the extent we fail, our people will not be nourished in the love of Christ which is expressed most fully in community.

To Become a Minister

In Ephesians 3:7, Paul reminds us that he, and thereby each of us, "was made a minister, by God's gift" (NEB). In fact, Paul knows that in his own life he had no business being called to such a task for he had been a persecutor and a sinner. But instead, he was "granted...the privilege of proclaiming...the good news of the unfathomable riches of Christ" (Ephesians 3:8, NEB).

One of my favorite writers, Frederick Buechner, offers these thoughts on the nature of ministry:

> The first ministers were the twelve disciples. There is no evidence that Jesus chose them because they were brighter or nicer than other people. In fact the New Testament record suggests that they were continually missing the point, jockeying for position and, when the chips were down, interested in nothing so much as saving their own skins. Their sole qualification seems to have been their initial willingness to rise to their feet when Jesus said, "Follow me."[5]

When Jesus sent those first ministers into the world they were without many of the traits one would expect them to have. But Jesus gave simple directions—to preach the kingdom of God and to be a healing presence. To do so does not require our perfection, our brilliance, our skills at communication, even our ability to always practice what we preach, for sometimes our proclamation of the truth outreaches our capacity to live it.

Instead, such a commission embraces our shortcomings, our fears and failures, our lack of knowledge and foresight. It requires only that we love one another, that we be honest about ourselves, sensitive to our own life journey and to that of others, and that we be willing to grow. For whoever we are, and wherever we stand, to do these things in the name of Christ is to be a minister.

Notes

1. Alan Walker as quoted in George G. Hunter III, *How to Reach Secular People* (Nashville, Tennessee: Abingdon, 1992), 45.
2. The following discussion on the secularization of culture draws substantially on the observations of Hunter, *How to Reach Secular People*.
3. Joseph Sittler, *Gravity and Grace* (Minneapolis, Minnesota: Augsburg, 1989), 49.

4. Alan Jones, *Sacrifice and Delight: Spirituality for Ministry* (New York: Harper San Francisco, 1989), 60-61.

5. Frederick Buechner, *Wishful Thinking: A Theological ABC* (New York: Harper & Row, 1973), 62.

SHEPHERDS
ABIDING
IN THE FIELD

Chapter 4

A Perspective on the Centrality of Christ

Anthony Chvala-Smith *

The gifts he gave were that some would be apostles, some prophets, some evangelists, some pastors and teachers, to equip the saints for the work of the ministry, for building up the body of Christ, until all of us come to the unity of the faith and of the knowledge of the Son of God, to maturity, to the measure of the full stature of Christ. We must no longer be children, tossed to and fro and blown about by every wind of doctrine.... But speaking the truth in love, we must grow up in every way into him who is the head, into Christ—Ephesians 4:11-15, NRSV

Values and Beliefs

Several years ago I wrote a brief article on the core values of the RLDS Church. That statement, however, gave only a partial picture, because we cannot speak adequately of our core values unless we also speak of our central beliefs. Our values—whatever we hold them to be—flow from what we believe to be true. Values are what we express when we have internalized and digested certain beliefs. For example, the "centrality of Christ" is certainly a core value of the RLDS Church, but it is so because we believe certain things, and not others, about Jesus of Nazareth. Likewise, behind a value such as "the acceptance of all people" lies a collection of beliefs about the nature of God and the human person, and what God has done in behalf of humankind.

* Appreciation is expressed to Charmaine Chvala-Smith who gave material assistance to the author in the production of this chapter.

If values clothe the body of Christ with flesh, beliefs form the body's skeleton. Beliefs give structure, form, stability; values give life, warmth, personality. If in our values we express that the gospel is the life, in our beliefs we express that the gospel is also the truth. The two cannot remain long separated. To suppose that the church can do well without speaking of its beliefs is like supposing that a hand can be a hand without bones. If we do not work at teaching our beliefs, they cannot be internalized and turned to values. We are then at risk of being "tossed to and fro and blown about by every wind of doctrine" (Ephesians 4:14). And the values we are then likely to express may be only those of the dominant culture, and not those of the gospel. For the sake of the health and maturity of the church, we must therefore learn again to speak of doctrine. The church will come to peace with itself as it learns to talk about both what it values and what it believes.

The Unity of the Faith

The basic elements of the Christian faith have not changed. Throughout the centuries and across diverse cultures, as Christians have thought about their message, the central themes of the gospel have consistently reasserted and proved themselves. Today the RLDS Church finds itself rediscovering this center. In this process we are gaining a new heart and new eyes, and a mind for what really matters.

From the start Christians have spoken of their basic beliefs by making simple declarations. A brief look at three of these declarations will show how the central themes of the gospel have remained constant through the generations.

In dealing with a crisis in his Corinthian congregation, the apostle Paul finds that he must remind these early Christians of the basic message he first taught them. He writes:

> For I handed on to you as of first importance what I in turn had received: that Christ died for our sins in accordance with the scriptures, and that he was buried, and that he was raised on the third day in accordance with the scriptures. —I Corinthians 15:3-4)

This is a simple statement of the faith of the earliest Christian community. Paul did not make it up, but received it and passed it on. We believe, Paul says, that Jesus is the Christ, God's anointed Son; his crucifixion was for our sins and thus had atoning power; his resurrection confirmed his identity and established him as the Lord of all things, who would come again. This is the message you believed, and which—if you hold fast to it—will bring salvation (I Corinthians 15:1-2).

In subsequent centuries Christians came to declare these beliefs in various creeds. In doing so, they were not departing from Paul's example in I Corinthians 15, but following it. (In fact, the New Testament has many other short creedal statements; see, for example, Colossians 1:15-20 or Philippians 2:6-11). These statements of faith became the best way to pass on basic beliefs. For the Western Christian tradition, the Apostles' Creed was one important means of passing on basic beliefs. This creed originated in the late second or early third century as a profession of faith made in baptism. Its second section restates the central claims of the Christian faith:

> [I believe] in Jesus Christ [God's] only Son our Lord; who was conceived by the Holy Ghost, born of the Virgin Mary; suffered under Pontius Pilate, was crucified, dead, and buried; he descended into hell; the third day he rose from the dead; he ascended into heaven; and sitteth at the right hand of God the Father Almighty; from thence he shall come to judge the quick and the dead.

These words restate the basic events of the gospel story and their meaning. It differs at some points from the declaration in I Corinthians 15. For example, it refers to Christ's descent into hell, which may be taken either as a reference to his proclamation to the dead (I Peter 3:19), or simply as an affirmation of the reality of his death. But the structure and content are markedly the same: Christ crucified, risen, and coming again. Here again we see what Christians have considered to be their most central beliefs.

This same center was reaffirmed in the early years of the Restoration movement. Section 17 of the Doctrine and Covenants declares these basic beliefs in language reminiscent of both I Corinthians 15 and the Apostle's Creed:

> Wherefore the almighty God gave his only begotten Son, as it is written of him in those scriptures which have been given of him: he suffered temptations but gave no heed unto them; he was crucified, died, and rose again the third day; and ascended into heaven to sit down on the right hand of the Father, to reign with almighty power according to the will of the Father.... — Doctrine and Covenants 17:5a-d

One could easily find these same basic beliefs expressed in the Book of Mormon, but the passage from the Doctrine and Covenants is instructive because it shows that the Restoration movement from the beginning sought to hold to the basics of the Christian faith.

61

These three examples span the centuries. The church can see and hear what is most central to its life by attending to what is constant in them. Here is the heart of the gospel: Jesus Christ is the Son of God, crucified for our salvation, risen in victory over death, coming again as Lord of all. He is Emmanuel, Sacrifice, Victor, and Goal. In him we find forgiveness of sins, reconciliation with God, the promise of life everlasting, and the hope for a new heaven and new earth. This is the apostolic faith, which has never been without witnesses, and which the Restoration boldly reaffirmed. It is from these beliefs that some of our most deeply cherished values flow. Thus what we believe and teach about Christ could hardly be more important to the church's future. For the only future for which the church can rightly hope is to "grow up in every way into him who is the head" (Ephesians 4:15).

This is the "everlasting gospel": Jesus Christ, crucified, risen, and coming again. These are the basics, the "ABC's"; and this is the bedrock of our movement. Let us look again at each of these elements of the faith.

Jesus Christ: Crucified, Risen, and Coming Again

Jesus Christ: Emmanuel

The New Testament witnesses speak in a variety of ways about Jesus' unique divine status. Christ who was in the image or form of God did not count his equality with God a thing to be grasped but emptied himself (Philippians 2:6-7). Thomas claims Jesus as "my Lord and my God" (John 20:28). Paul holds that in Christ "all the fullness of God was pleased to dwell" (Colossians 1:19). Through the Son, God created the worlds, and Christ is "the reflection of God's glory and the exact imprint of God's very being" (Hebrews 1:2-3). Jesus Christ is "our God and Savior" (II Peter 1:1), and is worthy of our worship (Matthew 2:11; 28:16 IV/ 2:11; 28:17 others). And the Gospel of John even calls Jesus "God the only Son" (1:18, NRSV). The idea that Jesus' divinity is a notion imposed by later centuries is simply not in accord with the apostolic witness.

This testimony appears in more subtle ways, too. The New Testament authors frequently transfer to Jesus that language the Old Testament reserved for God. At the end of the story about the calming of the sea (Mark 4:28-33 IV / 4:35-41 others), the disciples exclaim, "Who then is this, that even the wind and the sea obey him?" For those steeped in the Old Testament, as the first Christians were, this language had an unmistakable ring to it. These words recalled the Exodus, in which wind and sea were at the command of God. The disciples' question is meant to cause readers of the Gospel to see a unity of action and purpose between Jesus and God.

The Book of Mormon's testimony, as well, affirms this unity between Jesus and God. Jesus is "the Christ, the Eternal God, manifesting himself unto all nations" (title page). Jesus is the "Lord Omnipotent" (Mosiah 1:116) and comes in divine power to break the "bands of death" (Mosiah 8:35). Moreover, Christ's atoning work on the cross is nothing less than the merciful work of God (Alma 19:97).

Thus the scriptures take great pains to show that what the disciples experienced in Christ was nothing less than the presence, power, and being of the Living God. Jesus is Emmanuel: *God* with us. Jesus' value for us flows from this divine nature. Why does this matter for us today? There are many reasons, but the simplest is this: experience teaches that the very energy needed for discipleship cannot come from ourselves. What we need is divine energy, a power sprung from the boundless love of God. Only a divine source can supply it. When we call Jesus Lord and Christ, we can mean nothing less than that Jesus is the divine source of energy which finds expression in our discipleship. The power that works in and through us in Christ's name is the very power and presence of God. Nothing less will do; nothing less will save.

The Christ I have come to know in the RLDS Church is the same divine Lord I met as a child in the Methodist Church and as a young adult in the Baptist Church. When I first read the Book of Mormon, I knew I was on to something exciting. I also knew that the Lord who was speaking to me there was the one I had come to know in other places. And if Christ is big enough to be Lord of Methodists, Baptists, and the Saints, then Jesus is big enough to guide me through my darkest nights and deepest struggles. So, with the Christians of all ages, we celebrate that Jesus Christ is our God and Savior.

Crucified for Our Sins: Sacrifice

Something breathtaking and powerful happened on Calvary. The Gospels depict this great mystery with a simple story. At the trial of Jesus, Pilate offered the crowd a choice: I will set free either Barabbas the murderer or Jesus the king. The crowd chose Barabbas. In Aramaic, the language of first-century Palestine, "Barabbas" meant "son of Abbas." But it also meant "son of the father." And with this little word play, we begin to see what the Gospel writers believed was really happening in the crucifixion. An exchange was made: the guilty son of the father is released, and *the Son* of the Father dies. Or, as II Corinthians 5:14 puts it, "one has died for all."

The New Testament writings are filled with a sense of sheer wonder that God's Son would die for us. And yet there is also a sense that here is a profound mystery. The first apostles knew that the message of the cross was a stumbling block, that the greatest wisdom of the age could not penetrate it and would even be repulsed by it. "In the cross of Christ I glory" would have sounded to the Roman ear like "In the electric chair of Christ I glory" sounds to us. How could the instrument of judgment and death be at the same time the means of revealing God's glory and love?

The meaning of Jesus' death is not self-evident. Something must happen in us so that we may see what God is doing here. Grasping the truth of the cross requires a radical shift of perspective. Only the Spirit of God can lead us to the point of understanding what otherwise cannot be understood. And then as we comprehend, repentance and new life become possible. To grasp the truth of the cross is to learn that *I am Barabbas*. The exchange was made for me, for each of us.

The gravity of an illness may be seen in the potency of the medicine that cures it. The cross is the medicine God offers, and it lays bare the severity of the illness in our lives. Sin is the sickness unto death. And there is much in me that resists the diagnosis. Were I to claim that I did not need the Son of God to die for me, I should only be revealing how little I knew myself.

The sacraments of baptism and the Lord's Supper depict how utterly central Christ's death is to the Christian faith. These sacraments reveal that the meaning of our discipleship is to be found in the cross of Christ. In baptism I am crucified and buried with Christ. Baptism expresses that I must die to self, and find my new life in Christ. In the Lord's Supper the church proclaims Jesus' death as the ransom for many. As we eat bread and drink wine we also declare our willingness to live in self-emptying love for others. These two sacraments re-present the meaning of the cross for us.

Though for some the cross evokes disgust, for the church it evokes wonder, praise, and gratitude: "O Lord, by faith I see that Thou didst give thyself for me, to cleanse my soul from sin" (*Hymns of the Saints*, No. 332).

Raised from the Dead on the Third Day: Victor

There were many crosses in Roman-occupied Palestine. But only one was *the Cross*. The church knows the saving power of the cross and knows Jesus Christ as Lord only because of what happened on Easter Sunday. If Christ was not raised from the dead, as Paul holds, our message and our faith are vain, and death is the last word about our lives (I Corinthians 15:12-19). Everything we are and do in the name of Christ could be called into question if Easter Sunday had been a hoax perpetrated by the well-meaning followers of a martyred prophet.

The New Testament takes considerable trouble to show that this was not the case. There were witnesses—not of the actual event of the resurrection itself—but of the Risen One and the empty tomb. When Paul dealt with the haughty skepticism of some of his Corinthian converts, he recited for them a list of people to whom Jesus had appeared. The Lord was seen by Peter and the Twelve, and then by 500 disciples at once, most of whom are still alive, Paul adds. Then Christ appeared to James, then to all the apostles. Finally, Paul says, he appeared to me, despite my unfitness (I Corinthians 15:3-8). What we preach can be verified, says Paul. We have seen the Lord's glorified, transfigured body. And because this was the message that brought you life, its truth has already been verified in you.

When Palestinian Jews heard the early Christians proclaim that Jesus had been raised from the dead, they could only think of that in bodily terms. One could not go about saying "God raised Jesus from the dead" while the tomb was still full. A body in the tomb would have immediately falsified the proclamation. Thus it is interesting that even the church's early opponents concede that the tomb was empty; they simply put a different interpretation on it (Matthew 27:64-67; 28:10-14 IV / 27:62-66; 28:11-15 others).

Christian faith stands on a miracle, or better, a series of miracles: an empty tomb, men and women who saw the risen Lord, and lives transformed by the risen Lord's presence. Great effects have great causes. Something wondrous and marvelous happened on Easter Sunday. Apart from this event, the rise of Christianity and its continued transforming power are inexplicable. Without boasting, but without anxiety or hesitation, the church has always declared "he rose from the dead on the third day."

The power of the resurrection came home to me in the fall of 1990 when I was a teaching fellow in the Department of Theology at Marquette University. In one of my sections of Introduction to Theology, I had a Vietnamese student whose English was rudimentary. Christian theology was a foreign and difficult subject matter for him, so I worked hard to help him along.

Midway through the semester, we were nearing the completion of a unit on the New Testament. I asked my students to write a paper comparing either Matthew or Luke's Empty Tomb story with Mark's. This was an exercise in redaction criticism. The point was to assess how either Matthew or Luke modified or edited Mark's account, which, according to most scholars, was their primary source. My aims were basically literary and historical.

My Vietnamese student wrote a solid paper, but as I reached his concluding paragraph, I was surprised at what I read. He ended on a personal note. He said, "After reading these stories, now I understand about God. When I go back to Vietnam I will tell my father about this."

I cannot convey both my surprise and delight, and how much that experience has changed my heart and mind about many things. The New Testament's witness to the risen One had awakened in this student the very thing it has always awakened in people: faith in Christ. Christ is risen from the dead and reveals himself in the apostolic testimony: what a tremendous source of hope and life!

The Restoration movement has reaffirmed that Christ is risen. "And, now, after the many testimonies which have been given of him, this is the testimony, last of all, which we give of him, that he lives; for we saw him, even on the right hand of God" (Doctrine and Covenants 76:3g). Joseph Smith and Sidney Rigdon saw the risen Lord. Their experience gives an added confirmation to the testimony of the first apostles: he lives who once was dead, and in him we shall conquer death.

Coming Again: Goal

Hope is a cardinal Christian virtue. It is likewise a core value of our tradition. But in the testimony of the apostles and their earliest followers, hope is more than a positive attitude about the future. It has a specific content: the early Christians hoped for their Lord to come in glory. Indeed they rejoiced in Christ's risen presence already among them. But they knew this was not the end of the story, for their transformation was incomplete. They knew that all history and all creation must have its Easter morning, too. So they cried out in worship *"Maranatha!"* — "Our Lord, come!" (see I Corinthians 16:22; Revelation 22:20).

The doctrine of Christ's coming is not much talked about today. In some ways we are right to be cautious about it. Throughout the church's history, this belief frequently has been a source of great mischief. I once saw a Sunday school poster that depicted the so-called "rapture" in dreadful scenes of destruction. These scenes were hard for me to reconcile with the hope Christ's future coming gave the first disciples. Among other abuses of this doctrine are those useless calculations and speculations about when the Lord will come (which were, of course, forbidden by the Lord himself!). And some Christians have turned Christ's coming into an excuse for ethical and social irresponsibility: "Don't worry about pollution; once we've used everything up, Jesus will return" or "Nuclear catastrophe is God's way to cleanse the earth." Some of these statements would be laughable if they were not so monstrous. So there are many reasons why thoughtful Christians are suspicious of the doctrine of Christ's future coming.

The fact that people abuse or misunderstand a belief, however, does not mean it should be abandoned. We must instead look deeper and listen better. Clearly, the hope of Christ's future coming is found uniformly throughout the New Testament. It was not an afterthought, as though the disciples wondered what they should think about now that Jesus was risen. On the contrary, belief in Christ's future manifestation lay at the center of their hope. If this belief was so central to the apostles' message, then we must patiently and carefully attend to it. We must do our best faithfully and intelligently to teach it and live in its light. It is both fair and accurate to say that authentic preaching of the gospel must include the doctrine of Christ's future coming.

What difference can this make to our lives? An experience of the late Arthur Oakman suggests one answer.[1] In June 1939, while ministering to the Saints in Nazi Germany, Apostle Oakman was arrested by the Gestapo and accused of spying. The interrogation led to one all-important question: "What are you teaching our people about the second coming of Christ?" Oakman asked the officer why he wanted to know. The officer replied, "Because Hitler is building the Reich to last for a thousand years." Do you see the implications of that?

Oakman knew that if he had been teaching the imminent coming of Christ, he could have been charged with treason. So he carefully responded to the officer: "We teach that the kingdoms of this world shall become the kingdoms of our God and his Christ, and it does not matter how long the German Reich lasts, eventually every knee shall bow and tongue confess." Oakman and his traveling companions were released.

Oakman's experience teaches us something very significant. It is this: We must not give up any doctrine that makes despots and oppressors nervous! The doctrine of Christ's future coming teaches that the future does not belong to the Hitlers, Stalins, and Pol Pots of this world, but to the Lord Jesus Christ. If Christ is the end toward which the human story is moving, then the doctrine of Christ's coming can fill us with the power to resist all the little kingdoms human beings want to set up. It has always been on this basis that Christians have resisted evil power systems. So, at the very least, the doctrine of Christ's coming has *real* political implications for us.

What matters more than its relevance is its truth. We believe that Christ will come, for so he said and so the apostles taught. And so the Restoration movement has reaffirmed. The promise of Christ's coming has led the Saints to want to build, not tear down: "We have the promise that Jesus will come, Zion the beautiful beckons us on" (*Hymns of the Saints*, No. 316). To believe that Christ will come is to say that the joy, forgiveness, righteousness, and love we experience in such fragmentary ways will one day come in a fullness that knows no end. That day will be none other than "the day of our Lord Jesus Christ" (I Corinthians 1:8). That day will not come because we have become smarter and better; it will come because the Lord himself will graciously bring it.

Conclusion

The gospel is not a message we make up as we go along. We are responsible to God for passing on the testimony of the first apostles and prophets. Without this message, we would have no testimony of our own to give. Our testimony receives its life from these basics: Jesus Christ—crucified, risen, and coming again. By and in this proclamation the church has come to faith. We believe, and *therefore* we speak (II Corinthians 4:13). Values flow from beliefs; action springs from being; our task issues from God's gift.

Our task is not to "make" this gospel relevant for a new era. Such thoughts reveal our own egotism, showing that we presume the gospel to be *our* message. But it is not. The gospel is *God's* message. Our task begins with trusting that it *is* relevant. As the year 2000 approaches, the most meaningful gift we have to offer our world is "the faith that was once for all entrusted to the saints" (Jude 3). We need nothing more; we must share nothing less.

Notes

1. Arthur Oakman, *He Who Is* (Independence, Missouri: Herald House, 1963), 133–136.

SHEPHERDS
ABIDING
IN THE FIELD

Chapter 5
The Centrality of Christ:
A Comment

Paul M. Edwards

The church is continually aware of the call to be God's people in a harsh and difficult world. This awareness is reflected often in the question of identity. How do we see ourselves in this age of postmodernism? What does it mean to be a Christ-centered church?

One form of response is to identify values, doctrines, or forms of worship that depict us in a unique fashion. As far as this goes, it is probably helpful. But it is important to remember that values, like prejudices, are not inherent in themselves. Rather they are based on more centralized and primary assumptions that form the core of our beliefs: assumptions we have made about the nature of reality, of Divinity, and of knowledge. These assumptions are often hard to define and are always most difficult to trace, but they continually color our selections, affect our judgments, and foster our identification of, and dedication to, values.

Understanding and acknowledging these assumptions are central to our belief structure. Our assumptions/beliefs serve as the core around which our values are established. It is in the solidity of these beliefs that our response becomes more than the symptoms of our current inadequate age.

It would appear that if Christ stands at the center of our belief, it is because we assume certain things about him. If we base our values and behaviors on those beliefs, we must feel some interrelatedness between such beliefs and our expectations. In reality, such a belief must go far beyond the mere identification of an accepted myth.

Many believe the message of Christ but are less enamored by the traditional methods of identifying how that message is conveyed. This is made even more serious when people feel that traditional identifications interfere with the message.

The more traditional form of our acknowledgment is to adopt the terminology and the myths of those who first recorded their understanding of the event. The apostle Paul, for example, depicts the death of the Christ who died having been crucified between two thieves; he rose from the grave and ascended (after a short visit in hell), and promised that he would come again. It is around this description that Paul, and many others since, have identified Christ.

However, there are other means of identification. The concept of the Christ may best be seen as a symbol of faith that has evolved over the years. This symbol has addressed the needs of generations and is best described in a manner that, in its own way, reflects the age in which disciples are called into service.

All we know with any sort of assurance is that he, whom we call Jesus, is identified by birth narratives, crucifixion stories, and midrashic and evangelistic interpretations that arose from the silence that followed his death. The myths seem questionable, not so much because of their message but because of the media. They appear to tie the faithful to some particular course of action—actions that appear less than fulfilling to the promise of the event. Many wonder if there is only one model. A Christ described and identified by miraculous understandings and exaggerated interpretations seems strangely out of place in a world in which value is often a choice between evils. Especially when the affirmation of the story is seen as more important than participation in the promise.

Perhaps the tendency to insist on one particular model as *the* model moves us away from the assumption that we are the one true church, but it encourages the assumption that we are the one world religion. To me, the power of God seems present in other stories, other myths, and other identifications.

Perhaps more significant is the fact that our insistence on a single model encourages us in the tendency to memorialize rather than to celebrate Jesus Christ. That is, we remember rather than experience, we ritualize rather than recall; we consider Christ as he who was rather than he who is. The celebration of Christ should call us to participation, not merely affirmation.

* * *

Our collective beliefs, especially about the justification for our religious assumptions, are not necessarily compatible. One way to consider this is to acknowledge the difference between our faith and belief. The source of our faith lies in the abstract and absolute nature of concepts beyond our experience that we justify by acceptance. We build our beliefs on the limited nature of our immediate experience. Our faith becomes the source of our belief; our belief, the test of our faith.

In this manner we have come to accept paradox as a part of complexity. But the conflict between the myth of the powerful goodness of Divinity and the continual presence of evil and suffering leaves many to wonder if we have misinterpreted the concept of victory. This is confused further by the fact that the goodness of God is understood in the abstract and is acknowledged in our chanted affirmations. However, it is the immediate and experiential nature of evil that is the human challenge.

Much is said about the "Hound of Heaven": the God who searches out those in whom to plant the faith necessary to have faith. The initiative is God's, yet we are somehow responsible. Of interest in our age is the seeming absence of such a call. The Hound of Heaven has not sought us out. Thus it is not the death of God that is the person's wonder; it is the awesome silence.

Perhaps our understanding would be far more simple if the vast majority of people began their religious affirmation with the presence of a belief, especially if their belief was strong enough to cross denominational bickering and secure enough that one could construct on it a lifetime of values.

Unfortunately, many people seek God from the midst of their inability to deal with a world of pain. They are confused by the claims of this abstract God who, commemorated rather than celebrated, seems only to observe. They seek to absolve God from the anger and frustration imposed by a life over which they have lost control. They wonder about a God whose victories over pain and suffering are so rare they must be memorialized by stories in *Guideposts*.

To such a challenge the affirming words of the birth narrative, or the many interpretations of the resurrection, are less than fulfilling. Rather, the affirmation of the power of God, the presence of Christ, is found when the confirming presence of love is acknowledged. Are we not as disciples more to take love into the apparent absence of

God than to chant the ritualized memories of a time when people claimed to hear?

I find no fault with those whose affirmation of the birth, crucifixion, resurrection, and promised return is sufficient for their enlightenment. But I must agree more with William Fox who feels that the role of religion is primarily to provide strength for the living of these days. The call to the religious seeker is to identify value from living rather than to lose oneself in affirming the cerebrally satisfying, and inherently less frightening, proclamations of the meaning of life. The question of meaning is, more than we realize, that we are alive.

The belief that Jesus Christ is central to the values of the Restoration depends not so much on what we accept about Jesus Christ's mystical beginnings. Rather it is a means by which we format our lives—a life in which Christ is not the idol, but the heroic model, the silent friend, the fellow sufferer.

*   *   *

It is terribly important for the good people of the Reorganization to talk about belief and to dialogue, as well as affirm, what is significant. Such speaking must articulate the promise of our individual faith. It must consist of more than repeating the clichés of religious thought and reverting to dependence on the rituals, symbols, and myths that have perpetuated hope and thus held us in the past. It is time to stop pretending that our history is our theology.

While it is both easy to say and comforting to affirm that the basic doctrines of Christianity have not changed, it is unwise to ignore the fact that what has changed is our understanding of what *are* the basic doctrines of Christ. If we are not very careful in our dreary repetition of the stories and slogans, our essential message will be lost in the retelling. The source of our hope will become a distant Lord who is acknowledged but not followed.

My concern is not so much that Christ died for my sins, but that people today continue to die for my sins. If he died for my sins, why must you? What can I learn from the desired affirmations and my ritual attendance that will erase the soot my footsteps leave on the snow of other people's lives?

I do not identify Jesus as the Christ because of the stories told from the pulpit about his birth and death, or even his resurrection. Rather I acknowledge Christ in the presence of love at my side when I am afraid. To confirm Christ as a historical figure, to assume value only from tradition, places the source of the love far from the presence of the action.

Forgive me, but I do not know what many of these things mean that I am told I must affirm. The question I hear from the lips of the suffering is not that God can control the winds or the seas, but that the winds that beat upon the shore appear uncontrolled. Few from the Christian tradition doubt that Christ was victorious over death; rather they wonder why death visits the innocent; why the God who appears to have time to encourage the preacher cannot help the starving child, or why my church is often my judge and rarely my friend.

For more than thirty years I have urged the church to look at its theology. No one who knows me can believe I am urging either irrational or unquestioned acceptance. The theological inquiry, the philosophical challenge, and the historical investigation are essential; but they must move beyond the beautiful reaffirmations of old myths to which we have become unreasonably attached.

I have had people ask me, because they see me as a skeptic, how I can have any convictions at all. It is because I am willing to submit my beliefs to honest challenge that I am encouraged by the strength of those convictions that remain. My faith in the power of love emerges not from some abstraction about the nature of Divinity but from being loved. My belief in the sustaining power of a divine force does not emerge from a story or a myth or a proclamation but from the fact that I am sustained. Thus my conviction about the power of love and the ministry of presence is so powerful that it is expressed, when I am able, in experience.

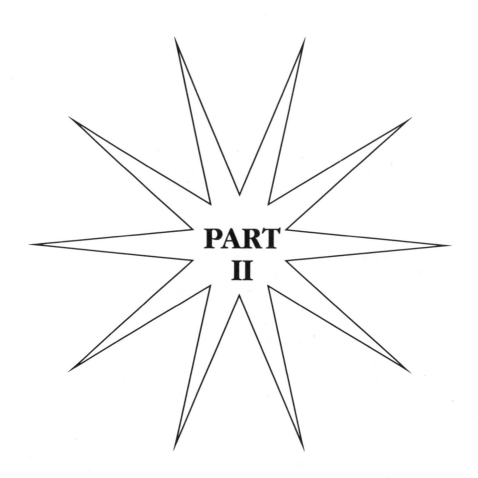

PART
II

The
Mission
of
Leadership

SHEPHERDS
ABIDING
IN THE FIELD

Chapter 6

The Servant Ministry of Jesus: Priesthood in Today's World

Joe A. Serig

When leaders are doing everything themselves, they probably are not leading. To be effective leaders in today's culture, we need to redefine leadership from "How much have I done?" to "How many others have I involved and supported?" If no one follows, who is leading?

One definition of the word "serve" is to put the ball in play. Think of this definition in terms of games such as tennis, Ping-Pong, or volleyball. As leaders we are called to put the ball in play. We cannot play all positions or win every game on our own. The servant leader gets the game started and helps other players participate. A leader keeps the ball in play. You don't make the rules. Leaders are not always the star player; you are more of a coach. Unless asked, you are neither the referee nor the scorekeeper. You put the ball in play and help the team to keep the ball in play. What, then, are characteristics of a servant leader?

Qualities of Servant Leaders

Some think of leaders as having a great deal of natural leadership personality. Both personal observation and solid research reveal that there is no single personality type that guarantees success as a leader. There are leaders who are personally warm and affable. Others may appear cool and aloof. Nor can leaders be stereotyped by the way they go about their work.

There are many different styles of leadership. Some lead by example. Others lead by sensing the direction of the group. Some are problem solvers who stimulate group decision. Others see potential consequences and relationships that may be overlooked. In complex human relationships those who are servant leaders learn to adapt their style to the needs of the group and to the issue at hand.

Flexibility and adaptability will need to characterize each of us in our specific role or task assignments. Personal commitment to Christ, to each other, and to the church as the body of Christ are common values from which we lead and follow.

Simply stated, servant leaders
- lead by example;
- focus on mission and common values;
- put people and their needs ahead of programs and buildings;
- expect the best, and give their best;
- avoid judgment (praise publicly, question in private);
- go the second mile in supporting others;
- are kind to themselves;
- set realistic and achievable expectations; and
- take time for personal renewal.

The Example of Jesus

A review of the Gospels indicates that Jesus' style of leadership was one of invitation, encouragement, and enablement. He was a facilitator (server), one who encouraged and stimulated friends to be responsible for their behavior. He challenged people to express the freedom they found in his message by sharing in the concerns of others. Jesus taught and demonstrated that the focal point of life for disciples is the worth of persons. This central value is to be lived out in the awareness of God's love for all. He confronted religious and social authority and structure when they denied or restricted growth toward community in God.

One way to examine the servant ministry of Jesus is to review the scriptural narrative referred to as "The Temptations" (Matthew 4; Luke 4). Three common tests of servant leadership are explored in the scriptural narrative.

First, Jesus was tempted to command stone to turn to bread. He was confronted with a fantasy that there are shortcuts to accomplishment or satisfaction. Jesus was hungry after fasting for forty days. His loneliness, his hunger for food, and the emotional pressure of this temptation could have combined to justify the demonstration of one bit of magic on his behalf. The possibility was at hand. Jesus' relationship with God provided the counterbalance that bread is earned or baked, not made from stones.

A test of servant leadership lies in the capacity to wait for a larger good, rather than to settle for a short-term satisfaction of an impulse or need. Every leader feels this temptation at some time to revert to authoritarian styles of leadership to get the job done quickly. The pressures for this compromise are real. In the long run human worth provides the corrective to this temptation.

Second, Jesus was tempted by the authority and glory of all the kingdoms of the world in one moment of time. In other words, he was tempted by the promise of preeminence of position without the long, hard journey that authentic strength requires for servant ministry and leadership. The status seekers in the world want to be the center of attention and to be recognized for their power, but the suffering servants are in the world to be ministers.

Third, Jesus was tempted with the illusion that he was an exception to the laws of physical and human nature. This may be interpreted as falling prey to the deception of the superhuman image of leadership. Jesus was tempted to throw himself down from a high pinnacle on the self-centered perception that he would not be physically harmed. In effect, he was confronted with the temptation to force God to guarantee personal safety and to support frivolous fantasies of power.

The writer of Hebrews states that the basis for Jesus' compassion for others was that he was tempted, just as they are, yet was without sin (see Hebrews 2:18). In other words, Jesus didn't give in to the illusions of self-serving power but used his gifts to minister to others. The exact citation reads, "Because he himself was tested by what he suffered, he is able to help those who are being tested" (Hebrews 2:17).

Sometimes in our anxiety to be perceived as real leaders and to get the job done we live out of the superhuman image. Often, this is at the expense of our families, friends, and fellow workers. We develop feelings of guilt because it is difficult to understand why things do not move rapidly, to our personal satisfaction. We are so busy doing so many good things for the church and for others that we forget our own humanness. We, in effect, give in to the temptation to tempt God to produce on our behalf because we are so busy.

Jesus' Response

After the experience we call the temptations, what was Jesus' response? He immediately returned to his home village. He was remembered there as the son of a local carpenter. When asked to read the scriptures in the synagogue, he chose this scripture from the Hebrew prophet Isaiah:

> The Spirit of the Lord is upon me, because he has anointed me to preach good news to the poor. He has sent me to proclaim release to the captives and recovering of sight to the blind, to set at liberty those who are oppressed, to proclaim the acceptable year of the Lord.—Luke 4:18–19 RSV

Our Response

Putting aside our illusions of power and authority requires daily renewal. We have feelings, needs, and thoughts that can be used to justify self-centeredness and authoritarianism. Like Jesus we need to go to our quiet places to keep our priorities straight. We are often prone to lead in ways that enhance our own status rather than serve the needs of those within the church and the larger community. Sharing this reality honestly and openly with friends will give us support to be honest with ourselves and others about our humanness. We can end the pretense that we are somehow superhuman and that our inappropriate actions are justified because "God understands."

The trilogy of temptations faced by Jesus is common to all leaders. To face them honestly is a genuine test of our moral leadership. Such honest self-analysis is painful but essential for effective servant leadership. The agenda proclaimed by Jesus by his intentional use of the prophetic reference to his own calling cannot be avoided. We may wish he had used a different reference point for proclaiming who he was and what he was about, but we do so at the risk of self-deception. Choosing an alternative to Jesus' agenda of ministry is an attempt to avoid the sufferings and disciplines required for an effective and clear-headed approach to leadership. Such efforts are but feeble attempts to permit ourselves to live in a world of our own making through our own fantasies, rather than the world of being, doing, and acting—identified, claimed, and loved by Jesus.

Our leadership styles must reflect a basic concern for the lives of other people. Program objectives and leadership processes are evaluated ultimately in terms of ministry given to people at their point of need in life. The search for personal significance and the meaning of life are deeply felt needs of modern individuals. Unless our focus is on this genuine cry for help, we miss our calling. Jesus met ordinary people in ordinary places doing ordinary daily tasks. The woman at the well, fishermen, a tax collector, mothers, soldiers, merchants—these reflect his connections with real people. The same should be true for us.

The principal ethical teachings of Christ are love of God and love of neighbor. These must be modeled in our lives if servant ministry is to be meaningful. An implication of this approach to leadership is that we intentionally foster, encourage, and stimulate participatory styles of church life. We center our ministry on the principle that people are freed from bondage to commitment to serve in community, never in isolation. We need each other. I cannot become what God intends without you, nor you without me.

We take this principle demonstrated in the leadership of Jesus seriously enough to incorporate it into our personal leadership. John (3:32 IV / 3:31 others) states that John the Baptist lived as an appropriate model of leadership in relation to Jesus. When asked by his followers what to do about Jesus, he said "He must increase but I must decrease" (3:30 RSV). God's intent for human fulfillment is ever so much more important than my ego needs or personal agenda. We must decrease so God in Christ may increase in the congregations, communities, and relationships of our lives.

The Vocation of Servant Ministry

The test of Christian leadership is whether or not lives are being changed toward godliness and whether or not society is being transformed into God's kingdom. Programs, agenda, and leaders are not ends in themselves; rather, they are means of enabling people and societies to accept, identify, and fulfill divine purpose.

The vocation Jesus claimed in Nazareth identifies *our* vocation. It is the same one to which congregations are called. In accepting this vocation, congregations discover their own true identity. Jesus' identity led him to a life of servant ministry in a world of uncertainty and pain. In today's world, we are called to that same vocation of speaking and living the good news. This leadership requires our very best.

Ultimately what we each have to give as disciples and leaders is ourselves—nothing more, nothing less. We ought not to be confused or intimidated by this reality. It has always been so. In the New Testament Peter is confronted by a man in need. Peter's understanding of the source of his ministry can guide us as servant ministers. "I have no silver or gold, but what I have I give you: in the name of Jesus Christ of Nazareth, stand up and walk" (Acts 3:6 NRSV).

In the early days of the Restoration Joseph Smith Jr. summarized a leadership training experience with church leaders in these words: "I called you servants for the world's sake, and you are their servants for my sake" (Doctrine and Covenants 90:8b). When two of Jesus' early followers argued among themselves about status, Jesus counseled, "Whoever wishes to be great among you must be your servant" (Matthew 20:27 NRSV).

Let us accept the challenge to be servant ministers in our world today. Congregations, families, and communities will be blessed as we demonstrate our commitment to the ministry of Jesus Christ.

SHEPHERDS
ABIDING
IN THE FIELD

Chapter 7

Overwhelmed with Compassion: Coping with Personal Needs Within the Congregation

Linda L. Booth

In this often crazy, scary world, compassion and hope may be hard to find. Occasionally, the sadness of life overwhelms us. To find comfort, we insulate ourselves from feeling others' hurts and pains. With our own burdens to bear, limited time, and scarce resources, we ignore or refuse to give compassionate support to those in need.

Let me tell you a true story about compassion and the hope it brings. About fifteen years ago on a freezing January morning, residents all over Olathe, Kansas, read or heard the horrifying news about the Duffield family. In the early morning hours while the mother, Carol, worked the night shift at the Olathe hospital, an intruder broke into their home where her husband and three children slept. He brutally beat her son, leaving him for dead. He killed her youngest daughter and kidnaped her oldest daughter. Three days later, the seventeen-year-old Duffield girl was found dead on the icy spillway of an Olathe lake.

Shock and horror spread across our secure, safe community. We asked, "How could this happen in our city?" As I lay in bed at night praying for the Duffield family, I wondered how a person could survive such a devastating tragedy and live a normal, productive life.

When our three active sons were growing up, it was not uncommon to take them to the emergency room. On a sultry, summer afternoon, our fourteen-year-old son, Ben, called me at work to say he thought he had broken his ankle. Because Ben had already broken several bones and become a "semi-expert" on the subject, I told him I'd be right home. I then called our orthopedic doctor who instructed me to take Ben to the emergency room to have his ankle X-rayed, and if it was broken, he would meet us there.

When we arrived at the emergency room, I knew a drama was unfolding. Later I learned that a teenager, with his younger brother and his brother's friend in the back seat, had pulled onto the highway in front of a heavy-construction vehicle. The younger boys died in the emergency room; the teenager was critically hurt.

As doctors and nurses ran from cubicle to cubicle, I watched a nurse with white hair comfort the parents and family who awaited word of their children. I saw her hold a disheveled father and a distraught grandmother in her arms as they sobbed. As I watched her compassionately care for those strangers, I knew I was witnessing the living Christ.

When the nurse came over to thank Ben for his patience and to tell us a doctor would soon help him, I looked at her name tag and read Carol Duffield.

Awed by the quality of her ministry and because I was the editor of a local newspaper, I called Carol for an interview. I wanted to understand how a woman who had lived through such anguish could place herself in a position to suffer with others.

Sitting at her kitchen table with the pictures of her three children on the wall behind her, Carol told me of the pain that nearly destroyed her and of depression's darkness. She also told me about a support group called The Compassionate Friends. Sitting in a circle with members of that group whose children had also died, Carol felt God's compassion as those people suffered for her. Because of that small band of caring people, Carol became whole and received hope.

In response to that gift, Carol goes to places where people hurt and shares in their brokenness, fear, confusion, and despair. Carol immerses herself in the painful condition of being human. As a result, her compassion brings hope to many people.

As congregations of Christ's followers, we are called like Carol to bear each other's burdens. Congregations experience hope when they seriously accept their mission to be as compassionate as Christ. As they reflect the living Christ to others, they become God's power in the world.

What is compassion?

Compassion is more than a general feeling of kindness. The word comes from two Latin words. When combined they mean "to suffer with." In Luke 6:36, Jesus calls each of us to be a compassionate person: "Be compassionate as your Father is compassionate."

Each of us has felt God's compassion. When is compassion most evident? Is it when someone gives advice? Perhaps. However, we more likely feel God's compassion in our moments of pain or suffering when someone is there for us, suffers with us, and helps us carry our burden.

Her name was Patricia. She was one of those church attenders who builds walls to keep people away. She was a professional woman, cool and aloof. On the surface, she seemed to have it together. But when you talked to her, you could sense she was troubled.

Then one day, she gave in. An older woman in our congregation kept inviting her to attend Wednesday night fellowship services, and she came. The love, warmth, and openness of those present touched her deeply. Later, she told me that something seemed to loosen within her heart, and she began to cry. Appalled at her vulnerability, Patricia stood up to escape the circle.

At that moment a young woman sitting across from her stood up, walked to her side, and held Patricia in her arms. The young woman simply said, "God loves you and is near." Patricia said that for the first time in her life she knew that was true because she could feel God's arms around her.

How to Be a Compassionate People

Sometimes we take for granted that compassion will flourish in our congregations. However, like faith, compassion doesn't just naturally happen. Compassion takes nurturing, encouragement, and commitment. People learn about compassion and are more likely to give compassion when they see and feel it lived out in the lives of their congregational leaders.

And just as congregational leaders make stewardship, Christian education, and worship plans, they need also to plan for ways to make God's compassion the cornerstone of their congregation's mission. For when a congregation responds to the individual needs of its members, those members are more able and willing to return that compassion to others in the congregation, as well as to go forth into their individual worlds, representing and sharing Christ's compassion.

The following suggestions will help your congregation live out its mission in compassionate ways.

1. Build relationships.

Building a caring family atmosphere takes more time than just meeting on Sunday mornings. It takes a plan created by your leadership team to provide opportunities for people to spend time together so they can get to know each other, care for one another, and then respond in compassionate ways. It also takes the commitment of many people who are sensitive to diverse needs and interests.

The following are just a few activities to help build relationships and strengthen your church family. Best results occur when monthly activities are well-planned, promoted, and everyone is encouraged to attend. It's also helpful to set aside, for example, the third Saturday night or the second Sunday afternoon of every month, so people can save those dates. These get-togethers provide opportunities to invite neighbors or assist community projects.

Gift and Talent Auction. Ask all ages to give a gift to be auctioned. A teenager can give a Saturday morning cleaning windows, or a retired woman an afternoon caring for small children. The money can be designated to go to the Red Cross, a community homeless shelter, or to assist a needy family. Most communities have professional auctioneers who are willing to donate their time and make the evening fun. Youth groups can earn money selling hot dogs, nachos, and drinks. The blessings of the Gift and Talent Auction continue long after the event—you get to know that teenager as he or she spends time with you cleaning windows, and the retired woman and the children in her care become more like "family."

Congregation Help Day. Check with local agencies, asking about needs they might have that your congregation could meet. For example, in our community Temporary Lodging for Children assists children in emergencies caused by neglect or abuse. Helping paint playground equipment or dorm rooms provides an opportunity to work side by side, get to know each other better, and help a worthy cause.

Fly a Kite. Spring provides a great excuse to make kites together and then fly them. Sometimes kites aren't easy to get up into the air. The blessings come as all ages work together to make sure everyone's kite is flying high.

Children's Day Picnics. A park or member's yard becomes dotted with blankets and conversation as church family members share food and good conversation. Games such as balloon toss and three-legged races unite all age groups.

Full-Field Softball. Everyone takes part in this ball game. Big and little people cover the field; no one is excluded. Some may choose to sit on the sidelines and cheer. Everyone becomes a winner in this noncompetitive affair. Laughter often outscores the runs.

Grand Birthday Party. Everyone's birthday is celebrated on one evening. In your fellowship room or eating area, people who share a birthday month sit together for a meal, complete with decorations and cake based on that month's theme. This is a great opportunity to get to know different people. Also, during the year designate someone to mail birthday cards to church family members.

2. Carry people in your heart.

My fondest childhood memory was spending the weekend at my grandparents' home. My grandmother made heavenly buttermilk pancakes, the kind that puffed up in the pan and melted in your mouth. One Saturday morning with the pancakes stacked on the plates, Grandmother told me to go tell Grandfather they were ready. I remember going outside, seeing Grandfather sitting in a lawn chair out under the pin oak tree, and running to him through the cool, green grass.

As I got closer, I knew something special was happening with Grandfather. He was sitting quietly, meditating. I went to his side and asked, "Grandfather, what are you doing?"

"I'm holding the people in my heart," he said.

I remember his words because as an imaginative child I pictured people sitting in his heart, side-by-side like on a school bus.

Today, I know what Grandfather meant as I carry people in my own heart. Those people I carry become my family. As I pray for them and think about them during the day, I grow to love them deeply.

Baron von Hugel wrote to his niece: "I wonder whether you realize a deep, great fact? That souls, all human souls, are interconnected, that we cannot only pray for each other but suffer for each other. Nothing is more real than this interconnection, this precious power put by God into the very heart of our infirmities."

As congregational leaders you can encourage this attitude of "carrying people in your heart" in many ways. I can promise you that when people pray for one another, they are changed and the congregation receives rich blessings. As we pray for one another, we become involved in each other's lives in new, powerful, and exciting ways.

Saturday Night Prayer. Ask several people to pray specifically and by name for people attending Sunday's service. Encourage presiders as part of their responsibilities to pray for those participating in the service and the congregation.

Sunday Morning Prayer Circle. List in your bulletin the opportunity to join others a few minutes before the service to pray that each person might know God's Spirit is near.

Share and Care. As part of Sunday worship, bring prayer concerns to the congregation's attention.

Prayer Chain. Have in place a calling tree, able to communicate emergency prayer concerns and make them a high priority in people's lives.

Spiritual Journey Classes. Make sure your church family, both children and adults, learns how to walk with Christ. Spiritual formation takes discipline and commitment. It's nearly impossible to be a compassionate people without the indwelling of the Spirit.

3. Accept and celebrate differences.

If we believe that each of us is created in God's image and understand that we all think and experience the Spirit in different ways, we can then encourage people to be their *real* selves. Too often, people come on Sunday mornings wearing masks. They disguise their thoughts and try to act like everyone else because they fear being shunned or excluded from the body if they are judged to be different.

As church leaders, value your people, respect their ideas even if you don't agree with them, and encourage tolerance. Provide opportunities, whether during church school classes or Sunday night chats, for a free exchange of ideas. Allow people to express their thoughts and spiritual experiences without feeling strange, weird, or even heretical. In a safe, caring atmosphere, mature together, even though the spiritual paths you might take are as diverse as the personalities God has created.

4. Value all gifts.

Your congregational home is more than a pit stop in the fast track of life. It is a place where people come to discover their gifts; where their gifts are nurtured and developed; where individual ministry is celebrated as a gift from God.

Every congregation is blessed with gifted people. Your challenge is to match gifts with church family needs. For example, there is a man in our congregation who senses his divine calling to greet people. I don't mean he just shakes people's hands and gives them a bulletin. By his attitude and concern, people know he loves them. As they see compassion in his eyes, they often tell him of the hardships they are facing. And just as frequently, his sensitivity alerts others to potential needs. Many children believe he *is* the pastor because his gift is to pastor people walking through the church halls who might normally fall through the cracks or be ignored.

Our congregational leaders value Ed's pastoring and depend on his compassionate nature to develop a sense of community in our church home. Every congregation has people of all ages like Ed, whose ministry isn't as visible as those standing up front to preside or preach. However, the Eds of our congregations hold our people together and minister in personal, transforming ways. Value and develop these quiet ministers.

5. Meet physical, emotional, and crisis needs.

As public relations and information director of a large school district, I attended a monthly crisis-management meeting. With nearly 19,000 students and 2,600 staff, our team wanted to be prepared for any emergency. Similarly, congregations can prepare themselves to meet the physical, emotional, and emergency needs of church family members.

Ministry Need Teams. As a leadership team, list all the emotional and physical needs that might be an issue in your congregation. Your list might include marriage problems, suicide, eating disorders, teenage conflicts, legal issues, hospital stays, drug or alcohol abuse, and difficult pregnancies. Then recruit people in your congregation to be trained and on call to handle these situations.

For example, in our congregation two women had difficulties in their pregnancies. A maternity nurse in our congregation gave them and their families emotional support and information. Another person in charge of pastoral care organized people to clean their homes, care for their children, and take in meals.

Mediation Teams. It is normal for church family members to disagree or hurt each other's feelings. Have in place a team of people, with ordained teachers and evangelists taking leadership roles, to help solve these problems before permanent damage is done to either person, or separation occurs.

This mediation team should be trained in the spiritual art of seeing with eyes of love. This doesn't mean to view life sentimentally through rose-colored glasses but to strive to understand both sides. Then help both sides experience a mutual compassion for each other. Buddhist monks call this practice "benevolent glancing," which means to train the eye to see with compassion. If two monks are fighting, they are brought together to resolve the conflict. Before they talk, they sit silently facing each other. Challenged to look into the heart of the other as if it were their own heart, they are forced to listen to the other's position and reach a compromise.

6. Give flesh to God.

Help each person in your congregation know that his or her mission is to be vessels of God's compassion, to make God real in others' lives.

There is a story in one of the *Chicken Soup for the Soul* books about a little girl named Sasha. When Sasha's parents brought her little brother home from the hospital, she began to ask them to be left alone with him. Because her parents were conscientious and had read that siblings could be jealous of new babies and shake, pinch, or hit them, her parents told her no. They did, however, include her in her baby brother's care. Sasha helped feed, bathe, and change his diapers. But this didn't seem to be enough. She continued to plead to be left alone with him.

So finally, because Sasha showed no signs of jealousy, her parents said she could. Sasha went into the nursery and closed the door. But because she was little, the door latch didn't catch. The door opened just wide enough for her curious parents to observe.

Sasha went to her brother's bed, and placing her head as close to him as she could she said, "Baby, tell me what God feels like. I'm beginning to forget."[1]

There are people in our congregations, homes, neighborhoods, and places of work and school who desperately need to know what God feels like. They desperately need to know they are not alone. You and your church family members may be the only ones who through compassionate care can share God's presence with others.

As communities of joy and God's people, we are called to be compassionate like Christ, to give flesh to the Spirit as we compassionately care for one another. As we take seriously this calling, hope will be alive and well in our congregations, expanding our mission and bringing others into Christ's compassionate fellowship.

Notes

1. Dan Millman, "Faci" as found in *Chicken Soup for the Soul: 101 Stories to Open the Heart and Rekindle the Spirit*, compilers Jack Canfield and Mark Victor Hansen (Deerfield Beach, Florida: Health Communications, 1993), 290.

SHEPHERDS
ABIDING
IN THE FIELD

Chapter 8
Talking Together about Difficult Matters

David Schaal

"And they lived happily ever after." I have always liked stories that ended that way, and based on the number of stories that do, I must not be alone. Perhaps these stories are popular because of our need to take a break from reality from time to time. Maybe they have appeal because they relate in some vicarious way to our personal fantasies. On a deeper level, though, I suspect that Loren Mead is correct when he says that we love the "happily ever after" stories because they preserve our dream of being in some sort of peaceful unity that endures.[1] The only problem, of course, is that the idea of living happily ever after in some undisturbed state of bliss is simply out of step with reality. Again quoting Mead (this time with his tongue firmly in his cheek):

> I wonder, for example, how Cinderella felt when the prince, now a 50-year old paunchy king, fell in love with a slip of a serving girl and ran off with her, or how the prodigal son felt after six months at home, plowing the back forty in the hot sun.[2]

Nevertheless, the idea of living in peace and harmony for any extended period draws at our hearts. It is also probably true that few organizations have a longer history of promoting the idea of peace and harmony than the world's religious communities. In fact, we often speak of the church as a fellowship wherein people can find the much needed peace of Christ. If the church, then, places such a premium on peace and harmony, does it not make sense that the church should be a place where people can come and find a reprieve from dealing with the difficult issues of our world? No, it does not.

This chapter deals with the reality that congregations will have conflict over difficult issues. Specifically, it is about the need to create environments where the congregation can discuss these issues effectively. We often call ourselves the family of God. If this is so, then we must acknowledge up front that healthy families play together, work together, worship together, and yes—have conflict together.

This chapter also affirms that conflict is not only unavoidable but has the potential to be a healthy source of great creativity, vision, and problem solving. The family of God has conflict, not always because something is wrong, but often because something is right.

Welcome to the family.

Why is dealing with difficult issues unavoidable in the church?

The answer to this question is found, at least in part, by examining our theology. At the heart of RLDS thought runs the Zionic vision which manifests itself in the affirmation that we are called to build community.

This includes the challenge to establish a fellowship together in which true community is lived out. To do so, we must wade in the waters of learning how to relate to one another in a more than superficial manner. Living in community means that we enter each other's lives, share each other's fears and hopes, and embrace one another as we are. This includes the likeable, easy-to-be-with portion of our being, as well as the shadowy, grumpy, not-so-nice aspects of our character. Moreover, we who are sisters and brothers in the faith are not cut from the same cloth in regard to our social, theological, or political values. Given all these things, it becomes apparent that living in community will *require* us to deal with difficult matters. The question is, will we do so honestly as fully human beings, or will we insist on wearing the masks that hide us from one another and present the illusion of perfection.

In addition to the foregoing, the church is not called to develop this sense of community by withdrawing from the world, but by engaging the world. As disciples of Jesus Christ, we should be found in the social, educational, economic, and political systems of our communities, nations, and planet. As congregations, it is unethical for us to reach out to others with the invitation of baptism if we are not equally concerned about the overall environment in which these people live out the majority of their lives. If we are serious about engaging our world redemptively with all of its variety, goodness, and sin, it becomes obvious that dealing with difficult matters is simply something the church cannot avoid. It is, in fact, what we do.

Why are difficult matters so difficult?

Issues may be difficult to deal with for many reasons. Some issues are difficult because solutions to pressing problems are simply hard to find, or require resources to which we do not have access. Sometimes they are difficult because we must make ourselves vulnerable to pain in order to address them. There are many reasons, but because this chapter has to do with talking about issues that may evoke conflict in the congregation, I want to focus on one reason in particular. That is, many issues are difficult for congregations to deal with because the issue itself threatens something we or someone else in the congregation values. What is more, the threat itself may never be consciously identified, even by the party feeling threatened. The following story is a good example.

I remember participating in a series of difficult congregational discussions about developing a worship program that addressed the needs of its members. As the first session began, it was apparent that the battle lines were clearly drawn between one group desiring to maintain a traditional form of worship and another group wishing for a greater variety of elements in the worship experience. When voicing their opinions on this subject, both groups quoted scripture, used religious language, and talked about the rationale behind their desires. Neither group, however, had yet been able to articulate what finally became apparent to those of us who were observers. Underneath all the logistics of their arguments, all parties were feeling personally threatened.

As later conversations confirmed, many in the more traditional group had found great meaning through the years in a particular set of symbols, styles, language, and music. This had provided an anchor during the stormy seasons of life, and was deeply cherished for its rich meaning. Changing the pattern of worship, for them, would be like losing an old friend, and it was a grief they did not want to bear.

The other group was threatened in a different way. They also loved the church but struggled to find ways to worship that contained language, styles, and music relevant to their lives and circumstances. The possibility of not changing the worship pattern of the congregation was a source of grief. This grief centered around the perception that the church they loved as children was becoming irrelevant to them as adults, and that too was a loss they did not wish to experience.

There are many types of difficult issues in the church. Some are theological, some are social, and some have to do with relationships. In each case, however, where a difficult matter is being addressed, it is a good idea for all parties concerned to examine the question: "What is being threatened?" Because we can really only answer this question for ourselves, it shall be dealt with later in the section on personal readiness. Still, we need to keep in mind that without our knowing it, any given issue may pose a threat to someone else. This is why difficult matters must be addressed rationally, and always with a pastoral heart.

So what do we do?

If difficult issues are unavoidable in the life of the church, it only makes sense that we should learn how to talk about them together. The remainder of this chapter is devoted to exploring three things that can help congregations talk together about difficult matters.

The Context of Community

I recall teaching a class of senior high students at a camp a few years ago in which the subject was sexuality. For five days in a row we met together and explored various matters related to sexuality, based on the questions the students wanted to have addressed. During the course of the class, a spirit of openness, trust, and sharing developed that was truly wonderful. On the last day I asked the class how many of them came from congregations where sexuality was ever discussed. Out of 240 students, seven hands were raised. I then asked how many of them could identify a minister back home with whom they would feel comfortable in discussing issues pertaining to their sexuality. Three hands were raised.

With obvious concern, I wanted to find out what it was about this camp that caused these young people to share their questions, observations, and concerns so openly, and why they were so hesitant to do so in their congregations. The answer, not surprisingly, had to do with the environment. There at camp they played together, worshiped together, socialized together, and were in classes and other groups where a conscious effort was being made to listen to everyone without condemnation and with genuine caring. In other words, they had established a sense of community.

It is this sense of community that we must foster as congregations if we are to talk together effectively about difficult issues. If we are truly going to open up to each other, we will need to feel safe in doing so. After all, if many issues are difficult because they threaten something we value, then honest dialogue demands from us at least a degree of vulnerability. This leads to a major probability—that is, we will not make ourselves vulnerable to those we do not know and trust. The opposite, of course, is that we will be more likely to self-reveal in those relationships where there is a high degree of trust. M. Scott Peck says this well:

> Vulnerability is a two way street. Community requires the ability to expose our wounds and weaknesses to our fellow creatures. It also requires the capacity to be affected by the wounds of others, to be wounded by their wounds....There is pain in our wounds. But even more important is the love that arises among us when we share.[3]

The point is this: Congregations will be able to talk about difficult issues more effectively if the congregation has fostered an adequate sense of community among its members. This includes personal trustworthiness, but goes beyond it to encompass the congregation's overall relational environment.

A while ago I was visiting with a small group of church members who were discussing their congregation's needs. One woman spoke up and said, "This congregation is made up of wonderful people. We just don't know each other." I found it to be an insightful observation.

It is one thing for the church to become a place where we routinely go for programs, classes, and worship. It is quite another, however, for us to experience the church as that place wherein meaningful relationships are built and lived out.

To be truly healthy, congregations need opportunities for its members to play together, do meaningful work together, socialize together, learn together, and worship together. Granted, this is no easy task, especially given the extremely busy lives people live, and there are many places wherein the traditional approaches to congregational social activity may no longer be effective. Yet the need is there to find relevant forms of play, work, socialization, and worship to help us become involved in each other's lives. This is best done when various demographic groups in the congregation are helped to create their own opportunities for socialization and learning (as opposed to congregational leaders attempting to come up with ideas that might appeal to these various groups).

There are some specific things we can do to talk about difficult matters effectively. If, however, the spirit of community is not being developed in the congregation, our actual talking about difficult issues will lack the trust, depth, and openness that is so vital for healthy dialogue.

Let's Talk

No matter what degree of community is established in the congregation, sooner or later difficult issues will arise that need to be discussed. It may be challenging to determine the best time to discuss a particular matter, but one thing is for sure: The time to talk about *how* we will discuss difficult matters is now.

In discussions with couples who are preparing for marriage, we always affirm there will be conflicts that will arise in their relationship. No couple can predict what all these conflicts will be, but couples can agree ahead of time about how they will choose to handle them when the conflicts arise. In doing so, they prepare themselves for dialogue, which is more effective than a simple knee-jerk approach where we immediately respond to conflict out of whatever state we are in at the time.

This principle holds true for congregations as well, but how do congregations actually get at it? One way is to design a special congregational activity specifically to discuss how to handle difficult issues when they arise. This can be a helpful process, and should include the following four considerations.

First, consider the environment for the meeting. Most people are unaccustomed to discussing difficult issues before one actually arises. Consequently, they may come to the activity with a bit of suspicion: "I wonder what issue is really lurking in the background?" With this in mind, the physical environment for the activity should be as celebrative as possible. Good lighting, refreshments, and balloons can send the message of meeting under conditions of hope and goodwill, rather than gathering to hassle over some particular conflict to be sprung on the group during the course of the meeting.

Second, the activity should be kept as informal as possible. It is not so much a program to present as it is a group of friends meeting to talk about their relationships.

Third, a portion of the time together should be spent discussing what it means to be a part of a faith community. This can be a good opportunity for people to share with one another what they value most about the fellowship of the church. It is also a good time to talk about why encountering difficult issues is unavoidable in the life of the church.

Fourth, the major focus of this activity should be on developing consensus as to how we will deal with difficult matters when they arise. The activity leader might present some guidelines for healthy, effective group discussion. Eight suggested guidelines are described below.

Number 1: Speak only for yourself. It is tempting to use terms such as "we" and "they" when discussing important matters. In healthy dialogue, though, we speak only for ourselves. I recall a heated conversation one morning at church in which one congregational officer stated that "the people" were upset about some things that had occurred recently. After pressing for more information, I discovered that "the people" in this case were this gentleman and his wife! We should not attempt to speak for others, nor should we assume what others are thinking.

Number 2: Everyone has the right to share his or her own point of view, or to disagree with someone else's. But no one has the right to call into question the motivation or integrity of anyone else.

Number 3: Never interrupt. Many of us were taught while growing up in our families and schools that interrupting was rude. It still is.

Number 4: Avoid unqualified generalizations. As children, we probably all attempted to seek our parents' permission at one time or another by saying, "But *everybody* else is doing it!" (In my house, that usually equated to a friend down the street who was busy using the same line on his parents.) *Never, always, everyone,* are words that typically distort reality and represent assumptions at best.

Number 5: Recognize that people will only know what we are thinking if we tell them. I remember receiving a scolding once from a member of the congregation who was upset that no one from church came to visit her in the hospital. "I'm sorry," I said, "I didn't realize you had been in the hospital. Who from the church did you tell?" She replied, "Nobody." We are not called to be mind readers. If we wish to make our feelings known, we should share them.

Number 6: No gossip or backbiting! The value of any meeting is greatly diminished if it is preceded or followed by people talking behind each other's back in ways that injure. Spreading gossip, criticizing others behind their backs, and attempting to "win" others to our way of thinking via behind-the-scenes campaign tactics is counterproductive to community building. Healthy congregations not only know how to talk about difficult matters, but when *and where* as well.

Number 7: All participants are valued equally. At a glance, this may sound like mushy sentiment. It is, however, a significant and not-so-obvious matter. Charles Cosgrove and Dennis Hatfield have written that people tend to replicate the family patterns they learned growing up and that current family systems influence how people relate to each other in congregational families.[4] They go on to suggest that in congregations, some people may think of themselves as *parents* (who believe authority should be deferred to them). Others may behave like *children* (who defer authority to others). Still others may behave like *independent children* (no one defers authority to them, but neither do they defer authority to others).[5] When the family of God comes together for dialogue, however, we need to acknowledge the equal worth of all present. This is difficult because congregational power systems are very real and people have been deferring authority to others for years. It is, nevertheless, something to work on.

Number 8: Listen first. We are typically so sure of our own point of view that our primary goal in dialogue is often to persuade, or to at least make sure that we are understood. In more mature relationships, though, our primary role in dialogue is to attempt to understand another person's point of view before we communicate our own. This does not mean we have to agree with it but that *we will put our agenda on hold until we understand where the other party is really coming from.* When this happens understanding is increased, conflict is reduced, and relationships are deepened.

After these eight guidelines have been presented and discussed, see if the congregation can mutually agree to use these guidelines to govern the way difficult issues are discussed when they arise. These guidelines should then be recorded and reviewed in the congregation from time to time. They can be written about in the congregational newsletter, and printed and practiced at leadership team meetings, priesthood meetings, etc. They could be presented to every new member of the congregation: "This is the way we deal with difficult matters in this congregation."

When a difficult matter does arise, these guidelines should be reviewed and everyone reminded that these will govern the way we talk about the issue at hand. Special emphasis should be made for guideline number 8, "Listen first," because this will be the easiest to forget in the heat of discussion. (Sometimes an issue is of such a nature that it is best to invite an outside facilitator to lead the discussion process. This can be an important option that should not be overlooked.)

This approach does not ensure that any difficult matter will be resolved easily (or even be resolved at all). It does, however, encourage the congregation to engage in genuinely helpful ways of relating to each other in processing difficult issues. Even with this, some individuals may choose to ignore these guidelines, and there will still be hard feelings, unchristian behavior, and self-centered motivations. However, as William Countryman has said, "God will be able to separate the good news in the church from the hypocrisy. We have to find ways to live the good out even in the context of a mixed reality."[6]

Personal Readiness

The fact you are taking the time to read this particular chapter indicates you have at least a degree of interest in how people can talk about difficult matters. While we may not be able to control how others approach debatable issues, we certainly can be intentional about developing a sense of readiness in our own lives. While there is much we can do in this regard, I suggest the following four ideas for personal readiness.

First, it is important to explore what our personal reaction tends to be in talking about difficult matters. Some may find conflict to be exhilarating, because of the dynamic and potential creativity that can occur. On the other hand, some may welcome conflict as a way to muscle their way over others or as an avenue to vent their anger. Others may avoid conflict at all costs, fearing the tension and hurt feelings that might result from it. Still others may see themselves as responsible for calming troubled waters and making sure that everything is OK with everybody. This latter group can be a blessing, but only if they understand that conflict is necessary and that people may have to experience a bit of pain before things can be OK. In other words, they need to be mature enough to avoid the temptation toward a "quick fix" approach to conflict resolution. A "kiss and make up" approach is short-lived at best and never really gets to the underlying issues.

With this in mind, it is important to ask ourselves: "When I become aware of the possibility of discussing an issue with people at church that may cause conflict, I tend to...." This question is important because knowing yourself is a vital aspect of engaging in conflict. Am I a person who looks forward to discussing difficult matters? Am I a person who dreads dialogue about difficult matters? What does my response tend to be?

Asking this question, however, is not enough. We also need to ask ourselves a companion question that, in many respects, is more difficult than the first. Once we articulate what our response to conflict tends to be, the next question is "Why?"

For example, I know a capable minister who appears to seek out conflict every chance she gets. From the time she was young, her life has been a litany of pain and emotional injury. While I cannot prove it, I suspect she has rarely had opportunity to truly grieve her losses with another caring person. Instead, her unresolved pain has caused her to be a bit stoic, and she tends to build walls between herself and others in an effort to protect herself. Consequently, others have, in turn, withdrawn from her. As the years have gone by, she has fallen out of practice, so to speak, in regard to warm, caring interpersonal behaviors. Still, her need for attention and emotional contact drives her to seek out interaction with others. Unfortunately, her approach to attention getting is through initiating conflict, which, to her, has become a security blanket of sorts. It guarantees her the attention she needs.

On the other hand, I have a friend who welcomes conflict for an entirely different reason. He grew up in a family in which conflict was either avoided or engaged in through screaming, yelling, and threats. He witnessed firsthand the inadequacy of these approaches, but through his work discovered the wonderful creativity that can result from conflict engaged in via healthy dialogue. He has learned the skills of discussing difficult matters and welcomes conflict as a means of healing and discovery.

All of us can identify individuals (perhaps ourselves) whose life history is such that they simply avoid conflict at all costs. The reasons for this are varied, ranging from childhood experiences to personal fatigue.

The point in all of this, however, is that we do ourselves a favor when we begin to understand why we behave the way we do in the face of talking about difficult issues. Once we know what has shaped us, we are in a better position to shape our future responses. Without so doing, we merely float into the future on the currents of our past.

A second suggestion for personal readiness has to do with practicing the principle of *listening first*, listed as guideline number 8 in the "Let's Talk" section of this chapter. One way to do this is to employ the following experiment with yourself.

Every week for one month, select a twenty-four-hour period in which you are going to be intentional about listening first. During this period, make the commitment that no matter what kind of discussion you are a party to, *you will not share your point of view until you thoroughly understand what the other party is saying and why they are saying it.*

Our desire to share an opinion, to offer helpful information, to make sure that we are understood is typically so strong that this little experiment will probably be more challenging than it sounds. In fact, even if you are a good listener you probably will be surprised at what you learn if you give this a try. Think for a minute about the various conversations that occur during a typical day. There is the conversation with a spouse about what color the new kitchen curtains should be. There is the conversation with a neighbor about how her favorite political candidate compares with yours. At work, there is the conversation with a coworker about how to best fix a broken piece of machinery, or how to best service a valued client. We engage in countless conversations every day that give us the opportunity to practice the skill of listening first.

This exercise is not meant to make every relationship an ongoing laboratory for experimentation. Neither is it to suggest that there is anything wrong with the good-natured bantering that goes on between friends. It is simply to suggest that intentionally experimenting with listening first for twenty-four hours, once each week for a month is a great way to learn an important skill that will only enrich our relationships. It also will help us to see how natural it is for most, if not all, of us to be more preoccupied with our own opinions than to truly work to understand another person. Try it for a month and see what you learn.

Here is one more suggestion regarding this experiment in listening first. It can be an excellent experience for a group (Sunday school class, leadership group, etc.) to agree to do this for a month, and then debrief their experiences together. Talking together about what was hard, what was easy, and what was learned can be helpful in cultivating the ground for discussing difficult issues in the future.

A third idea relative to personal readiness has to do with a rather difficult aspect of introspection. I have stated earlier that many matters are difficult because they threaten something we value. When such an issue for discussion comes along, we do well to ask ourselves, "What do I value that is threatened by talking about this matter?" Many times we (particularly men) will reject such a notion and brush aside the suggestion that such a threat exists. If nothing is threatened, though, why do we find the issue difficult?

I remember speaking with a friend once about an issue in her life she was needing to talk about but was avoiding. Her avoidance struck me as strange because she had the capacity to be a rather courageous soul, sometimes taking on challenges that would be difficult for anyone, and was rarely afraid to speak her mind. As we talked she began to tell me some things about her life and relationships with loved ones. In each relationship she described, she painted a picture of herself as a caregiver, a strong individual on whom others could lean. This, she said, was who she was supposed to be. In fact, she was told from the time she was little about her personal inner strength and of her capacity to be strong. Her parents praised her for this quality, as did others. The problem was that the issue she was avoiding was one she could not effectively discuss without exposing personal weakness and admitting her need for help. The issue, which seemed relatively commonplace to me, threatened her very identity. If she could not be strong and self-sufficient all the time, was she betraying who she was really to be? She had not yet learned to be fully human, and the threat was very real.

Not all difficult matters are so because of such long-standing life issues. Sometimes what is threatened is simply the relative peace we have been enjoying that we do not wish to have disturbed. Whatever the case may be, it is good to slow down just a bit before we go flying off into conversation or avoidance, and ask ourselves, Really, why is this a difficult matter for me?

One final suggestion regarding personal readiness. The culture that many of us live in is saturated with hurry, overcrowded schedules, and stress. Consequently, when difficult issues arise, we may discuss them with each other out of fatigue, hurry, and frustration. With this in mind, it is vital for us to cultivate a personal *center* of peace and stillness out of which we can draw strength. I do not recall who said it, but I remember someone referring to a particularly skilled teacher: "He is effective," this person said, "because he always teaches from the center, never the periphery." How easy it is to enter the fray of discussing difficult matters from the rush and distractions of the periphery. How important it is, though, to cultivate a quiet center within us, out of which can flow reason, calm reflection, and a more balanced perspective. The disciplines of meditation and contemplative prayer should be a daily part of the lives of those who would talk together about difficult matters. Without them, our personal readiness is incomplete.

Summing Things Up

We live in a culture where the *quick fix* is honored as a virtue. If television were our tutor, we would understand that there is hardly a problem that cannot be resolved in thirty or sixty minutes (although the really difficult ones may require up to seven days if the episode is to be *continued*). We know, however, that real life is not so. With this in mind, let us remember that talking effectively about difficult issues is not a matter of finding an easy formula. It is, however, a matter of creating a congregational environment wherein trust can be fostered and difficult matters discussed. To do so, I have suggested that we become intentional about building community, agree on eight specific guidelines to inform our discussion, and that we engage in four specific exercises in personal readiness.

At this point I should also say that these three suggestions are all ongoing and are not to be thought of in some essential sequence. For instance, some congregations are in great need of engaging in dialogue "right now" and do not have time to "build community first." If, however, they honor the eight guidelines in their discussion, pursue the process of community building, and engage in the disciplines of personal readiness, their sharing together is more likely to grow in depth and effectiveness through the years.

One final thought. Given that scripture plays a central role in church life, it is good to take a look at the scriptures in dealing with difficult issues. As we do, we notice something striking—that time and time again the great insights of the scriptures have come in response to humanity's wrestling with difficult issues.

In the tradition of scripture, the church, if it is faithful, will always be challenged to deal with difficult matters. It is simply what happens when we choose to care for one another and our world. If we do so creatively and in love, we have every reason to believe that divine insight will arise once again from our efforts, and we will learn even more about the blessing and challenge of establishing the kingdom of God in the places where we live.

Notes

1. Speed B. Leas, *Moving Your Church through Conflict* (Bethesda, Maryland: The Alban Institute, 1985), 5.
2. Ibid.
3. M. Scott Peck, *The Different Drum: Community Making and Peace* (New York: Simon and Schuster, 1987), 69–70.
4. Charles Cosgrove and Dennis Hatfield, *Church Conflicts: The Hidden Systems Behind the Fights* (Nashville, Tennessee: Abingdon Press, 1994), 12.
5. Ibid., 33–56.
6. L. William Countryman, *The Good News of Jesus: Reintroducing the Bible* (Valley Forge, Pennsylvania: Trinity Press International and Crowley Publications, 1993), 101.

SHEPHERDS
ABIDING
IN THE FIELD

Chapter 9

Peace Like a River:
Everyday Issues of Human Justice

John Billings

Footprints of Wisdom

From the earliest moments of recorded history through our present age people have been concerned about issues of human justice. Words of wisdom and insight have been recorded all through that history to provide footprints that might guide us along the way. Listen to a few of the voices speaking to us regarding issues of justice.

The author of Luke writes:

> The Spirit of the Lord is upon me, because he has anointed me to bring good news to the poor. He has sent me to proclaim release to the captives and recovering of sight to the blind, to set at liberty those who are oppressed, to proclaim the acceptable year of the Lord.—Luke 4:18-19 RSV

The Jewish tradition offers these words in the writings of the Talmud:

> Whoever can protest against the injustices of family, community, and the entire world but refrains from doing so, should be punished for the crimes of the family, community, and the whole world.[1]

The prophet Amos provides this admonition:

> Take away from me the noise of your songs; to the melody of your harps I will not listen. But let justice roll down like waters, and righteousness like an ever-flowing stream.—Amos 5:23-24 RSV

Martin Luther King Jr. writes: "True peace is not merely the absence of tension; it is the presence of justice."[2]

Pope Paul VI proposed: "If you want peace, work for justice."[3]

Cardinal Suenens in an address to the United Nations in 1963, made this statement: "Peace among peoples requires: Truth as its foundation, justice as its rule, love as its driving force, liberty as its atmosphere.[4]

Sam Keen provides this observation: "The powerful have always been willing to baptize the status quo and name it 'peace,' and the impotent are regularly accused of being troublemakers when all they seek is justice."[5]

J. Andrew Bolton, author of the Herald House book, *Restoring Persons in World Community*, writes: "The World Church is an international fellowship working for a global vision that calls us from our sins of parochialism and self-centeredness, to be accountable to each other for peace and justice."[6]

Footprints of such great significance, yet here we are, examining again, issues that have faced the people of our world for all of history. Will we, as people of faith, be left with the legacy, "I had the opportunity to make a difference, yet lost it as I turned my back on some of the very issues that call for our attention again today"?

Justice Claims Our Attention

When we turn our hearing to the prophetic voice of Micah, the centuries-old words ring loud and clear again: "He has told you, O mortal, what is good; and what does the Lord require of you but to do justice, and to love kindness, and to walk humbly with your God?" (Micah 6:8).

Walter Brueggemann proclaims that Micah 6:8 is "commonly recognized as a very peculiar and precious summary of the demands of God."[7] Brueggemann continues,

These expectations are not general norms, but they are specific expectations placed on God's covenant partner. In this well-known triad of expectations, it is no doubt important that the first element is to do justice. In biblical faith, the doing of justice is the primary expectation of God. Everything else by way of ethical norm and covenantal requirement drives from this, for God is indeed a "lover of justice" (Psalm 99:4). Israel is here commanded to attend to the very thing which God most values, namely justice.[8]

This command of God found in Micah is the foundation, the theology, that drives the claim for our attention to do justice.

Perceptions of Justice

There are many different ways to examine and perceive justice. Aristotle said, "Justice is rendering to each person his or her due."[9] Many voices suggest there is an essential connectedness between peace and justice and propose that for there to be peace in our world, the injustices that separate people must be eliminated. Yet other voices would say that justice lies in the controlling and authoritarian voice of those who should rule supreme.

A recent personal experience vividly portrays this contradiction in the perception of what justice really is. I had an incredible experience marching arm in arm with friends, black and white, at a recent birthday parade and celebration for Martin Luther King Jr. As we marched, the words "Keep the dream alive" were sung, chanted, and shouted while sharing in the hope of a peace and justice that brings people together on the basis of equality and the worth of all persons. A counter-gathering was taking place at the same time as our parade. The Ku Klux Klan was holding a rally for the justice they claim to be true.

My original plans had been to return home after the Martin Luther King Jr. parade and celebration. However, my path took me within a block of the KKK rally. So, having never been that close to a KKK gathering, I decided to see what was happening. What I witnessed was incredibly disturbing. I have never seen such hatred portrayed in the voices, language, and actions of people. It came from those representing the KKK and from many of those who gathered in opposition. It was hatred and violence promoting more hatred and violence.

The KKK was proclaiming a justice that from their eyes sees white supremacy, white control, and white dominance over people of color. It is a misdefined justice that diminishes self-determination, laughs in the face of the belief that all are equal and free in the Spirit of Jesus Christ. It is a justice that calls for hatred and intolerance rather than a justice based on peace, truth, love, and liberty. Even to speak of justice in this way seems terribly incongruent. It is true that those opposing the KKK also were party to words and actions of violence as well. This is not justice either. It is also a delinquent reaction to the KKK voices.

Let Justice Roll

Let me propose this principle from the Zoroastrian scriptures, the Zend-Avesta, as a basis for viewing justice:

> To enjoy the benefits of providence is wisdom; to enable others to enjoy them is virtue. Those who are indifferent to the welfare of others do not deserve to be called human. The best way to worship God is to ease the distress of the times and to improve the condition of humanity. This is true religion....[10]

This truly is justice. Justice from this perspective promotes the values that will help correct the many issues of human injustice that challenge us everyday.

Understanding Issues of Justice

In a recent conversation I approached a friend and colleague with this question, "What do you see as everyday issues of human injustice?" Scott shared many thoughts and experiences that were confronting his community and family. They may be similar to your own. They certainly rang true for my experiences as I have traveled through many of the large cities and smaller rural communities in Kentucky, Indiana, Illinois, and Missouri.

Scott spoke of racism and prejudice, recalling the church burnings, crosses burned on lawns, and swastikas painted on buildings. He spoke concerning the employment practices of businesses that discriminate against people of color, homosexuals, and others who are judged as "less than." He told me about an effort by a community group called P-FLAG (Parents and Friends of Lesbians and Gays) to promote some community dialogue regarding issues of homosexuality. They had hopes of curbing some of the hate crimes stemming from a spirit of prejudice and intolerance present in his community. He related that two national network-affiliate television stations refused to cooperate. They would not allow any public service time for this effort. Our conversation centered on issues relating to racism, poverty, intolerance (a societal and religious intolerance), and a rigid parochialism present in the community where he lives.

Scott also shared some of the good news from his area. "There are those trying to make a difference," he said. He talked about some congregational and community efforts to care for the hunger needs of children, provide clean running water for homes, shelter those without homes, and efforts to create an atmosphere of acceptance and tolerance rather than self-centeredness and hatred. He shared that the major religious faith groups in his area were coming together hoping to foster a better understanding of each other. They also hope that a result might be cooperation and partnership as they endeavor to care for community needs.

In your daily life, what are the everyday issues of human justice and injustice? Your experience and involvement in church and community will be your best resource for answering this question. At least that seems to be true for me.

I became more acutely aware that this was also true for people around the nation when I attended the "Call for Renewal" conference held in Washington, D.C., in February 1996. This conference was developed by religious leaders around the country concerned that our churches and individual members were not in touch with the realities of the justice issues within our communities. It was an effort to lay the foundations for a "new politics" rooted in spiritual values beyond the old categories of Right and Left. I came away from this conference with new insight to both the scope of justice and political issues that face each of us and the need for a renewed grassroots effort in our churches and communities to respond in positive ways to these issues.

What are the everyday issues of human justice?

Is there one particular list that is best for our consideration? If so, which list: yours, mine, or that of my low-income neighbor in the city? In the list that follows are World Conference resolutions that have been approved over the past twelve years. These resolutions provide a window into the thinking and concerns of many church members around the world. They represent quite well everyday issues of human justice.

1986

Domestic Violence
Human Rights Committee
Apartheid

1988

Racism
Ministry to Persons with AIDS/ARC
Health Ministries
Day of Prayer and Fasting for Peace

111

1990

Urban Ministries Task Force
Stewardship of Ecology
Towards More Environmentally Sound Practices
Our Common Future—A Sustainable Global Perspective
Temple Ministries for Peace and Justice

1992

Peace Promotion
Earth Stewardship Committee
Human Diversity
Our Pursuit of Peace
Interfaith Organizations
International Human Rights Award for Service to Humanity
Apartheid in South Africa
Peace in El Salvador
Children's Advocacy

1994

Pursuit of Peace and Reconciliation
Older Adult Ministries
Exploratory Peace Committee

1996

Nurture of Children

The World Church also has several working committees addressing many of the issues raised in the above list of resolutions:

World Church Committees

Earth Stewardship
Human Rights
World Hunger
Peace
Race and Ethnicity
Human Sexuality

From the list of resolutions and World Church committees it is evident that issues of justice appear to focus on peace, human rights, the environment, poverty and hunger, health concerns, ministry to children and older adults, domestic violence, racism, and urban ministry.

A Closer View of the Issues

Realizing that this is a broad scope of justice issues which confront us each day, how do we give a face to such concerns? Indeed this is vitally important. As the old saying goes, "That's where the tire hits the road." The answer lies with you and with me as we become involved with the issues listed. All these matters remain only a list unless we become concerned enough to venture into our neighborhood or community through opportunities of service and action. Then and only then will these issues become personal.

Principles Regarding Issues of Justice

What can we do in our communities and families to bring justice into our everyday world? First, there must be some foundational principles and values that guide any action we might take.

Realizing that any list is likely to be incomplete, I wish to offer the following collection of principles I believe are important as a guide for the challenges we face each day and for the action we might take as individuals, churches, and community groups. These principles are grounded in a tradition of religious and social teaching.

The Worth and Dignity of All Persons

This certainly has been a principle promoted by the Reorganized Church of Jesus Christ of Latter Day Saints. We actively sing hymns like: "Help Us Accept Each Other"; "This Is My Song"; "In Christ There Is No East or West"; and "The Cause Of Zion Summons Us." The words of each of these hymns call us to claim the dignity and worth of all people. We have an active statement on human diversity (WCR 1226) on the books. This statement affirms human worth and calls for the celebration of the rich diversity of human life.

Human Rights and Responsibilities

In 1984 the World Conference delegates passed WCR 1184, saying:

> [W]e affirm that all persons have essential rights, including the right to peaceful assembly, free speech, specific cultural identities and self-determination, the formation of intentional mutually cooperative human communities, freedom from fear and threats to personal safety and well-being, and the right to fulfill personal potential through continued growth and development."[11]

The statement also calls the church membership to "support those organizations and movements which specifically work to secure the human rights of those whose rights are being violated."[12]

113

The Call to Values in Community and Family

We have heard the statement recently, "It takes a village to raise a child." This statement clearly promotes the ideal of family and community joining in partnership to care for the needs of our communities. The mission statement of the Reorganized Church of Jesus Christ of Latter Day Saints also lifts up this principle in these selected words:

> The purpose of the Reorganized Church of Jesus Christ is to help families and congregations develop the likeness of Christ in each person.... We embrace an unconditional love for all and seek with them a faithful relationship with God.

This principle is also emphasized in our shorter mission statement: "We proclaim Jesus Christ and promote communities of joy, hope, love, and peace."

Improve the Lives of Poor Children and Their Families

The RLDS community is challenged to ensure dignity and care for poor children and their families. For those within the scope of welfare reform in the United States, the focus of reform should be on the issue of reducing poverty and dependency. This point calls us to the task of strengthening family life, protecting the dignity of human life, preserving a safety net for the most vulnerable, and encouraging partnerships within the public and private sectors of our communities. This task may be applied to our outreach to poor children and their families throughout the world.

Togetherness with Others in Our World

The hymn "The Love of God" (*Hymns of the Saints*, No. 107), offers a clear description concerning the conditions of disunity we have in our world: "There are walls that keep us all divided; we fence each other in with hate and war. Fear is the bricks and mortar of our prison, our pride of self the prison coat we wear." The RLDS Church is called to be an example and promoter of the principle that we are one human family despite differences of culture, race, economic condition, gender, age, sexual orientation, and mental or physical disability. Loving our neighbors, both far and near, is the challenge of those hoping to promote communities of joy, hope, love, and peace.

Personal Commitment to the Issues of Justice

I have several posters on my office walls. They remind me about where my priorities should lie as I try to remain true to being a person of faith.

- "Ways to Make Kids Count"
- "Brothers and Sisters of Mine Are the Hungry"
- "Peace Works"
- "AIDS. It's About Life"
- "How Can You Buy and Sell the Earth?"
- "Diversity"

I also have a personal mission statement that helps guide my life. It says:

> As a person of faith, I believe I am called to love my family and my neighbors, to share God's abundance—especially with the "least of these" my sisters and brothers who are hungry, poor, lonely, or hurting—and to seek peace and justice for a better world. I believe faith calls me to have compassion, requires action, and that acts of charity must be linked with the search for justice.

So what? Words on a poster, a personal mission statement, a list of issues are only words. Moreover, they will remain just words unless I become an active part of those religious and community organizations that are working to bring resolution to the issues of human justice. The same is true for you.

What do your posters say? What does your personal mission statement say? Then, most importantly, what part of the community is calling for your attention? What part of your life are you giving to address these everyday issues of human justice?

Are we a church of justice?

The continuing challenge to be a church of justice, to be a "prophetic neighbor," [13] is not an abstract ideal for us, but an urgent task for the Reorganized Church. We certainly face many important issues. We have been blessed with extraordinary opportunities, resources, and strength. We have accomplished much together as the church has responded to the issues of justice around the world. Yet the summons continues. We are confronted with important decisions as to the appropriate response to urgent everyday issues of human justice. Who will we be in this search for justice?

Will we be in the forefront of the endeavors to create a world of justice? Or will we leave the legacy, "I had the opportunity to make a difference, yet lost it as I turned my back on the everyday issues that call for our attention?"

- Will we respond to the haunting needs of defenseless children in our communities?

- Can the Reorganized Church impact the need to bring together in partnership the strengths within our communities to confront poverty and dependency?
- How can we partner with others to combat continuing prejudice and discrimination, overcome divisions among people, and heal the open wounds of racism?
- How can we support the tradition of family, as well as value the relationships within different family systems that provide moral roles and opportunities of self-determination?

Can the Reorganized Church join with others as they challenge the systems of government that appear set on balancing budgets on the backs of the poor? Who will ensure that all people have real opportunities for decent education, housing, and health care?

Will we be able to pursue the values of justice and peace in a world often branded by violence and human rights violations?

Will the Reorganized Church resist the temptation to withhold leadership from the very ministries that can move us forward in our response to issues of social action and justice?

Will we make the necessary appointments that ensure our presence at the tables of decision and action around this nation and around the planet?[14]

Will the Reorganized Church speak out for the voiceless in our lands?

Will the Reorganized Church be true to its claim to be disciples of Christ? Will we be true to the mission of Jesus as it is given to us in his reading of Isaiah 61:

> The spirit of the Lord God is upon me, because the Lord has anointed me to bring good tidings to the afflicted; he has sent me to bind up the broken-hearted, to proclaim liberty to the captives, and the opening of the prison to those who are bound; to proclaim the year of the Lord's favor.
> —Isaiah 61:1–2 RSV

The cry for renewal of our communities is before us. The task is at hand. Yes, our task is for "modest proposals,"[15] meaning taking those everyday steps that will make a difference. Yet at times there must also be extreme responses that carry us to far-reaching consequences of social action and justice, maybe even to a healing of people and a healing of our land.

Two final thoughts: From the words of Israel A. Smith, "It is yet day when all can work. The night will come when for many of my people opportunity to assist will have passed" (Doctrine and Covenants 142:5b). And from Dorothy Day, cofounder of Catholic Workers, "No one has a right to sit down and feel hopeless. There's too much work to do."[16]

Notes

1. Steven Scholl, ed., *The Peace Bible: Words from the Great Traditions* (Los Angeles: Kalimat Press, 1986), 62.
2. Ibid., 66.
3. Carrie Leadingham, Joann E. Moschella, and Hilary M. Vartanian, *Peace Prayers: Meditations, Affirmations, Invocations, Poems, and Prayers for Peace* (San Francisco: Harper San Francisco, 1991), 77.
4. Scholl, 66.
5. Leadingham et al., 130.
6. J. Andrew Bolton, *Restoring Persons in World Community* (Independence, Missouri: Herald House, 1986), 107.
7. Walter Brueggemann, Sharon Parks, and Thomas H. Broome, *To Act Justly, Love Tenderly, Walk Humbly: An Agenda for Ministers* (New York: Paulist Press, 1986), 5.
8. Ibid., 5.
9. Robert McAfee Brown, *Unexpected News: Reading the Bible with Third World Eyes* (Philadelphia: Westminster Press, 1984), 70.
10. Scholl, 64.
11. *Rules and Resolutions, 1990 Edition* (Independence, Missouri: Herald House), 85.
12. Ibid.
13. Helen Bruch Pearson, "The Church and Social Action: Justice or Just Us?" in *Theology: Justice or Just Us?*, ed. Richard A. Brown (Independence, Missouri: Graceland/Park Press, 1996), 20.
14. Ibid., 22.
15. Ibid., 23.
16. Dorothy Day, source of reference unknown.

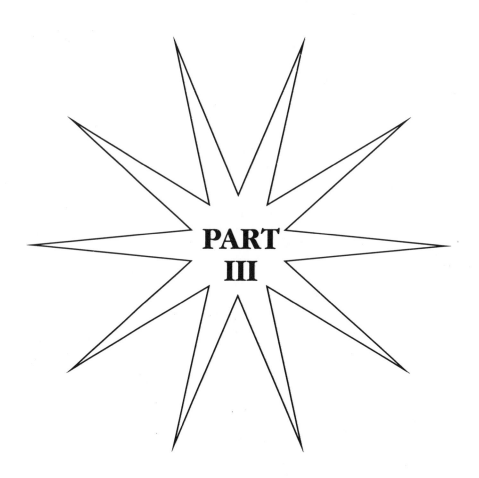

PART III

The Celebration of Pastoral Leadership

SHEPHERDS
ABIDING
IN THE FIELD

Chapter 10

From Balloons to Tears:
Achieving Balance in Worship

Mary Jacks Dynes

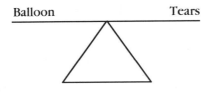

My dad died January 4, 1996. Scattered about taped on the surface of his desk for several years before he died were various 3x5" cards on which he had written "Inexplicable Joy!" In the moments I shared with him seated at his desk during the Christmas before he died, he tried to explain to me just what those words, "Inexplicable Joy," meant to him. The joy that was difficult or impossible to account for happened in the times Dad had experienced God and had felt the presence of the Divine in his life. These instances took place many times in worship as well as other moments throughout his life. At the time Dad seemed to want to really emphasize to me that experiencing and encountering God was what worship was all about. The source of this inexplicable joy came from encountering God in worship.

Maybe what Dad had in mind is similar to what Paul Lynd Escamilla expresses when he says that "worship gives us a window upon joy. It is the joy of our complete reconciliation with God and creation."[1] This joy of reconciliation and "at-one-ness" was what Dad experienced.

Most certainly Dad emphasized that joy was not the absence of sorrow, for there was pain and sorrow in his life. Joy for him was, rather, the recognition of God's presence and the love emanating from that experience no matter how unworthy Dad felt. This is what worship is all about—our encounter with God.

In interviewing individuals who have left the Christian church, William D. Hendricks found that they expressed a need to meet God in worship. Ultimately people go to church because they hope to find God there.[2] If this is the case, we should look at our worship services and try to meet this primary need of those who come. To make this encounter happen, then, worship needs to be focused on God as experienced in the life of Jesus Christ. And it needs to be faithful to our best understandings of the gospel.

Because diverse people come to worship and desire to encounter God and Christ, each brings a unique self with a variety of needs. And so for vital worship to happen for a variety of people, balance needs to be addressed. Vital worship is intimately related to balance.

Because individuals worship in their own way, we have spent many years emphasizing the need for worship to touch each person, if not all in one service, then over the span of a few services. That's why we don't promote having separate worship services for children. We have said that we are all a church family and should all worship together. Our free-form style of worship encourages this with the result being a balance in all segments of worship between: innovative and traditional, contemporary and historical, celebrative and reflective, transcendent and immanent. Even the elements of worship should reflect this balance between: participation and observation; silence and sound; standing and sitting or kneeling; use of children/youth and adults; the verbal and nonverbal; movement and stillness; worship leaders and congregation; priesthood and laity; word and sacrament. The list could go on and on.[3]

Several years ago two colleagues and I attempted to put a service together that would be innovative and Spirit-led. Being new at worship planning, we were stunned after the experience because the service did not meet our expectations, nor was it a moment when the worshipers met God. I remember how disappointed we were. Yet when I look back at the experience, I realize that there was not much of a balance. To achieve this balance, good planning and preparation are vital.

Peter Judd, former director of the Temple Worship Center, points out that even though we plan, the results of our efforts are often unpredictable. Nevertheless careful attention to the planning task does pay off in most cases, and a thoughtful, conscientious approach to planning a service generally will provide the kind of setting where people who have come prepared and expectant will indeed have a meaningful encounter with the Divine.[4]

This encounter with the Divine could be considered the focus of all our planning. If we were to go on and express the balance of various facets, this encounter with God could be expressed as the fulcrum. The fulcrum is the point or support on which the balance takes place. Without the fulcrum there would be no balance. Without God and Christ, there would not be worship. Encounter with God as expressed in the life of Jesus Christ or the gospel is the central support from which all planning for worship takes place. If the beam is out of balance Christ, God, and the gospel will not be the center of our worship. If one side is too heavy the fulcrum will not be in the center.[5]

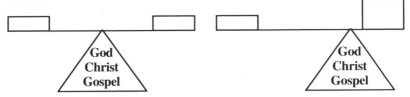

There are three major beams that need to be balanced, with one having three minor beams, that rest on the fulcrum of the gospel of Jesus Christ. As these are presented, study the character of your congregation's worship services by using these beams to review what is going well and what needs to be strengthened. On analysis you may see things you need to strengthen and change. Many times worship leaders have made changes in worship with the best of intentions without any thought about the consequences of the changes being instituted. It is my hope that these examples can help you find your way to a more revitalized and healthy worship life.

In *Ministry and Imagination* Urban Holmes III suggests two facets of experience essential to the vital spiritual life of a community.[6] One of these facets represents the secure elements of our worship that communicate assurance, order, clear definition, dependability, and things under control. Having a bulletin every Sunday gives a sense of structure. Singing well-known hymns also gives us that sense of control. Liturgical forms such as the baptismal statement, the Lord's prayer, the prayers of blessing on the bread and wine, the prescribed marriage covenant, and a similar order of worship each Sunday give worshipers a sense of continuity. Each congregation also has unique worship forms it has developed over the years that are important to them. Forms help establish community by creating church family traditions, so valuable for people whose present situations change by the minute. Adapting Holmes's insight, Thomas H. Troeger and Carol Doran call these elements the "structure"—the ordering and defining characteristics of our worship.[7]

Beam #1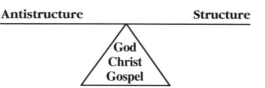

On the other end of the beam are the more elusive, mysterious, and uncontrolled aspects of worship where resides a richness of meaning and a depth of feeling that words cannot express. This is the awe that we experience at the celebration of a sacrament or when hearing music. These elements draw us, as Troeger and Doran explain, to the "antistructure" and remind us that no matter how satisfying the "structure" is for order and control, the God we worship is far greater than any of our established forms.[8]

Both antistructure and structure are essential to vital worship in our congregations. Healthy, meaningful worship is a continual interweaving of both these elements. We need a certain amount of form in our worship together. At the same time, we also need to feel engaged by the elusive mystery of the living Spirit of God. There must be a movement back and forth between antistructure and structure: personal communion and group experience, feeling and thinking, Spirit and word, ambiguity and certainty, spontaneous and in the bulletin, abyss and familiar ground, story and doctrine, insight and principle.[9]

This balance was pointed out to me so very well at the Central Illinois District reunion at Brush Creek recently. An eight-year-old boy whom I didn't know came up to me and shared that he really liked the stories that I had told. I was impressed with his forthrightness and genuineness, especially when I asked his folks if they had coached him to tell me. Their answer in the negative emphasized to me the importance of this balance between structure and antistructure, and how stories seem to offset doctrine and principle in capturing this balance.

The balance of these two elements, antistructure and structure, should be reviewed by worship planners. By analyzing several services using past worship bulletins, I found that it may be possible to discern the rhythm of worship and to assess whether one element has dominated or excluded the other. Many times when I was presiding, I gave instructions that were not necessary, because they were quite clear in the bulletin. This intruded into the sense of prayerful worship in the congregation. Other times, as presider, I needed to help the congregation understand just what they were to do, because it appeared to be unclear. It is a matter of balance.

Troeger and Doran stress that if such needless chatter is dispensed with, generally there will be a greater sense of antistructure. The structure will still be present in the order of service and established customs of the congregation. But by not focusing attention on the ordering elements of worship, the congregation can be led to the boundary of mystery and wonder.[10]

Beam #2

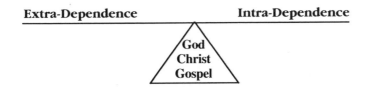

Extra-Dependence   Intra-Dependence

God
Christ
Gospel

Another beam to be balanced is that of extra-dependence and intra-dependence. Just as before, in worship it is important to move back and forth between these poles.

Most adults are intra-dependent, that is, dependent on themselves, in control, responsible, taking care of themselves and others. Intra-dependence is quite demanding, and so humans must move out of that role from time to time. In these moments we need to receive instead of give, to surrender control instead of taking control—in other words, become "extra-dependent" and depend on others.

During worship each congregation invites people to become dependent on God and Christ. When worship is vital, those in the congregation are renewed by the experience of extra-dependence so they can return to their daily lives and take responsibility for using the gifts God has given them.[11]

Let us return to my example as the presider giving intrusive instructions. When this happened, the worship process became tightly controlled and never moved into a state of extra-dependence on God. Possibly a sense of boredom set in as worship became just one more intra-dependent activity and worshipers ceased to expect an encounter with God.[12]

Yet opposite problems also must be avoided. Too much extra-dependence can lead us to avoid taking responsibility for our lives. Also, worship can become nothing more than an escape from a life that seems too overwhelming. Both pitfalls point to the issue of relevancy. We come to worship to encounter God and to gain a sense of the holy. Yet we also must be equipped to apply what we experience to daily living. Leaving church, we should feel empowered for witness. This is the point at which a congregation's worship feeds its life as a community and its mission to the world.[13]

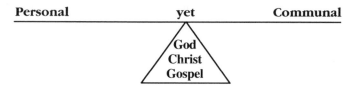

| Personal | yet | Communal |

Vital worship balances needs for both privacy and community within human nature. Worship needs to be structured so there is time for personal reflection and expression. Yet we cannot emphasize the personal at the expense of the communal because we are individuals within community. A balance between the two must be found.

To be communal, worship should provide opportunities for shared expressions of faith. Responsive readings, skits, dramatizations of the scripture reading, and acting out the children's moment in mime are a few examples. If a skit or dramatization could be done as a group with each group member giving his or her personal testimony, both the personal and the communal dimensions would occur.

Another meaningful way to provide an experience that is personal yet communal is through the use of an item as a focal point. Nails on Good Friday, a hymn sung together, a responsive reading where individuals fill in their own responses, and a candle that each person holds and then blows out together can provide a touch of both the personal and the communal. Repeating the Communion prayers after the presider reads them is another way to make the Lord's Supper more personal yet corporate. The focal point brings everyone together in community and also provides that needed personal dimension to worship.[14]

In *Exit Interviews*, William Hendricks points out that one of the common desires expressed by worshipers is not for more entertainment but for more participation in worship services.[15] Wise leaders will provide worship experiences that are both personal yet communal.

To be relevant, vital worship needs to be emotional yet instructional. Apostle Paul, referring to speaking in tongues, explains that emotional expressions of the Spirit are not beneficial to the larger group when emotion gets in the way of understanding (see I Corinthians 14).

The heart in Old Testament times included the whole being—the intellectual and the emotional.[16] We need both and they must be in balance. The cognitive, intellectual, or instructional is important, yet can become routine and stagnant if we overlook the emotional impact worship also can have. If worship is alive, there will be an emotional residue left behind to intermingle with the cognitive and allow us to see in new ways how we are to live our lives after we leave the doors of the sanctuary. It is as if during worship the spotlight has shown on some aspect of our life that we have seen but never really examined, and we walk away a different person. We have been impacted and changed.

On the other end of the balance beam is the instructional dimension. Oftentimes the worshiper is brought to tears, but the act of wor-

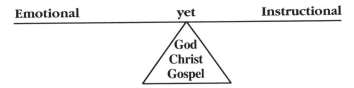

ship has no effect on everyday life. Worship that is emotional and also instructional is other-centered and points toward service instead of being an end in itself. Richard Schowalter notes that to achieve this balance there is usually very little to change. Emotion must not merely be directed inward, but toward the outside world where there is an opportunity to live out the challenge of the worship experience. Balanced worship sees the outside world as an opportunity for the worship experience to be completed, not as an unwanted intrusion into sacredness. We distort worship's true significance when emotion does not lead us out into the world as a positive expression of the love of Christ.[17]

Stories can capture this balance of the emotional and the instructional leading out into the world. Telling stories of real-life experiences, whether personal or otherwise, emphasizes the instructional and puts an exclamation mark on the emotional. Many times I have had children with their honesty and forthrightness ask out loud if the story I was telling was true. It was as if the truthfulness made the instructional more emphatic. One time after a service in which I shared a story about a wolf, I met Andrew with his mom at the grocery store. He said he just had to stay in the service and not go to children's church. Normally children left after the children's moment. I had displayed a picture of a wolf and had mentioned before the children left that I would be telling a story about a wolf. Because the story had captured him so much emotionally, he had to tell me.

Inspiration is often emotional. But everything that is emotional is not always inspiring. Inspirational worship often uses symbols to elicit emotional responses. Even though our experience with God or Jesus

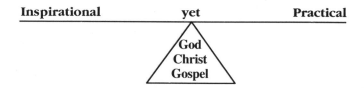

Christ cannot be quantified, the experience of the Divine is most often an experience of symbols. Symbols point beyond themselves. Although the presence of the Holy One cannot be seen, the essence of symbols is that they point us to the reality of God as an experienced hope. So symbols point us to the reality of hope in Jesus Christ because they point us to what cannot be seen. Therefore congregational worship that utilizes symbols is a patient, waiting style of worship filled with hope and expectancy.[18]

I am reminded of the candles representing God and Christ that were used at the opening worship experience during Renaissance Week at Graceland College in February 1996 when John Billings and I were guest ministers. The candle was a symbol of God's presence that touched our spirits and brought us into a relationship with the God we could not see. Testimonies were shared of how God had brought light into the darkness and warmth into the coldness of each life. The symbol of the burning light allowed the worshiper to experience the reality of God in many of God's attributes in a physical and tangible way.

Our scriptures are rich in symbols that have the potential to be used to invite a sense of the spiritual into our congregational worship. The waters of baptism and the bread and wine of Communion are obvious spiritual symbols. Many times we take the symbolism for granted, and we need to explore more meaningful ways to express these symbols. As Doctrine and Covenants 158:11c reminds us, we should look to the sacraments to enrich the spiritual life of the body.

Other sources for inspiring practical spirituality are music and prayer. Music is symbolism for our ears and can lift our spirits, speak to our emotions, and give information to our minds that we can take home with us. Prayer also can bring about the power of spirituality and yet be practical in worship. Having a moment for concerns where several people offer prayer for those in need promotes these aspects of worship. Prayer request cards and a time of silent prayer are also ideas to enhance inspiring, practical spirituality.

The more the senses of seeing, smelling, tasting, touching, and hearing are involved, the more vital the worship will be. The sacraments are good examples of how the senses are used to bring about a powerful impact in the lives of the people. When we become aware of

Beam #3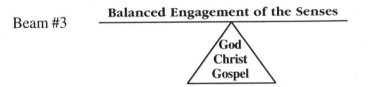

this fact, we can use the sacraments more effectively in our worship services. Tactile experiences need to be incorporated more in our worship. I will never forget the impact of sprinkling water on "my friends" as I shared what living water has come to mean to me and how I want to share this with those I love. First of all, there was the sound of moving water as my hand dipped into it and the element of surprise as I lifted up the water and went around the room sprinkling "my friends." They saw, heard, and touched while absorbing in a very powerful way what I was trying to say. The more the senses are involved the more the people of God are worshiping.

Having taught for twenty-six years, I became very aware of the science known as "neurolinguistic programming" or NLP. This science suggests that individuals receive and interpret messages three different ways: visually, audibly, and kinesthetically. Even though each person operates in all three modes at one time or another, usually one dominant mode stands out for each individual. Just as I once tried to use this knowledge to become a more effective Spanish teacher, I also think this awareness will enhance and enliven our worship.

Richard Foster points out: "God calls for worship that involves our whole being. The body, mind, spirit, and emotions should all be laid on the altar of worship. Often we have forgotten that worship should include the body as well as the spirit."[19] After our closing worship at MAST '96, which centered on the theme "Casting Our Net," we went out of the chapel and formed a net with our arms outstretched to each other. This captured the interconnection between each of us, the sense of community, and the call for us all to cast our net of discipleship into the deep. In a physical and tangible way this activity emphasized, by the positions of our bodies, what we had heard and expressed the entire weekend. This action put the final exclamation point on the weekend!

These are a few ideas on how to achieve balance in worship. By no means are they complete. One thing is clear: as John 8:3 reminds us, the Spirit blows as it will. To feel the fresh wind of the Spirit blowing through our congregations would make all the extra preparation and planning worthwhile. Worship doesn't just happen. A balanced worship, which is the result of extra effort, greatly increases the chances of opening windows to the Spirit.

As a little girl I often played with members of my family among the tall redwoods along the Pacific Ocean shores in northern California at Prairie Creek Campgrounds. As we strolled, we came across a river that fed into the ocean. Later we camped alongside the creek which led into the river. Traveling up the creek I asked my dad where the creek began. He replied that usually a creek starts with a spring or is the runoff from snowfall high in the mountains. I remember wondering where one began and the other ended. The ocean is the spring and the spring is the ocean. As Toreger and Doran remind us, tradition is like that—the source is the flow, the flow is in the source.

Congregational worship may take new forms and in doing so change the shape of the culture through which it runs. At the same time it is changed by that culture, yet the taste of its originating spring is the same. This taste is the persistent need of the heart to break forth in prayer and song for the joy of being in the presence of the Divine and to give thanks and praise for what God has done for us in Christ. But when we stop only at the ancient wells of inspiration or settle farther down the creek with the words and music of our own time, we reduce tradition to a still and stagnant pond.

Healthy, vital congregational worship is always in touch with tradition and openness to new things, from the spring to the ocean, from the past to the present. We must travel the whole river from the spring to the ocean and back. We must open the windows to the Spirit.[20] We must maintain balance in our worship. In doing so we will find joy. *Inexplicable Joy!*

Notes

1. Paul Lynd Escamilla, "Sometimes Bigger Than All of Us: *Koinonia*, Fruitfulness, and Joy in the Worship of God," *Weavings* (July/August 1995): 30.

2. William D. Hendricks, *Exit Interviews: Revealing Stories of Why People Are Leaving the Church* (Chicago: Moody Press, 1993), 282.

3. These thoughts were taken from notes and conversation with Eileen Terril in the Temple Worship Center office.

4. Peter A. Judd, *Worship in a Diverse Culture* (Independence, Missouri: Herald House, 1995), 97-98.

5. I am grateful to Jack Hedal, bishop of Seattle Stake and the Pacific Northwest Region, for his idea of the balance beam and fulcrum.

6. See Urban Holmes III, *Ministry and Imagination* (New York: Seabury Press, 1981).

7. Thomas H. Troeger and Carol Doran, *Trouble at the Table: Gathering the Tribes for Worship* (Nashville, Tennessee: Abingdon, 1992), 94.

8. Ibid., 95.

9. Ibid., 101.

10. Ibid., 98-100.

11. Ibid., 101.

12. Ibid., 102.

13. Ibid., 102-103.

14. Richard P. Schowalter, *Igniting a New Generation of Believers* (Nashville, Tennessee: Abingdon, 1995), 81-82.

15. Hendricks, 260.

16. Paul J. Achtemeier, ed., *Harper's Bible Dictionary* (San Francisco: Harper San Francisco, 1985), 377.

17. Schowalter, 85-86.

18. Ibid., 86.

19. Richard J. Foster, *Celebration of Discipline: The Path to Spiritual Growth* (San Francisco: Harper San Francisco, 1978), 147.

20. Troeger and Doran, 135-136.

SHEPHERDS
ABIDING
IN THE FIELD

Chapter 11

Bear Witness of the Hope of the Gospel

Stephen M. Veazey

"Uphold me according unto thy word, that I may live; and let me not be ashamed of my hope."—Psalm 119:116

The "lively hope" of the New Testament saints was apparent and evoked questions. In light of this, the followers of Jesus Christ were admonished to "...be ready always to give an answer with meekness and fear to every man that asketh of you a reason for the hope that is in you" (I Peter 3:15). This scripture challenges disciples of all ages to be ready and willing to share clear witness of the hope of the gospel when evangelistic opportunities present themselves.

My basic testimony is that the gospel of Jesus Christ generates and sustains hope in my life. The gospel enables me to live beyond the confines and struggles of present circumstances in "earnest expectation" of the fulfillment of God's purposes in my life and in creation. This foundation of hope is very important to me because I, like you, live in a time when anxiety, insecurity, and despair are rampant. I strongly suspect that without the hope of the gospel, I would easily slip under the waves of cynicism, disillusionment, and gloom that overcome so many people today.

Frankly, I do not fully understand all the reasons why the gospel has this "hope effect" in my life. Many aspects of hope remain a mystery to me, beyond my ability to fully comprehend or explain. In fact, I believe that in the final analysis hope can only be seen as a gift of the Spirit that comes through the grace of God. However, as I reflect on the meaning of the gospel, my own experience with it, and the experiences of others, I can identify some reasons for the hope that lives in me and motivates me to engage in the mission of the church.

Hope for This Life

Wherefore, if a man have faith, he must have hope; for without faith there cannot be any hope.—Moroni 7:48

I believe the affirmations and principles of the gospel are an effectual source of hope for those who accept them and faithfully apply them to their lives. The basic tone and content of Jesus Christ's message and ministry reveal the love and concern of God for those who are discouraged, marginalized, and experiencing other forms of physical and spiritual suffering which drain hope from life. Through acts of purposeful presence, compassion, healing, and insightful teaching, Jesus revealed the divine perspective on human worth and the possibility for new life through repentance, forgiveness, healing, and reconciliation. Christ's death and resurrection present dramatic evidence of God's love and eternal purposes for humankind. Those who embrace the precepts of the gospel today find new beginnings, spiritual growth, increased capacity to love others, and hope for their lives.

I recently visited a young family who found hope through the basic tenets of the gospel. During our visit they recounted their story of coming to the "edge" of despair through a series of unfortunate life reversals, including job loss and impending bankruptcy. The stress and isolation they experienced were almost unbearable and caused them to wonder whether there was any hope for them and their children.

After moving to a different area in an attempt to find employment, they were drawn into the fellowship of a small-group ministry sponsored by the church as part of a church planting project. Through sensitive, caring relationships, relevant scripture study, sincere testimony of God's love, and practical financial help grounded in stewardship principles, they were, as they put it, "saved." As we discussed their experience, it became clear to me that they were not using the term "saved" in the usual sense. They meant that they had been "saved" in the present tense from hopelessness, despair, and near fragmentation of their family.

Near the end of our visit, the husband announced his decision to follow his wife in baptism. His countenance radiated with joy and hope. He and his family had found new lives and a hopeful future through the basic principles of the gospel and the caring ministries of the church. Because of experiences such as this, I am convinced that the basic principles of the gospel are an effectual source of hope for those who embrace them.

The core of the "good news" is that the future, in terms of the direction and quality of one's life, does not necessarily have to be a continuation of the past. That is a message of hope. Once you have seen the life-transforming impact of that message in the lives of people, there is no doubt that evangelistic ministry is worth every ounce of the time, energy, and resources we can possibly offer.

Hope Not for This Life Only

[B]ut the gift of God is eternal life through Jesus Christ our Lord.—Romans 6:23

Many people fear death as the end of life. Lack of belief in the possibility of eternal life often leads to a sense of anxiety, despair, and hopelessness. As a result, some choose to live for the moment only, absorbed in self-gratifying pursuits without any thought given to the long-range consequences of their behavior. For others, the imposing shadow of death mocks investment in causes that will not likely find fulfillment in their lifetimes.

The gospel presents a dramatically different perspective on the nature and potential of life. The apostle Paul highlighted this aspect of the gospel when he wrote, "If in this life only we have hope in Christ, we are of all men most miserable" (I Corinthians 15:19). In the scriptural context, the apostle was presenting his witness of the resurrection of Christ as a "reason" for having faith in our own eventual resurrection and eternal life. The testimony found in I Peter that God has "begotten us again unto a lively hope by the resurrection of Jesus Christ from the dead" (I Peter 1:3) echoes this central theme of the gospel as proclaimed by the New Testament church.

Faith in the resurrection of Christ gives rise to the understanding that there is more to life than mortal existence. A central theme of the gospel is the opportunity afforded people to develop lives of growing character that find fulfillment in the eternal realm of God's creation. While we cannot fully comprehend this lasting dimension of life, we can live in hopeful assurance of it as we grow in response to God's love. By choosing to live hopeful lives of increasing faithfulness and responsiveness to God, the principle of resurrection begins to work in us in the present, raising us to new levels of purposeful living.

The hope-instilling impact of the principles of resurrection and eternal life was impressed on me during the few hours preceding my grandmother's death. As I slept fitfully, waiting word of the outcome of her heart surgery, I awoke with a sense of calm assurance that God conserves and renews life in the eternal realms of creation. Though I was deeply saddened by the news a few hours later that she had died early that morning, and struggled to find the words to tell my grandfather, I found hope in the assurance that life continued in dimensions beyond the reach of physical death. I am aware of many others whose faith and hope have been sustained by similar insights and experiences.

It is important for me to state that I do not believe that my hope for eternal life is just a welcome balm in times of grief or an antidote to nagging anxiety regarding my mortality. Rather it is an expression of my openness to a future that includes the fulfillment of individual being in God. And, if the fulfillment of individual being is to embody the kind of Christlike love that loses itself in serving others—as the gospel clearly teaches—then I express my hope in eternal life by growing in love and service to God and others in the present.

Hope regarding eternal life is an important aspect of proclaiming the gospel in an age when cynicism and doubt hold many captive. While interest in this topic should not lead to unwise speculation regarding the details of eternal life, a message of hope "not for this life only" is an important facet of our witness to people struggling to understand the nature of death and the meaning of life.

Hope for the World

And God shall wipe away all tears from their eyes; and there shall be no more death, neither sorrow, nor crying, neither shall there be any more pain, for the former things are passed away.... Behold, I make all things new.—Revelation 21:4-5

Conditions in the world today can lead quickly to the conclusion that the future of humankind and the planet earth is not too promising. We appear locked in accelerating cycles of poverty, disease, and violence that threaten a majority of the world's population. Racial, ethnic, and regional conflicts are on the rise. Shortsighted consumption of natural resources and pollution of our environment move us toward exceeding the "carrying capacity" of the earth. Beyond this, we are conscious of the destruction that can be released in an instant through the horrors of nuclear and biological weapons. Our common future hangs in jeopardy. Is there any real basis for hope for the world?

Beyond the individual implications of the gospel, there is a faith perspective on the ultimate future of creation that provides a basis for hope, responsible living, and involvement in efforts to make the world a better place to live. The Christian faith is undergirded by a belief that humankind and creation are destined to find their consummation in God because God will ultimately triumph over all that seems to threaten the future. This view of the end toward which creation moves offers assurance that death and destruction will not have the final word, but that a "new creation" of peace, wholeness, and balance—the kingdom of God—is coming into being even now. In fact, a major theme of Jesus' message was that people can experience the kingdom of God in the present as they embrace God's will and live out the values and hope of the kingdom in their daily lives.

Several years ago I had an experience that brought new insight to my understanding of this aspect of the gospel. I was having deep struggles arising from a difficult situation in which I could see no good resolution. I became bogged down in anxiety about the future and mulling over "worst case scenarios." I became stuck in fear and pessimism.

During a time of meditation and prayer a phrase from a sermon that I had heard a decade before came to mind and bored its way into the very core of my consciousness. The phrase was: "Live as if what will be already is." At the same time I sensed that the future, while possibly difficult and challenging, was not to be feared. I also understood that the encouragement to "live as if what will be already is" was not just referring to a particular situation, but that it was the perspective a person of faith should have all the time. Disciples of Jesus Christ, grounded in the meaning of his life, death, and resurrection, should live in the present as people of resilient hope who sense the nearness of the kingdom and express their confidence in that future by living the vision of the kingdom now.

When such determined and far-reaching hope is taken seriously, passive surrender to fear, suffering, or despair is not a viable option. Commitment to the hope and vision of the coming kingdom of God challenges disciples to seek ways to participate with God in bringing the kingdom to fuller expression in their time. While there may be some situations that are so difficult or overwhelming as to present no real options for response, hope may still be expressed as an "active waiting" for new options to emerge in due time.

> Waiting, in the Christian context, is not merely "waiting around," for want of something better to do to pass the time. Rather it is the active, receptive attitude that allows the maturing of the situation, the development of the appropriate resource, or the strengthening of the self until the time is ripe. The hoper realizes that time is often needed to outlast the opposition, consolidate its gains, or cultivate the gifts appropriate to the task.[1]

Obviously, this kind of hopefulness should not be confused with apocalyptic views of the "end of time" that await a violent destruction of creation from which the "pure and righteous" will be spared. That view leads all too easily to attitudes of escapism and spiritual elitism that avoid responsibility for transforming the world in anticipation that one will soon be leaving the world and that the world will be annihilated anyway.

Restoration theology affirms that the earth is the primary locus of God's creative, reconciling, and redemptive activity. The "great and marvelous work" is essentially the call extended to each generation to go into the world to partner with God to bring forth divine purposes, including actively proclaiming the hope of the gospel to the "ends of the world" (Doctrine and Covenants 1:4) and seeking "to bring forth and establish the cause of Zion" (Doctrine and Covenants 6:3).

The "cause of Zion" is a powerful symbol of hope in our movement. It challenges us to engage in community-building ministries that evidence our commitment to the realization of God's kingdom on earth. Application of Zionic principles moves us squarely into the world to address conditions that are contrary to God's will for peace and justice for all people.

Furthermore, adherence to a doctrine of "continuing revelation" simply does not allow us to sit idly by with the assumption that it is "all but over" and that there is nothing we can really do to impact the future. In fact, recent revelation to the church calls the Saints to become even more actively involved in witnessing and peacemaking pursuits, not to sit back and wait for the end of the world.

I recently read some comments made by Sojourner Truth, a nineteenth-century African-American social activist, to an assembly of churchgoers who were anxiously awaiting escape from the "impending" destruction of the world. Her comments reflect a kind of hope-based commitment to involvement in ministry with Christ that challenges and inspires:

> Hear, Hear! ...Here you are, talking about being changed in the twinkling of an eye. If the Lord should come, He'd change you to nothing, for there is nothing in you. You seem to be expecting to go to some parlor way up somewhere, and when the wicked have been burnt, you are coming back to walk in triumph over their ashes—this is to be your new Jerusalem. Now I can't see anything so very nice in that, coming back to such a mess as that will be, a world covered with the ashes of the wicked! If the Lord comes and burns—as you say He will—I am not going away; I am going to stay here and *stand the fire*, like Shadrack, Meshach, and Abednego! And Jesus will walk with me through the fire, and keep me from harm. No, I shall remain.[2]

The desire and determination to "remain to minister" with Christ in the midst of suffering and despair is the epitome of what it means to me to be a Latter Day Saint.

Ministries devoted to individual and societal transformation that reflect hope for the future based on a vision of God's coming kingdom are urgently needed in a time when many wonder whether hope for the future is possible. In fact, a compelling vision of a hopeful future, coupled with opportunities to actually become involved in ministries of compassion, witnessing, and peacemaking, may prove to be very attractive to a number of people who desire to recover hope and make a difference with their lives.

Communities of Hope

> If we claim that the gospel offers hope to the world, we must offer a living witness to that reality. The church lives out its call most fully when it is a community of faith with arms around a community of pain.[3]

The various strains of hope outlined above come together for me in the fellowship and ministries of congregations of the church that embody and reveal the hope of the gospel. Ironically, the greatest evidence of the church's capacity to be an agent of hope typically comes from people who appear to have the least reason for hope.

What does the gospel really have to say to people who suffer in conditions of abject poverty, hunger, disease, and oppression? It is easy to lay claim to the hope of the gospel when one is relatively well-off with access to food, shelter, medicine, and opportunities to pursue personal development. But what is the source of hope for those who do not have such blessings?

That question recently pressed me with new intensity when I was visiting a small village in Honduras. Having been asked to preach that night, and being very much aware of the hardships facing those who would be present, I questioned what I could share that would bring any real hope to their lives. In the depths of my struggle, as I wrestled with the essence of the gospel, I came to understand that my calling in that place was not what I could say, but it was to be "as fully present as possible" with the people in the circumstances of their lives.

The people gathered for worship, having walked for many miles in a light rain. They greeted us with hospitality and openness that transcended language and cultural differences. They began singing spirited songs of praise and thanksgiving to God. Then they shared testimonies of God's love in their lives. I was surprised and deeply moved by the strong spirit of joy and hope that permeated the congregation. What was the source and reason for this hope in the midst of suffering? The event was the opportunity to be together. But the source, I came to understand, was awareness of the presence of the living Christ in the loving relationships of that community of faith. The assurance that one does not suffer alone—which would be the ultimate form of isolation and reason for despair—and the awareness that Christ truly has companionship with the poor and sick, is a precious source of hope beyond words.

I received a gift from the people of Honduras that night. It was a deep appreciation for the calling of congregations of the church to serve as "communities of hope" in a world of suffering. I believe that we experienced the presence of the risen Christ and a "foretaste" of the kingdom of God in that experience of worship and deeply caring fellowship. That glimpse of divine presence and possibility for the future brought assurance and encouragement. Being in that community left me with more than good memories; it actually enlivened hope in me.

Hope grows in the presence of hope. Hope needs the experience of Christ-centered community to thrive and grow. Throughout my life I have been nurtured and blessed by congregations of the church that have revealed, affirmed, and enfleshed the hope of the gospel. Because I have found the church to be a community that instills and sustains hope in the face of the difficulties of life, I want to invite others to share in that community also. To do otherwise is to keep for myself that for which others desperately yearn.

Hope to Action

Because of the despair that is rampant in the world, I view my faith-rooted hope as a blessing from God. That awareness is the primary motivation for me to share the gospel with others. If I have received the source of "lively hope" through the grace of God in the fellowship of the church, the only way I can genuinely respond to that blessing is to share witness of the hope of the gospel with others.

Recent revelation to the church indicates that we are in an unusually opportune time to share witness of the gospel with those who have yet to respond. Doctrine and Covenants 153:9 asserts that God's Spirit is moving to open the lives of many people to receive the gospel and the ministries of the church. Section 154:7a states: "If you will move out in faith and confidence to proclaim my gospel my Spirit will empower you and there will be many who respond, even in places and ways which do not now seem clear." In recent words of counsel to the church encouragement is given to be "courageous and visionary, believing in the power of just a few vibrant witnesses to transform the world."[4]

The evident action of God's Spirit to prompt, guide, and support missionary ministry through the church is an indication of the continuing movement of God to fulfill the purposes of creation. Awareness that "God is reaching out even now," and that "a few vibrant witnesses" can make all the difference in the world, is as sure a reason for hope and increased evangelistic activity as any I can imagine.

Notes

1. Geoffrey F. Spencer, *A Brightness of Hope* (Independence, Missouri: Herald House, 1996), 73.
2. Pamela Cooper-White, "Women and Conflict," *The Living Pulpit* (July–September 1994): 45.
3. John M. Perkins, "The Authentic Church," *The Other Side* (September–October 1993): 46.
4. W. Grant McMurray, statement to the closing session of World Conference on Sunday, April 21, 1996. For the full text see the *Saints Herald* 143, no. 5 (June 1996): 8.

SHEPHERDS
ABIDING
IN THE FIELD

Chapter 12

Celebration of the Simple

Barbara Howard

Centuries ago, the prophet Micah spoke to the issue of injustice and God's punishment of the people for their lack of compassion for those in need. His description of the people of his time clearly describes the futility of our own modern consumerism:

> You shall eat, but not be satisfied, and there shall be hunger in your inward parts; you shall put away, but not save....You shall sow, but not reap; you shall tread olives, but not anoint yourselves with oil; you shall tread grapes, but not drink wine. —Micah 6:14–15 RSV

In 1854 Henry David Thoreau wrote the following counsel, echoing Micah:

> Our life is frittered away by detail.... Simplicity, simplicity, simplicity! I say, let your affairs be as two or three, and not a hundred or a thousand.... Why should we live with such hurry and waste of life? We are determined to be starved before we are hungry.[1]

In a humorous monologue describing his life in New York City, Garrison Keillor comments on Thoreau's call to simplicity by observing wryly, "But Thoreau didn't live in a New York City co-op apartment and have to worry about plumbing."

Keillor catches up the frustration many people experience in these last years of the twentieth century. Life seems dreadfully complex. It is easier to develop theories about simplicity; it is difficult to live simply.

In an attempt to order their chaotic lives and perhaps simplify schedules, many people use a daily "organizer," their activities prioritized, sometimes to the minute. One of our friends began work for a firm and during her first week attended workshops on how to use her daily planner. "I didn't think I would ever want one," she said. "Now, if I lost it, I'd be desperate. It makes life so much easier." The planner helps her keep her extremely busy life under control.

But at times, my friend said, woefully, "The organizer controls me." To embrace simplicity, then, is not always simple. Strange, isn't it? A desire to have less, to be free from a stress-related life which accompanies acquisitiveness can be complex. Simplicity may mean a conscious effort to change radically the way we think and live.

Simplicity as a lifestyle is countercultural. It defies the economic systems of developed countries. It may require a new way of looking at life and faith, and could entail risk. But in some instances, it is a life-and-death decision.

Emblazoned on one of our grandson's t-shirts is the admonition, "Live simply, so that others may simply live." The greedy consumption of the latter part of the twentieth century is juxtaposed against the hunger and suffering of millions who starve and live in abject poverty. Simply living for some is not an option. The bare essentials of life are denied them. Their lives are founded on complex social systems that contribute to their deprivation.

Compassion alone does not change those systems. But compassion is essential. So, where does the compassionate Christian begin?

One place might be to engage in the practice of simplicity, for centuries considered one of the classic spiritual disciplines. Yet, of all the disciplines, it is most subject to misinterpretation and dismissal. Richard Foster suggests that it is easy to oversimplify simplicity itself. Simplicity cannot "function independently of the rest of Christian devotion," Foster writes. It is "the most outward of all the Spiritual Disciplines and therefore the most susceptible to corruption and the greatest corruption is to isolate it."[2]

One way of isolating the discipline is to talk and write about it, rather than making one specific change. The rhetoric of change is easier than acting out change. It is much easier to talk about (even to write about) simplicity than to practice the discipline. But the doing is the living. I am not what I speak or write; I am what I do. And so, I begin at whatever point I can to reorder my hectic life.

Sometimes when I am preparing a meal, I will have several things going on at once. This can be disastrous. I love to cook, and in order to have the joy of celebrating the beauty of the food, it is imperative to do one task at a time. I can then savor the flavors, the fragrance, the sheer beauty of the vegetables or fruits. When I come to the meal, having communed with the creator of the food itself, the meal is different. When our children were small, "harried" and "frenetic" seem weak terms to describe the chaos of meal preparation. I wanted to blame this on the size of our family and our schedule. The real source of the chaos was in me, however. In recent years I've learned to simplify what we eat and to enjoy the preparation. Cooking is sacramental to me at this stage of my life. It is a small step, but a way of changing behavior. Theodore Rosak gives me encouragement:

> Even if one only goes a few steps out of the mainstream to redesign some small piece of one's life.... It is a sign...that something better is possible, something that does not have to await the attention of experts but begins here and now with you and me. In changing one's life one may not intend to change the world; but there is never any telling how far the power of imaginative example travels.[3]

To continue to redesign, we begin with a new way of looking at our world. Rather than compartmentalizing each segment and spending a great deal of energy trying to keep all those compartments in balance, another way of living is to see God in every aspect of life, and the entire world as a whole, under the love and compassion of a constantly creating God.

In this holistic world what we have understood as contradiction can be seen as paradox. These parts of life that appear to be in conflict will, instead, be understood as working together. For instance, if life is a continuum, with poverty at one end of the spectrum and wealth at the other, and these are fixed positions—as some present-day economists suggest—then the poor would, by definition, be poor in every aspect of their lives and the wealthy, rich in all of life. As Foster points out, "Paradoxes...are only apparent contradictions, not real ones. Their truth is often discovered by maintaining a tension between two opposite lines of teaching."[4] One need only look at the spiritually impoverished people in wealth and the deeply spiritual folk in poverty to see the paradox. Not all wealthy are spiritually impoverished, nor are all poor people deeply spiritual, but the truth is that wealth and poverty are related to much more than economic status.

Poverty/Wealth

Matthew, Mark, and Luke describe an encounter between Jesus and one of the "ruling class" who wanted to be sure of eternal life. He assured Jesus that he had kept all the commandments since he was quite young. When Jesus heard this, he counseled the man to sell all his possessions and distribute his wealth to the poor. Then he invited the man to follow him. In each account of the story, the man turns away, saddened by Jesus' commission.[6]

In Hermann Clementz's classic painting of this account, the German artist portrays the encounter in a portico, beyond which is a street where poverty and want await relief. The painting illustrates the conflict of the young man who holds closely to his brocaded robe, both hands closed. The face of Jesus invites the young ruler to consider his choice.

The greatest sadness in this story is the young man's bondage to his possessions which rob him of the freedom to follow Jesus. He does not own his wealth; it owns him. Neither poverty nor wealth are virtuous. Both can imprison. Jesus defined freedom: "Where your heart is, there also is your treasure." We choose our treasure. A story from India helps me understand Jesus' words:

> The Sannyasi had reached the outskirts of the village and settled down under a tree for the night when a villager came running up to him and said, "The stone! The stone! Give me the precious stone!"
>
> "What stone?" asked the Sannyasi.
>
> "Last night the Lord Shiva appeared to me in a dream," said the villager, "and told me that if I went to the outskirts of the village at dusk, I should find a Sannyasi who would give me a precious stone that would make me rich forever."
>
> The Sannyasi rummaged in his bag and pulled out a stone. "He probably meant this one," he said, as he handed the stone over to the villager. "I found it on a forest path some days ago. You can certainly have it."
>
> The man gazed at the stone in wonder. It was a diamond, probably the largest diamond in the whole world, for it was as large as a person's head.
>
> He took the diamond and walked away. All night he tossed about in bed, unable to sleep. Next day at the crack of dawn he went to Sannyasi and said, "Give me the wealth that makes it possible for you to give this diamond away so easily."[6]

I need to hold this concept of freedom in my mind. My idea of wealth is to be surrounded by books. When I was a child my favorite place in the world was the local library. Dick and I courted in used book stores, and I ended up—joy of all joys—working for a publishing house for most of my adult life. At Herald House, I would walk through the press room just to smell the printer's ink. I delight in the way words look on paper. I enjoy the variety and feel of books, and many books have enriched my understanding of God, others, and myself. As any bibliophile knows, getting rid of books is traumatic. So, here I am, surrounded by stacks of books, writing a chapter on simplicity. I read about the Desert Fathers, about St. Francis of Assisi, and ask myself, "But where did they keep their books?"

We moved to Georgia in 1995, and for months it seemed as though my life was absorbed by concern about possessions, particularly our books. What to keep; what to throw away? I did a poor job of paring down, and now facing another move in a year or so, I have begun to sort through countless boxes of books to see which ones can be given away. My hands, holding some volume by a favorite author, resemble the hands in Clemenz's depiction of the rich young ruler.

Then, in the quiet of the night I discover my true treasure: The forest behind our house is filled with large oaks and dogwood trees. Nearly every night the moonlight shines off the leaves and shimmers through our bedroom window onto the walls where we have our display of family photographs. Sometimes when I awaken in the night I can hear the soft, regular breathing of my sleeping husband beside me; the moonlight illumines the photos of the faces of our children across the room; I begin my gratitude ritual and the faces of others—beloved friends beyond my immediate family circle—fill my mind. In this quiet moment I sense the inexplicable wonder of God's love. I am rich beyond words. If my beloved books were destroyed, if there were nothing but this moment, I would be richer than I could ever deserve. I stay very still. Keep this moment in your mind, I say. Remember this, and you will not want. This is your treasure; here is your heart's desire.

Wealth or poverty is not measured in monetary terms alone, but certainly money is one of the complexities of our modern life. Richard Foster writes that we can learn from the monastic and the Puritan response to money. The monastic orders, such as the Franciscans, "renounced possessions in order to learn detachment." They can teach us, says Foster:

> We need to hear their word today: we who love greed more than we love the gospel, we who live in fear, and not in trust. We need to hear their word today: We who define people in terms of their net worth, we who push and shove to gain an ever larger piece of the consumer pie.

Foster, however, writes that the Puritan response to money is seen in their emphasis on industry. For the Puritans, their work was an expression of their spiritual life. They, too, can teach us, says Foster:

We need to hear their word today: we who find work meaningless and dull, we who are tempted by sloth and laziness. We need to hear their word today, we who are workaholics, who take multiple jobs in order to move up the economic ladder.

Then Foster recommends a vow beyond that of poverty or industry:

> It must be a vow that will reject the modern mania for wealth without a morbid asceticism. It must be a vow that calls us to use money without serving money. It must be a vow that brings money into obedience to the will and ways of God.[7]

Secular/Sacred

Richard Foster's challenge underscores the Restoration principle that "all things are spiritual" (Doctrine and Covenants 28:9a).

Joseph Smith Jr. spoke to the privatistic age of Jacksonian democracy and called for people to live out the gospel imperatives in every aspect of life. There was nothing in life that was outside of God's concern. This Restoration principle reminds us that in the midst of our frenetic lives, we are called to discover God, to find the divine presence in every moment. Annie Dillard describes such a discovery:

> One day I was walking along Tinker Creek thinking of nothing at all and I saw...the backyard cedar where the mourning doves roost charged and transfigured, each cell buzzing with flame.... It was less like seeing than being the first time seen, knocked breathless by a powerful glance....I had been my whole life a bell, and never knew it until at that moment I was lifted and struck.[8]

Dillard's experience in that Virginia forest reminds me that God will speak to us whenever we are willing to listen. Not only in nature, but in all creation.

Modern science has shown us that everything in the universe is connected. In an IMAX film at the National Air and Space Museum in Washington, D.C., a viewer may see the interrelationship of the entire cosmos—from the inside of an atom to the edges of space. God the Creator interpenetrates all worlds "without end."

If I want to simplify my life, one place to begin is to listen and look for God in the ordinary moments of my everyday life. I will need to develop other disciplines if I want to do this. I will need time for quiet: silence. When Jesus went into the wilderness, it was not to escape responsibility.[9] The time there freed Jesus to draw from the divinely placed inner well of power.

The human Jesus was also the divine Christ. This secular carpenter was Godself. Jesus experienced the wilderness as a sacred temple—a place "charged and transfigured" as a revelatory site.

Some Bible scholars focus on Satan's role in the wilderness, but others define this event as a time of definition for Jesus. Here, in the wilderness, Jesus chooses, owns, his source of power, and defines himself.

My need for clear insight about my calling draws me to wilderness places where I discover that what I seek, seeks me. That all my life, I, too, have been "a bell, and now I am lifted and struck."

Giving/Receiving

In Helen Keller's book *My Religion*, she describes the power when Annie Sullivan spelled the word "water" into her hand and pumped the water into a cup in her hand: "All at once there was a strange stir within me—a misty consciousness, a sense of something remembered." Once cut off from communication and now open to a new world, this child wanted to receive. But the more she received, the deeper was her commitment to sharing. Keller learned the inestimable joy of giving. Her blindness became a gift to others. "When I review my life," she wrote, "it seems to me that my most precious obligations are to those whom I have never seen."[10] Keller's life exemplifies the giving/receiving principle. All communication requires a giver and a receiver. In loving relationships, each person is both.

If I am living in the spirit of openness and love, everyone who touches my life brings me a gift. The gift may not always be welcomed, but it is often helpful. A number of years ago I took a course in theology where I was required to write several papers. My professor was particularly pleased with one of them and gave me the addresses of several journals. "This should be published," he insisted. Delighted, I sent the manuscript away to three journals. Two simply sent back the form letter of rejection, but the third sent back the rejected manuscript with two and half pages of criticism. When I first read the critique I was defensive and hurt. Then I read it again, and another time. The person who critiqued my manuscript knew a great deal more about my subject than did my professor. I learned much from the critique. I kept that manuscript with the critique for many years in my desk at my office.

Helpful criticism is different from negative judgment. Negative judgment intends to demean the person. I learned another wonderful tool from a counselor friend. "Just take the negative judgment of yourself and see it wrapped as a gift handed to you. Then see yourself handing the gift back to the person whose negative judgment was hurtful. See yourself saying, 'No thank you. I do not need this. You may have it back.'"

I've treasured that wise counsel. If I am to be true to my calling, then I must develop the skill to learn. My own tools need to be sharpened, but I do not have to subject myself to mean-spirited judgment. Simply receiving requires response. I am the one who must then give. The freedom of simplicity helps me discern between helpful criticism and negative judgment.

Perhaps the simplest truth about giving and receiving is that the giver is always a receiver. "Love keeps no score," Paul wrote to the Corinthian saints. A gift, freely given, has no requirements, no strings. And the giver of such a gift experiences a joy beyond measure. I believe that in the moment of giving, the giver is always the first to receive.

When our youngest son was nine he had a bank where he faithfully placed coins for a longed-for bicycle. He was close to his goal when one evening we had supper with the Neff family, our across-the-creek neighbors. Charles had just returned from Africa and spent the evening telling us about the amazing way some of the people there lived on so little. He spoke about the work of Outreach International and described the hope brought into areas of great need. Our son listened intently. When we arrived home that evening, he went to his room and came down again with a bandanna filled with the money from his bank. Off he headed again for the Neffs. His face shone when he returned. On many occasions when we shared favorite memories, Kip recalled the delight of dumping all his savings on the Neff's kitchen table "for the people in Africa." No person who received any help from Kip's funds could have known greater joy than he in the giving.

Letting Go/Holding On

In a lecture on public television, Deepak Chopra described how elephants are trained in India. In the beginning a large chain is used to secure the young elephant's hind leg to a large tree. In a short time, the elephant is so used to the chain that it doesn't struggle for freedom. Then, the trainer reduces the size of the chain. Gradually, the elephant has accepted the restraint, and the smallest rope can be used to restrain it. It is not the chain or the rope that controls the animal, it is the elephant's belief that it is restrained.

Everyone is in bondage in some way by beliefs that keep them confined and limited. Letting go is a vital part of simplicity—not simply letting go of acquisitive patterns, but releasing ideas and attitudes that chain us to an unhealed past or fear of the future. Letting go, however, is not a "once and for always" act. There is a rhythm in letting go, and sometimes the process must be repeated—perhaps in a new setting, but repeated.

Sue Bender describes her experience following the publication of *Plain and Simple*, her account of time spent in an Amish community:

> "I'll never write another word," I thought with relief when *Plain and Simple* was published. I felt complete—exhausted and satisfied....
>
> At first my days were unhurried. I enjoyed whatever I was doing. The spirit of the Amish was all around. On those days I felt grateful.
>
> Then hardly noticing it, I started getting busy, saying "yes" to the many things that were offered. Suddenly I had too much on my plate. I had slipped back into an old groove, frantically scurrying to get everything done, crossing things off a never-ending list, and feeling the constant weight of all that was left undone.[11]

Bender uses the metaphor of bowls, to record her insights about letting go and holding on, about being empty and being filled. In one section she offers these insights:

> I heard a story about three bowls.
>
> The first bowl is inverted, upside down, so that nothing can go into it. Anything poured into this bowl spills off.
>
> The second bowl is right side up, but stained and cracked and filled with debris. Anything put into this bowl gets polluted by the residue or leaks out through the cracks.
>
> The third bowl is clean. Without cracks or holes, this bowl represents a state of mind ready to receive and hold whatever is poured into it.
>
> Sometimes I am that first bowl, so busy being "productive" that I don't notice when the very thing I want presents itself. Sometimes I am the second bowl, with such a fierce judging voice that focuses on what's *not* working that I'm unable to see or appreciate all the things that are going well. And sometimes, wonderful times, I am the third bowl, able to be present and absorbed in what I am doing, whatever it is.[12]

Perhaps the most significant way to simplify life is to be present and absorbed in what we are doing. Several years ago I was driving to my office at Herald House, about a mile from our home. As I drove up the hill I organized all the papers on my desk, planned my morning's activity, chose which manuscript I would finish, and suddenly heard a train whistle. I looked out my rearview mirror to see that my car had just barely crossed the tracks before the train's arrival. I was shaken by the realization that I had been so inattentive to my driving that I had barely escaped being hit by a train. My mind was not in the car, only my body. My mind was at the office, at my desk.

When my life is packed with activity, it is easy to be other places in my mind. How, then, does God's Spirit infuse my present moment if I am somewhere else?

One way to be immediately present is to practice a healthy form of holding on. I need to let go of those qualities that keep me in bondage to fear, greed, ignorance, and hopelessness. But I need to hold on to faith, hope, love, joy, and peace.

"Let this mind be in you, which was in Christ Jesus," the apostle Paul counseled the saints at Phillipi. What an act of letting go and holding on. Holding on to complete confidence in God's redeeming power, Jesus identified with our human condition. Jesus let go of anything that would separate God from us. And later Paul describes God's ultimate act of holding on: "Nothing can separate you from the love of God..."(Romans 8:39).

We can discern more clearly what is vital and what may be discarded when our hearts and minds are centered in God's love. The chances of my holding on to unnecessary ideas or objects are reduced by my attentive offering of myself to God.

I have a friend who is dying. He is one of the most alive people I've ever known. "What is important comes clear," he says.

I shared the remarkable quality of my dying friend with another friend who is a nurse in the oncology wing of the hospital. "I see it all the time," she said. "Sometimes I have been with patients just before they die and they seem more alive than I. It is as though all of their lives have come into focus in that moment. And then, most remarkably, they seem to know when to let go."

Yet I know people who could well be described as "the living dead." They long ago forgot the joy of life and live in bitterness, resentment, and unhealed rage. Sometimes they remember "the good old days," but for the most part even their past is filled with rancor and distrust.

Living every moment of our lives requires the ability to hold on to the past to learn from it, and when needed, to let the past go. To hold on to life until it is time to let go.

Holding on and letting go are issues related to all of life. In 1977 Marie Augusta Neal, a Roman Catholic nun, published a small book calling for the churches to address the inequities in the distribution of wealth.[13] It did not become popular with any church that I know of. But in urging a Year of Jubilee for poor nations, for wealthy Christians to give up power and possessions, she addressed one of the central questions of holding on. Can I relinquish my wealth so that others may live?

Yes/No

In every moment of life we are deciding: "The first and easiest way to make a decision is to be knocked off a horse, as was Paul.... In less dramatic fashion, in the absence of such divine intervention, there is sometimes simply a profound sense of peace or rightness about a decision that does not demand a careful weighing of each side."[14]

But every choice we make changes us. When we were in Australia in 1995 we had a conversation with a couple who had, just a few years before, faced horrific economic struggles. Betrayal by a business partner left the man without a job and with enormous financial burdens. They ultimately had to sell their beautiful home and move into a small house on a busy street. "It was hard at first, but I treasure every lesson we learned from this," the woman said. "What is important in our lives is the gospel. We have each other. We have a loving church family. And we weathered the difficult times. We are strong."

Their story is repeated in many places as "downsizing" joins the vocabulary of our age. Unemployment has hit many middle-class families. "When I lost the job I loved, I learned to love the job I had," said a young man in one of our workshops.

We do not live in a simple world. The social and political structures are not just those of family or neighborhood. We live in a complex world of international relationships that often overwhelm us. In a Public Radio broadcast from Sarajevo in the summer of 1992, a woman said, "I long for my children to have an ordinary day—a day when they go to school, come home, practice music lessons, play, have dinner, go to bed." Then she described the horror of living in a city where 10,000 people were slaughtered before the war's end.

One young Bosnian man said, "You get used to it...dead bodies and blood...it becomes normal. Maybe sometime you are walking and you see there is a lot of blood in front of you, but you don't think about it. You think about it like it is water, like rain...."[15]

Bosnia's tragedy reminds us that we can become inured to human suffering. We can go about our everyday lives with no thought that in another part of the world people are starving, dying.

Our church's commitment to world peace is proactive. We are called to care about what is going on in all the world. Guilt because I have food and someone else is without will not ease the hunger of the world. Eating healthily, learning about the politics of food—the relationship between what we eat and world peace—is a beginning. Actively seeking to support agencies that alleviate world hunger is another step.

Each act, each choice is important. In every home we visited when we were with our church community in Australia, we saw a compost container on the kitchen counter. Creating compost for gardens was routine, not a burden. I was also impressed there with the number of people who owned clothes dryers but used clotheslines whenever possible. Simple choices to save rather than use.

Richard Foster encourages churches to teach and practice simplicity. He offers some specific actions for the church including opening ourselves to the possibility that God may want to use us in a large way; learning about our neighbors in other countries, including those where great suffering is happening; becoming advocates of the powerless and exploited; supporting relief agencies; influencing public policy; writing letters to editors, articles, and hymns of social justice; and praying.[16] Justice, Emily Townes reminded the women at the 1993 International Conference of Women, is not "just us." The need to stand against powers and principalities that rob others of their human dignity has always been God's call to discipleship. Justice calls for change.

Christian justice transcends the definition of Byzantium's sixth-century emperor Justinian I: "giving to each man his due." The scriptures enrich our understanding of justice:

> In the Old Testament there are two Hebrew words for justice, *mishpat* and *tsedageh*. *Mishpat* is equated with...legal or retributive justice. ...*Tsedageh* means, more precisely, *righteousness* and refers not only to one's attitude. We are righteous before God when, for the love of God and neighbor, we minister to the poor, the hungry, the naked, the stranger, the prisoner, without expecting anything in return, without determining what is "deserved." This concept is far more radical than any meaning of secular justice.
>
> Biblical justice, then, is concerned with *equity* rather than *equality*. It is righteousness....It requires us to love not only brothers (and sisters) and neighbors, but strangers and enemies as well.[17]

At a World Church level, we have supported justice issues in specific ways. One recent example was the Peace Symposium of 1995 at which Marian Wright Edelman, a children's advocate in the United States, received the International Peace Award. Edelman advocates action on behalf of children who are unable to act for themselves. She particularly urges churches to become involved in the political issues that rob children of needed governmental support. The biblical injunction to act justly requires us to stand with the dispossessed and powerless.

Simplicity is more than an option. It is an essential choice if we hope to preserve the planet:

> If the inevitable changes are to come about in our society voluntarily and without ghastly catastrophe, nothing will achieve them but a profound change of public opinion. Our Western malaise is one of attitudes, values and expectations rather than of methods and systems. Yet, inasmuch as the systems often impose the attitudes, we have to defy them also; and this calls for a counter-culture of families and groups that cannot be...manipulated because they simply do not accept the accepted values or pursue the ambitions...expected of them. We must try to live by the divine contrariness of Jesus.[18]

In his counsel to the church at the April 1996 World Conference, President W. Grant McMurray presented a number of challenges. Several passages seem particularly apropos for those who struggle with the paradoxes inherent in simplicity:

- Journey in trust....
- Be faithful to the spirit of the Restoration, mindful that it is a spirit of adventure, openness, and searching.
- Laugh and play and sing, embodying the hope and freedom of the gospel.
- Open your hearts and feel the yearnings of your brothers and sisters who are lonely, despised, fearful, neglected, unloved.
- Reach out in understanding, clasp their hands, and invite all to share in the blessings of community created in the name of the One who suffered on behalf of all.
- Be tender and caring. Receive the giftedness and energy of children and youth, listening to understand their questions, and responding to their need to be loved and supported as they grow.
- Do not be afraid. Be courageous and visionary, believing in the power of just a few vibrant witnesses to transform the world. Love will overcome the voices of fear and division and deceit.

In the Roman Catholic tradition each bead of the rosary is a prayer. When a faithful Catholic says the rosary, each prayer has particular importance. If we are truly committed to simplicity we can each create a "rosary" reminder. Grant McMurray's statements above are filled with rich imagery; each is like an earnest prayer. Every person is at some time caught in the paradox of wealth/poverty, secular/sacred, giving/receiving, letting go/holding on, and yes/no.

The way is not always clear, and we are somtimes confused, frustrated, indecisive. And so we listen to the direction to "be courageous and visionary." As we discover what it means to practice simplicity as a spiritual discipline, we shall discover new power to love and heal the world God calls us to serve with new freedom and new hope.

Notes

1. Philip Van Doren Stern, ed., *The Annotated Walden: Walden; or, Life in the Woods*, by Henry David Thoreau (New York: Clarkson N. Potter, 1970), 222.
2. Richard Foster, *Freedom of Simplicity* (San Francisco: Harper and Row, 1981), 11.
3. Theodore Roszak, *Where the Wasteland Ends* (London and Winchester, Massachusetts: Faber & Faber, 1973), 43.
4. Foster, *Freedom of Simplicity*, 6.
5. Matthew 19:16-26, Mark 10:17-27, and Luke 18:18-30 RSV.
6. Anthony deMello, *The Song of the Bird* (Garden City, New York: Doubleday, 1982), 140.
7. Richard J. Foster, *Money, Sex and Power*, quoted in *alive now!* (May/June, 1986): 51.
8. Annie Dillard, *Pilgrim at Tinker Creek* (New York: HarperCollins, 1988), 35.
9. Matthew 4:1 IV—"Then Jesus was led up, of the Spirit, into the wilderness, to be with God."
10. Helen Keller, *My Religion* (New York: Doubleday, 1927), 153-156.
11. Sue Bender, *Everyday Sacred; A Woman's Journey Home* (San Francisco: Harper San Francisco, 1995), 2.
12. Ibid., 12-13.
13. Marie Augusta Neal, *A Socio-Theology of Letting Go: the Role of a First World Church Facing Third World Peoples*.
14. Katherine Marie Dyckman and L. Patrick Carroll, *Inviting the Mystic, Supporting the Prophet: An Introduction to Spiritual Direction* (New York: Paulist Press, 1981), 71-72.
15. Scott Anderson, "Bosnia's Lost Generation," *The New York Times Magazine* (September 6, 1992): Section 6, p. 51.
16. Foster, *Freedom of Simplicity*, 182.
17. Eugenia Smith-Durland, *Alternatives, Voluntary Simplicity: Study-Action Guide*, 14.
18. John V. Taylor, *Enough Is Enough* (Minneapolis, Minnesota: Augsburg, 1977), 69.

SHEPHERDS
ABIDING
IN THE FIELD

Chapter 13

Taking Care of the Shepherd: Developing a Healthy Spiritual Awareness

Carolyn Brock

When I was in my mid-twenties and on a vacation visit to my family's home in central Oregon, I went out early one evening, sat on a large rock at the edge of the pasture, and watched the sunset. I'm not sure if I was living in Portland or Denver at the time, but at any rate, it was city living, and the calm quiet of the family "homestead," seven miles from the nearest town, began seeping into me with its familiar centering serenity. If you can imagine looking across twenty acres of fields and another twenty miles of flatland and foothills to view the Cascade mountain range outlined against a flaming sky, you will have an idea of what was before my eyes. The Three Sisters stood dead-center in my view: Mount Bachelor to the south, Mounts Washington and Jefferson to the north—rugged peaks of deepening purples and blues against salmon-rose cloud wisps.

I've always been prone to locating places to sit and look at, listen to, and experience the natural world. It's one way I find nourishment for my soul. I sat there a long time, letting the colors fade and deepen around me, feeling the changing temperatures of a slight breeze that stirred the grasses and brushed across my skin, listening to distant sounds from neighboring homes, watching the animals move about in the field. It was an experience like many over the years—one of slowing down, breathing deeply, paying close attention, and becoming immersed in the reality of the moment.

When it was nearly dark, I walked slowly back to the house and entered the bright warmth of the kitchen. I remember my father commenting to me in a half-teasing tone that I was the weirdest of all his kids, because I liked to sit on rocks out in the field with only sheep and cows for company. He found it unfathomable that this strange behavior had any productive merit. I give this example for two reasons: to introduce the concept of mindfulness (to be explored later) and to begin our discussion with clear acknowledgment that spirituality comes in multiple flavors and forms. I think of my father as a deeply spiritual person and we share many common beliefs and bonds, but we express our spirituality in unique ways. As in every other arena of life, people are diverse spiritually, and this reality can either separate or enrich us. Diversity always presents us with the possibility of being both delightful and difficult.

Spirituality is a core issue for congregational leaders. Our entire quest is centered in spiritual questions, spiritual identity, spiritual development and joy. Knowing where we are spiritually, identifying and nurturing our own spiritual life is essential if we are to provide guidance and support to people in our congregations. It is also essential if we are to keep our lives in balance and on the growing edge.

Let us begin by discussing some principles that are foundational to healthy spiritual awareness and then move to a discussion of specific practices that foster spiritual growth and health.

Inhabiting a Spiritual Universe

Restoration scripture provides wonderful language for describing the spiritual reality in which we live, move, and have being.

> The elements are eternal, and spirit and element, inseparably connected, receiveth a fullness of joy; and when separated, [man/woman] cannot receive a fullness of joy.
> The elements are the tabernacle of God; yea, [man/woman] is the tabernacle of God....—Doctrine and Covenants 90:5e, f
> And the light which now shineth, which giveth you light, is through him who enlighteneth your eyes, which is the same light that quickeneth your understandings; which light proceedeth forth from the presence of God, to fill the immensity of space.
> The light which is in all things; which giveth life to all things; which is the law by which all things are governed.—Doctrine and Covenants 85:3

These words written by Joseph Smith Jr. speak of the spiritual nature and connectedness of all things, including our human selves.

Spirituality is our birthright; it is integrated into our biochemical makeup.

What is intriguing about these statements is their correlation with current thinking in physics about the energy and light-based nature of the universe. When seen through the eyes of quantum physics, the world of matter appears to be made up of "dynamic patterns continually changing into one another—the continuous dance of energy."[1] Scientists in health care and other disciplines are asking questions such as these: "Does consciousness exist at cellular levels? Are our bodies more than an aggregate of chemicals? Is there a 'God particle' that provides the key to unraveling the mystery of life?" The solid, "soul-less" world of science is confronting issues that push it up against the spirituality of the universe it seeks to understand.

Some have suggested that the earth or even the universe may be God's body. Beyond a simplistic animism, such images may help us in understanding God as existing in and through all that is—the consciousness and love that continues to create, heal, and transform the universe. This may be what Joseph perceived when he spoke of the light that is in all things, that gives life to all things, that fills the immensity of space.

These concepts lead to the affirmation that we live in a spiritual universe, that indeed all things are spiritual, because they are permeated and inhabited by God in an as-yet-unknowable fashion. On this basis we are led to acknowledge that the universe itself, and we ourselves are sacred.

Spirituality is about waking up to our spiritual identity. The fullness of joy for which we hunger comes as we experience ourselves as sacred and intimately related to the God who has given us both our spiritual and physical existence.

As indicated above, we live in a time when science and religion appear to be moving toward common ground in understanding the nature of body, mind, *and* spirit. Wouldn't it be interesting if the existence of the soul and the Divine eventually become indisputable, because we have gradually developed the capacity to perceive and measure their effects? Physician Larry Dossey, in his book on prayer, predicts that in the future:

> This soul-like quality of human beings will no longer be just an assertion of religions, to be accepted only through blind faith; it will be considered a legitimate implication of rational, empirical science.[2]

This is not to imply that we should wait for science to prove its merit before investing ourselves in the spiritual life, but rather that the concepts of God and the sacred emerging from this process may expand and clarify our spirituality in unexpected ways.

The coming together of science and religion will also bring healing and growth to many people who have had their soul-life in the closet or on hold. For centuries Western culture's themes of science and secular materialism have caused it to discount all that could not be physically measured, observed, proved, or consumed. Pursuit of spirit, or nourishment of soul, was dissected from the flow of life and placed within the walls of buildings that we could visit when we wanted to feel spiritual. However, current trends indicate that this long exile of spirituality from its proper place as integrating core of life may be coming to an end.

We live in a time of great spiritual restlessness and hunger. The soul sickness of our society is evident in our fascination with violence, our obsession with things, our emphasis on competition and control, dysfunctional family systems, and our willingness to give the formation of life values over to the media and entertainment industries. Many of us resist these tendencies, yet find ourselves influenced and affected by them to greater or lesser degrees.

Paradoxically, in the midst of what appears to be spiritual bankruptcy and moral decline there is a dramatic resurgence of interest in the life of the spirit. Books, workshops, speakers, and gurus articulating concepts of soul and sacredness abound. Health professionals are exploring the healing effects of meditation, prayer, touch, social support systems, church attendance, art, music, and laughter. Perhaps we are trying to come back home to our true identity and heal the wounds we have inflicted on each other and the creation.

Spiritual Diversity

On a warm Sunday morning in Kinshasa, Zaire, we were asked to kneel on the cement floor of the modest home of a local physician where seventy people had gathered to enjoy a lively service of testimony, praise songs, and preaching. At this culminating point of the worship, we were asked to lay our concerns before God in nondirected communal prayer. I felt uncomfortable trying to sincerely reveal the needs of my heart to God in a roomful of strangers all talking at once in French, Luba, or Lingala.

At first there was a low murmuring of voices floating up from

158

bowed heads. Then language became more intense and one could detect anxiety, anguish, and passionate energy surging through the voices "conversing" with God. I began to feel connected with this sea of sound that was carrying our needs and desires to the shores of God's consciousness. We prayed intently for several minutes and then as if instructed by a conductor's baton, the voices began to subside, decrescendo, become a hush, then fade into silence.

It was an amazing experience that I had entered with polite skepticism. It smacked of emotionalism, and I feared a breakdown into chaotic Pentecostal expressions. Instead I found myself perceiving a reverent cord of connectedness in our simultaneous speech, unplanned synchronicity emerging out of apparent disorder.

I have felt spiritually alive and connected in a wide variety of settings: in the beautiful open spaces of nature, at a root feast celebration in a long house on the Warm Springs Indian Reservation in Oregon; with exuberant youth singing and dancing their way into a conference gathering in Zambia; while in the deserts of northern Kenya placing hands on bowed heads to confirm Turkana nomads as members of the church; in the presence of sacred music and spoken word echoing off the stained glass windows of the Stone Church sanctuary; sitting beside a single candle; listening to the early morning silence in my living room.

The human hunger for God is expressed in myriad melodies and rituals, symbols and sacraments, disciplines and dances. Each of us has a spiritual worldview that has developed within the context of our family, religious, and cultural experience. Even within the RLDS Church, spirituality is understood and expressed in a wide variety of ways.

Because of this reality, pastoral care needs in congregations may at times center on conflict, alienation, or lack of fulfillment which may result from our diverse spiritual needs and expressions.

Those who lead and guide need to have a spiritual worldview that is well defined, yet open to growth and accepting of what speaks to the hearts of others. Awareness of diversity and its potential for either enriching or separating us into frustrated camps is a primary concern for pastoral and worship leaders.

In her book, *Discover Your Spiritual Type*, Corinne Ware identifies four major spirituality patterns or personalities. A simplified and adapted overview of these types is found below:

Head Spirituality: People with strengths in this arena are charterized by "a love of order and a desire for things to be logical and consistent."[3] They see God as revealed and knowable primarily through the word, whether written or spoken and are spiritually nourished by the powerful sermon, the well-articulated idea, the study of scripture. Their motto might well be the title of a book my husband keeps trying to get me to read, *Thinking the Faith* (by Douglas John Hall).

Heart Spirituality: People in this group see God as knowable primarily through a personal relationship with Jesus Christ. The strength of this type is the "richness of feeling" they bring to their spirituality and "their ability to experience God in the present moment, to revel in what is happening around them, to be in the present tense."[4] Heart folks enjoy music and worship that is emotionally expressive, and testimonies of an intimate walk with Jesus are central to their spiritual growth.

Mystic Spirituality: Mystics are on a perpetual spiritual quest with the God they view as mysterious and transcendent. More concerned with being than doing, mystics tend to focus on the inner life and thrive on spiritual disciplines like silence, contemplative prayer, and meditation. They believe that God can be apprehended best by emptying ourselves of distracting, egocentric thoughts and listening for what God may choose to reveal.

Kingdom Spirituality: The least common group, this spirituality type is represented by people of visionary action. Their focus is on obedience, witnessing of God's coming reign, and the transformation of society into God's kingdom on earth. People in this group tend to involve themselves in peace and justice issues, sometimes to the point of sacrificing their lives for such causes. Kingdom people equate prayer with action, and their motto might be, "I pray with my hands and feet."[5]

Ware's emphasis is on the gifts and strengths each spiritual type brings to worship experience and congregational life. She believes that a well-rounded spiritual life is open to learning even from those we find to be our direct spiritual opposite. Her assessment tool and book may be a valuable resource for assisting congregational leaders in understanding their own spiritual journeys as well as the interplay of spiritual styles and strengths in our faith communities.

Healthy spiritual awareness includes the principle that we do not all find the same degree of spiritual nourishment from the same things. If we and others in our congregations are to continue to grow, we may need to ask ourselves questions such as: Is our personal spiritual preference or that of worship planners or other leaders preventing people of different spiritual types from meeting their needs or expressing their gifts? Are we stuck in one worship style and program track that shuts out the development of other avenues of spiritual exploration or outreach?

Dialogue and insight into this area of diversity may help our congregations to be inclusive and creative in new ways.

The Learner Stance

No matter what our spiritual type, it is important to remember that God cannot be confined to the thoughts, terminologies, or even theologies we may choose to apply. These may reflect our human personalities and preferences more than they define God. It is threatening to confess that none of us really knows for sure what and who God is. We can have a most profound spiritual experience and still have only perceived a millisecond of God's timeless presence, a micro-burst of God's infinite power. We cannot expect to be able to package God in our preferred words and produce the latest, updated version of the Creator of the universe.

For this reason it is helpful if we can approach the spiritual quest with a healthy naïveté, an open and questioning heart. To be a student, a learner, to have what Eastern thinkers call "beginner's mind," seems an important basis for continued growth.

Though I come from the mystic's contemplative bias, I believe mystery is an important concept for all of us to embrace. When all is said and done, God is beyond us yet before us, around us and within us, intimate yet unknowable, closer than our breath, but also the energy that sustains the movements and changing form of the universe. Words adapted from a beautiful children's book called *Old Turtle* express it eloquently:

> God is indeed deep...and much higher than high....
> He is swift and free as the wind, and still and solid as a great rock....
> She is the life of the world....Always close by, yet beyond the farthest twinkling light....
> God is gentle and powerful. Above all things and within all things....
> God is all that we dream of...all that we seek...all that we come from and all that we can find.[6]

If there are not moments when we are struck utterly dumb, absolutely and reverently silent by the apprehension of God's "awe-ful" reality, then perhaps we have not begun our journey with sufficient innocence and emptiness. If there are not moments when the mind is left receptive and attentive, waiting for a fleeting glimpse, a barely perceptible whisper, an unexpected touch, perhaps we are still afraid of giving up too much of our control to God's unconstrained movement in us.

One of my favorite quotes speaks to the ways we attempt to capture God in our spiritual framework, then miss the whole point while keeping God carefully locked inside a safety net of words and worship orders. If you haven't read Annie Dillard's work (*Pilgrim at Tinker Creek*, *Holy the Firm*, *Teaching a Stone to Talk*, and others), you might want to introduce yourself to her reflections on life, nature, God, and suffering. Here's what she has to say about the dangers of playing church:

> Does anyone have the foggiest idea what sort of power we so blithely invoke? ...The churches are children playing on the floor with their chemistry sets, mixing up a batch of TNT to kill a Sunday morning. It is madness to wear ladies' straw hats and velvet hats to church; we should all be wearing crash helmets. Ushers should issue life preservers and signal flares; they should lash us to our pews.[7]

Spiritual development is risky business when we think of being encountered and transformed by the sort of God Dillard portrays. While one of the main goals of the spiritual life is intimacy with God, let us not make God so "user-friendly" that we forget our limitations in comprehending the mind and heart of Divinity.

Grace and Transcendent Moments

Though we speak of spiritual disciplines and the need to "work on" our spiritual lives, we must acknowledge that God is not "on tap" like the water in our kitchen sinks. Spiritual practices may make us more receptive to perceiving the Divine, but they do not put us in control of how, when, or where God will reveal Godself. Sometimes "a light surprises" in the midst of a very ordinary, "unspiritual" day or place (if there can be such a thing).

I remember the day I was shopping for shoes with our daughter, Emily (then six), at a mall in Independence, Missouri. After several weeks of single-parenting and other stresses, I was feeling impatient and grouchy (I know, some of you single-parent *all the time*!). Earlier in the day, I had prayed to be more loving and see Emily in new ways, but I was totally caught off guard as she rode the carousel in the mall without a safety strap (a big deal to her). It was like seeing her again for the first time. Her whole body sat erect and energized, smiling from her eyes to the tips of her toes, a kind of proud, holy power radiating from her face each time she circled round on her horse and looked at me. I wept as I felt myself flooded with her awesome beauty; sweet, sad joy at having been given such a gift and only seeing her this profoundly for nanoseconds at a time.

Abraham Maslow has called such experiences, "peak" or transcendent moments. In my own words, these are the moments we can't explain or self-create that open us to a new way of seeing and sensing reality. It is as if a veil is pulled away, a door opened, a light projected onto ordinary stuff so that we can see its sacred dimensions and meanings. Everything is clear. We feel connected and become aware of our oneness with God, the universe, nature, or another person in ways that don't ordinarily seem possible. We understand what is truly important and may be filled with a profound sense of awe, compassion, or insight.

Such moments are certainly gift and grace. They are beyond our thoughts or adequate explanations. Yet they cause us to perceive, if only for a brief time, the deeper meanings of life, the milieu of spirit that encompasses the simplest of events, the ebb and flow of our daily patterns and struggles.

One of the goals of a healthy spiritual life is to nurture our awareness of holiness, meaning, connectedness in the process of our living. We cannot control revelation or coerce God into blessing or touching us. I have a suspicion, however, that God always is waiting for us to pay attention to what is happening in the present moment with enough awareness and care that we can be blessed with a sense of wonder and gratitude on a more continuous basis. Transcendent moments may be gift, but perhaps they also can be cultivated by living in the present moment with our eyes, ears, and hearts open to God's surprise.

One gift from Eastern spirituality is the concept of mindfulness. The basic premise of this practice is to wake up to whatever "is" in the moment. Receiving the present moment with attention and appreciation is the basis for "the art of conscious living" which allows us to experience the richness of life in new ways. Jon Kabat-Zinn, a physician who teaches mindfulness meditation at the University of Massachusetts, says that mindfulness "is liberating in that it leads to new ways of being in our own skin and in the world." It is also empowering in that it "opens channels to deep reservoirs of creativity, intelligence, imagination, clarity, determination, choice and wisdom within us."[8]

Some of us feel nervous when a particular spiritual practice does not include a lot of "God-talk." We think it may be leading us away from God rather than into God. If, however, we accept the premise of the Restoration that God is the light and presence in all things, slowing down and waking up to the unfolding of life around us can provide profound moments of connection with the creative presence of God. My personal preference is to incorporate my own God-language into such practices, so I begin with the premise that I am being mindful so I can wake up to God in new ways.

Transcendent moments and spiritual awarenesses are not limited to RLDS or even Christian experience. If God is omnipresent and gracious in all creation, pieces of spiritual truth must be embedded in the stories of all peoples. Believing that we can learn from other spiritual traditions without diluting or discounting our own frees us to an expansive, enriching approach to spirit rather than a fearful, protective stance.

Healthy spiritual awareness takes seriously the hymn phrase that tells us God has yet more light and truth to break forth into our awareness. It also acknowledges (as the Book of Mormon indicates in Moroni 10) that all peoples on the planet have received the word and Spirit of God in different ways. As a spiritual movement that began with the questions of a seeker and proclaims revelation ongoing, perhaps we should see ourselves as a people in process rather than those who are content with fixed points and final answers.

As we learn about the spiritual worldview of other cultures and individuals, we will want to keep a balance between openness and discernment. With open mind and heart we can ask ourselves how particular "truths" or practices are in harmony with our faith tradition and the teachings of Jesus. We can discern how these practices may be part of our healing and growth, our ability to see and minister more deeply and freely. Without openness we consign our spirituality to stagnation and risk missing the growth God may be inviting us to embrace.

Discernment can also help us identify those tenets and practices that are not in harmony with the inviolable principles of God's love, justice, and concern for the worth of all human beings. Recognition that all cultures, all religious systems, all fallible human beings fall short of the truth and "see through a glass darkly" is a healthy perspective to preserve. At the same time we rely on God's Spirit to help us find our way through this sometimes confusing maze of voices and viewpoints.

Spiritual Disciplines

If you're like me, your mind is preoccupied and chattering away with "self-talk" 90 percent of the time. We like to be in control, and one way we do it is to think and talk all the time. Perhaps we are not aware of transcendent moments more often because our brains are so full of our agendas, and so busy with the perpetual flow of information that floods our sensory systems. We allow God only tiny spaces of silence and brief moments of our focused attention in which to work. This human tendency brings us to a discussion of our need for spiritual disciplines or practices.

Developing a pattern of regular spiritual practices is a way of saying yes to what God would like to create from the "stuff" of our lives. It is saying that if I am to fulfill the measure of my creation, I must be taught by the One who created me. Spiritual disciplines provide us with opportunities to yield ourselves to God, give up our compulsions as the ego-identified, self-made individual our culture so admires. Regular attention to spiritual care is a choice to develop what some have called the deeper, true, or larger self.

Spiritual disciplines are practices that help us change the channel, shift the gaze. Through them, we intentionally create a space of quiet, focused attention on God's presence and movement in our lives. Depending on our spirituality type, we may find particular disciplines most appealing and others less helpful in this process.

Excellent guides to spiritual disciplines are available in a number of resources. Richard Foster's classic, *Celebration of Discipline*, is always a good place to begin. Temple School courses such as Spiritual Disciplines by Bob Slasor and Laurie Gordon, and Discovering Your Personal Spirituality by Joni Wilson provide valuable tools for exploring our spirituality on a personal or corporate basis. The 1996 adult reunion text, *To Journey with Christ* by Bob Slasor and Laurie Gordon, also provides an abundance of material for ongoing dialogue. And Dave Schaal has provided a helpful overview of spiritual disciplines in the Aaronic Priesthood manual.

Rather than attempting to create a complete list and description of spiritual disciplines, I will mention specific practices that I have found meaningful.

Meditation on Scripture

Praying the scriptures or "*lectio divina*" is a classic form of going deep into a scriptural passage to learn what it has to teach us. It involves a four-step process that appeals to most spirituality types. An adapted summary of Corinne Ware's guide is found below.[9]

> **Lectio** involves reading the passage for sequence and detail. Try to enter the scene and allow it to become real by imagining the sights, sounds, smells, people, and interactions.

> **Meditation** is approached by reading the passage again and asking why, what, how questions. Why is this recorded? What does it mean? How does it help us understand God? Who am I most like in the characters of the passage?

> **Oratio** puts us in touch with our feelings about the passage as we read it again. What emotions (fear, joy, sorrow, anger, guilt) arise as we contemplate the meaning of the scripture? In this phase we are asked to open our heart and talk with God about the feelings the scripture awakens in us.

> **Contemplatio** asks us to let go of thoughts, questions, or analysis and sit silently with the scripture. Breathing deeply and regularly, we try to quiet the inner self and listen at a heart level. Be aware of impressions or awarenesses that come then re-focus on being quietly open. If no impressions come, you may want to return to the scripture again. When you feel your meditation is complete, open your eyes and be aware of being refreshed and grateful for what you have experienced.

Of course, one does not have to follow this format to meditate with scripture. Anytime we prayerfully engage a passage of scripture or reflect on the word reverently with a readiness to learn, this is meditation.

Meditation on Creation

Connected with the practice of mindfulness, this meditation is a focused, grateful attention on a tree outside your window, the sounds of the birds or the wind, the sky at sunset or sunrise, the spider spinning its web. As we open our senses to these grand and simple gifts, we are moved to praise, gratitude, and wonder toward the One who is Source of all. This form of meditation can be done looking out a window, walking along a sidewalk, sitting on the deck or back porch, planting a garden, or fishing on a quiet lake.

Journaling

Keeping a spiritual journal is a way of processing and recording our spiritual questions, insights, experiences, and desires. Journals can be used to write prayers, poems, psalms, letters to God, quotes or scripture passages that speak to us, conversations with a spiritual mentor or friend, insights that come to us from meditation and the process of daily living. A valuable resource for the practice of journaling is a book by Anne Broyles, *Journaling: A Spirit Journey*.

Some people enjoy journaling as a response to a scripture story or an imagery exercise in which they are encountered by Christ in their mind's eye. This form of combined meditation and journaling can be a powerful tool for accessing our feelings about ourselves and our relationship to God and Christ. As long as we remember that the messages we feel we receive during this time are subject to our human wounds and wishes, needs and limitations, I believe this practice can bring healing to many who search for an intimate connection with God. This type of journaling appeals especially to those of the "heart spirituality" type.

Breath Meditation

Using breath as a symbol of God's Spirit is a powerful way to focus on God's indwelling presence. With eyes closed, I like to think of God filling me, waking each cell of my body as I inhale, then cleansing me and releasing unhealed emotions, distorted thinking, and pent-up stresses as I exhale.

Silently praying simple phrases in concert with the breath helps focus attention on opening to God in the present moment:
- I breathe in your love, I breathe out fear.
- I breathe in your grace, I breathe out shame.
- I breathe in forgiveness, I breathe out anger.
- I breathe in your light, I breathe out darkness.

Provide your own words to match the needs and desires in your life with God at this point.

Palms Down, Palms Up:

Richard Foster combines breathing practices with a "palms down, palms up" exercise. With palms placed down on our knees, we breathe out things we need to release or repent of (worries, unreconciled relationships, demands, and pressures). With palms up and open on our knees, we breathe in God's forgiveness and help with the issues we have attempted to release. For a complete description of this exercise, see Foster's book *Celebration of Discipline*, pages 30 and 31.

Sacred Word or Breath Prayer

Similar to the use of phrases described above, this practice begins with quieting the mind and body and asking God to help us listen for a word that expresses our deep spiritual yearnings at this point. As we let go of the mind's chatter and hear ourselves and God more clearly, we let the word arise in us. The word or phrase is then repeated with the breath cycle as a way of emptying the mind of all other agendas and distractions. What comes may be a single word like "grace" or "love," or it may be a scriptural phrase or line from a hymn that has meaning for us ("Be still and know that I am God"; "My peace I give unto you"). An excellent guide to this practice is found in Father Thomas Keating's book *Open Mind, Open Heart*.

Contemplative Prayer

This prayer form focuses on listening rather than with words of praise or petition. Contemplative prayer seeks to still the sound of our own voice—clear the airways, if you will, of our controlling clamor. By relinquishing control, contemplative prayer opens our mental and spiritual wave lengths to God's mind and voice.

I find I must approach this prayer form by gradually quieting myself with the breath and word prayers described above. As we let go and listen at deep levels, even the centering words slip away and we are left resting in a vast empty space of silence saturated with a sense of God's gracious, eternal calm. I have only been fortunate enough to experience this space on a few occasions, but find myself drawn back to seeking it again and again. It feels like I have finally found the way back home and nothing could ever make me feel afraid, lonely, or lost again.

Retreats

When Dave and I moved to Africa in 1983, I did not expect it to make me more of a mystic. To my surprise the Catholic, Quaker, and Mennonite friends we had in Nairobi contributed to my spiritual growth in numerous ways. One of those ways was by introducing us to the practice of spiritual retreats. Again to my surprise we found beautiful retreat centers with old stone buildings, fireplaces, libraries, and acres of green lawn on the outskirts of Nairobi and in the highlands where tea is grown. The Jesuits, Benedictines, and Episcopalians had all been there for years, providing places where people could draw apart, meditate, walk, pray, journal, sit looking at the earth, and become more mindful.

Some retreats were completely silent and involved a community of strangers living in the same space, yet respecting each other's need for quiet and privacy. Always, the retreaters were left to journey in their own way with God, without input from staff or requirements to share a particular doctrine or attend services offered. I find these same kinds of ministries and facilities available in Independence, in the larger Kansas City area, and in many rural and urban settings of the United States and throughout the world. I also have dreamed, with fellow mystics in the church, of people in our denomination developing retreat centers and programs offering spiritual nurture and guidance.

When I am feeling spiritually drained, disconnected, or have come to a plateau or turning point in my spiritual life, spiritual retreats have provided a time of intense searching, opening, and reconnecting with God. When we're filling up our yearly calendars, we might want to consider the benefits of scheduling a spiritual retreat day or weekend, alone, with our spouse, a friend, or the entire family. Those involved in congregational leadership and pastoral care are prone to stress and spiritual burnout. A retreat may be just what we need to keep us from slipping into patterns of depression, fatigue, or resentment.

Family Spirituality

In October 1995 our family of three headed to St. Joseph, Missouri, to spend the weekend on the farm of our good friends, the Carliles. We were left free to roam the ninety-three acres of wooded hills; gather leaf bouquets of dusty browns, muted golds, brilliant red-oranges; sit on the swing in a circle of huge oaks; or nap in the hammock. We sat around a small table in the basement, lit a candle, sang songs, and wrote earth prayers which we read to each other. Another important task during our weekend retreat was to discuss what we want our family to be like and stand for. Out of that discussion we were able to write a family mission statement.

It was a wonderful time, particularly for our daughter Emily who often finds herself with both parents shuttling off to weekend events or dealing with Dave's three- to four-week trips away from home. I don't think we realize what a gift we give our children by offering them our undivided attention in a time of slowed, reflective sharing about feelings, values, and meanings.

Usually quick to become bored, Emily was content to lie in the hammock, watch clouds in the sky, and sing for several hours at a time. She went on several haywagon rides around the farm with Dave Carlile, floated a homemade boat on the pond, and helped create the dramatic campfire lighting for our wiener roast supper. Mostly I was struck by how happy she was without the usual noise and activity level to which we grow accustomed and then subtly addicted.

In those moments I wanted more than anything to nurture and keep alive the spiritual wonder I perceived in my daughter. I vowed I would find ways to do this, but find I too struggle to incorporate time for stopping, wondering, seeing, listening, praying together.

We at times feel compelled and justified in spending large amounts of money and time on feeding, clothing, and grooming the physical bodies of our children or developing their musical, athletic, and artistic talents. We want our children to have a competitive education and access to an assortment of entertaining and stimulating toys, games, and literature. It's fairly easy for most of us to enumerate the ways we promote the mental and physical growth of our children, a little less clear to list the ways we specifically provide for care of their souls, fostering of their spiritual growth, and identity formation. Of course body, mind, and spirit cannot be separated into neat little compartments, but they are distinct dimensions of our experience that need distinct kinds of attention and stimulation.

Our children desperately need help in establishing a deeper set of values than looking good, wearing the right clothes, being athletically gifted, or preparing to move into a financially successful career when they graduate from college or learn a vocational skill. These are the messages they hear from everyone around them, and they are perhaps not bad messages in and of themselves. But they are *limited* messages, surface messages that teach them how to be mentally and physically acceptable in our culture. In the long run, they do not bring deeper identity as a soulful, sacred person with a clear sense of purpose in God's universe.

It is a challenge for congregational leaders to nurture spiritual well-being in their families. When we choose to create space for spiritual formation in already busy schedules, we almost certainly will feel we are swimming upstream. A torrent of work, school, media, and peer messages will keep pushing us back into the comfortable habit of not having time. Yet, by allowing ourselves to do so, we are making choices that affect the most ultimate and central meanings in our lives.

As congregational leaders we may find ourselves so busy dealing with other people's life crises or spiritual issues, we forget that wholeness begins at home. We cannot offer healing ministry out of personal chaos and family stress. We cannot offer wholeness to others if our own life is out of balance and consumed by the need to help others, work harder, accomplish more. But we can journey with others in our common brokenness and need. This capacity comes as we acknowledge our own need for healing and begin to see spiritual practices as necessary not only for our ministry but for our mental, physical, and spiritual survival.

The development of family rituals is an important aid to meeting our need for spiritual care. A yearly spirituality retreat together can involve a time of cooperative, creative planning and play for everyone. Nightly routines that contain a hint of holiness and a natural blend of humor and shared story can be very appealing to young people and adults alike. One of our favorite practices is to light a candle or make a fire in the fireplace, turn out all the other lights, talk about what was the best thing that happened to each of us that day, then end with a song and prayer over what we have shared. Candles and firelight provide a warm glow of mystery that calms both body and spirit.

Whenever our bedtime routine begins to seem a little too flat and familiar, I notice humor (usually from Dave or Emily) creeping in to reenergize it. "God, thank you for flowers and Frisbees, flutes and frogs, fritters and foghorns" (to paraphrase one of Dave's alliteration prayers). We all laugh and start adding words to keep the litany going, hoping God appreciates our "clever" way of expressing gratitude.

Children and youth can be trusted to create family worship experiences that can be quite enjoyable and meaningful for adults. If you're sick of congregational worship planning but feel guilty about the lack of sacred moments in your family life, try assigning one or more of your children to plan a worship experience at home. You may be surprised at the results. Emily and her cousin, Andrea (both age ten) have spent an hour or two of intense preparation to come up with an order of worship that included songs, prayers, scriptures, poems, and offerings. Such experiences connect kids with their ability to enter and make sense of the elements of the spiritual world. Watching our children grow in this arena is a wonderful way to relieve stress and refresh our spirits.

A designated and appropriately decorated "peace and quiet room" or area of the house is another way to make spiritual health and awareness an identified priority on a personal and family level. If everyone knows that there is a place where they can go to sit quietly, pray, meditate, or journal, these practices are more likely to find their way into the daily scheme of things. Children learn what they see being lived out by the adults around them. Our "walking the walk" is the most profound lesson we can teach about the place of spirit in our lives.

Transformation

We are created for community. We are biologically programmed to need unconditional love and intimate relationship with others. But we live in a world where true community is rarely experienced, and in which war, racial tension, economic and political competition are commonplace. We live in a world where acceptance too frequently must be earned, and human worth too often is measured in terms of productivity, education, earning power, gender, or skin color. We do not see each other with "sacred eyes" as L. Robert Keck discusses in his intriguing book by the same title.

We do not see each other with sacred eyes because we see ourselves with clouded vision and define ourselves in distorted terms. Somehow we have not understood what our creator has been trying to tell us since the beginning: You are the beloved. I am in you and you are in me. Your names are written on the palms of my hands. I am with you until the end. Perfect love casts out all fear. There is enough and to spare (if we have the will to use it wisely and justly).

Until we know and live these truths from a place deep in our hearts, we will continue to fear rather than trust, compete rather than cooperate, consume rather than conserve, wound rather than heal. Some have said that we live in this way because we have a hole in our souls that can only be healed by divine touch, filled by divine compassion. At times it seems that the human family has a chasm in its collective soul out of which flows darkness and depraved cruelty unleashed on the innocent and evil, the powerless and corrupt, the good and the not so good, seemingly without discrimination or care.

Jesus came to be God's love in the midst of our darkness; to pour the oil of grace on our self-hatred and fear; to breathe healing into our soul wound, our infinite chasm; to speak the word of peace into the hot winds of our anger and violence.

Jesus stayed true to his ethic of love and justice because of the extraordinary quality of his spiritual life. He stayed intimately connected to God through practices of solitude, prayer, fasting, service,

172

and obedience. He has shown us a way, a consuming passion, a spirit-driven dream, a dying to self, a bowing to the sacredness, an obedience to the life of the Wounded Healer. If we are to follow and do the things we have seen him do, spirit must become a central priority in our lives.

Spirituality is the path we must walk if we are to find healing and embrace wholeness. It is the discipline we must pursue if we are to be empowered in bringing a ministry of wholeness to our congregations and communities. It is the chief concern of a church commissioned to pursue peace. Spirituality that penetrates to the psychospiritual core of our lives will transform us into compassionate, courageous people, a people of prayer, a people of prophetic action. May it be so with us, and may we find ourselves restored and refreshed in the journey by the One who is both its beginning and end.

Notes

1. Fritof Capra, quoted by Margaret J. Wheatley in *Leadership and the New Science: Learning about Organization from an Orderly Universe* (San Francisco: Berrett-Koehler Publishers, 1992), 32.
2. Larry Dossey, *Healing Words: The Power of Prayer and the Practice of Medicine* (San Francisco: HarperSanFrancisco, 1993), 206.
3. Corinne Ware, *Discover Your Spiritual Type: A Guide to Individual and Congregational Growth* (Bethesda, Maryland: The Alban Institute, 1995), 85.
4. Ibid., 86.
5. Ibid., 43.
6. Douglas Wood, *Old Turtle* (Duluth, Minnesota: Pfeifer-Hamilton, 1992), 23.
7. Annie Dillard, *Teaching a Stone to Talk: Expeditions and Encounters* (New York: Harper and Row, 1982), 82.
8. Jon Kabat-Zinn, *Wherever You Go, There You Are: Mindfulness Meditation in Everyday Life* (New York: Hyperion, 1994), 8-9.
9. Ware, 107.

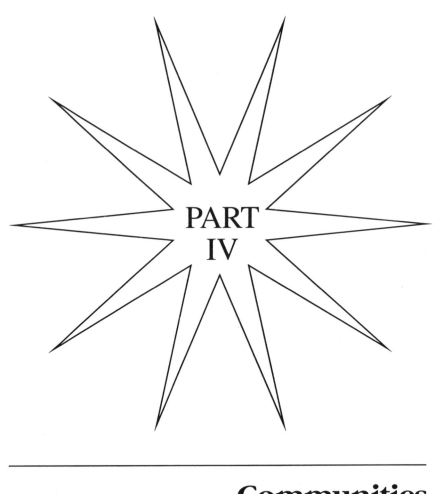

PART
IV

**Communities
of
Joy,
Hope,
Love,
and
Peace**

SHEPHERDS
ABIDING
IN THE FIELD

Chapter 14

Building a Community of Joy

W. Grant McMurray

The theater was crowded and noisy, I was alone, and I had never even heard of the movie that was about to begin. If anything, the presence of groups of exuberant young adults seemed to highlight the fact of my solitariness, and I hunched down in my seat so as to avoid being noticed and thought a poor fool. I didn't know why I had come to this particular place, except that its presence and my presence just seemed to converge at this moment. It was here and so was I.

It was not that I was feeling deeply sorry for myself. I was in Denver for an official purpose and my aloneness was a temporary situation that would be resolved when I returned home in a few weeks. It just seemed a bit awkward, that's all, and, had I my druthers, I would just as soon have been enjoying the company of friends or family. But here I was in a trendy little gathering place, choosing at a whim to enter a little theater with a high-brow name, and watch an artsy film called *Harold and Maude*, about which I knew nothing and cared nothing.

As the film began I realized it was a kind of dark comedy about age and love, life and death, all with a sharp edge, and a goodly dash of pretty serious humor. As the craziness and exuberance of the film began to unfold, I found myself caught up in its celebration of life. More than that, I found myself bonded to a community of strangers seated around me, all laughing hysterically along with me as we rejoiced in the message and spirit of this nutty movie.

I can rarely recall laughing so long and hard, and being pulled so suddenly and unexpectedly from a condition of self-pity. I left that theater with many friends, though I had spoken to none of them. I left filled with a sense of joy that I knew would never leave me.

When I called home, I excitedly tried to convey what had happened. But somehow I just couldn't explain it over the phone satisfactorily. If only they could see *Harold and Maude*, then they would understand what I was trying to say. I would grab the first opportunity to see it again, and take as many friends as I could get to go with me.

All of this was in prehistoric times, before VCRs. Back then, you had to either wait for the movie to come around to the theaters again, a vain hope usually, or scan the television section in the hope that some night the late show might carry it. A long time passed, probably several years, before I saw *Harold and Maude* listed in the *TV Guide*. My heart warmed and I could feel just a twinge of the joy I had experienced that night in Denver.

"You've just *got* to see this," I told my reluctant wife. "This is the funniest movie I've ever seen. You'll love it." The film unfolded just as I remembered it. But something was wrong. It was amusing, clever in places, insightful in spots. But it didn't jump off the screen at me the way it had before. Perhaps it was just my familiarity with it, the fact that I knew what was coming.

"What did you think?" I asked Joyce when it was over. "Pretty good," she said, awakening from a sound sleep. I was perplexed, and felt a bit betrayed. How could this film which had touched off such a joyful response some years before seem so ordinary, so spirit-less, so common?

Over the years I have frequently discovered the difficulty of recreating moments of profound joy or happiness or even sadness. Indeed, such moments, revisited, seem to not only lose the qualities that made them so powerful but make me wonder why it was that they seemed remarkable at all. Stripped of their original setting, or the constellation of feelings that made the moment unique, occasions that led to great joy have seemed only pleasant interludes or moments of small pleasure.

Time is an insidious temporizer. It moves us farther and farther away from those all-too-infrequent moments when our spirits soar, when our hearts are aflame, when our minds are alive with new understandings. As time pushes us away, the spirit slowly sinks to earth, the embers of the heart begin to dim, the mind loses once again its radical openness to the new. And soon, that which seemed so profound, so compelling, now appears altogether ordinary. Or at the least, it leaves us wondering what it was we got so excited about.

Christmas is kind of like that. We know that if we have survived that hectic season with a song still on our heart, it won't be there for long. The time of the year that is so full of reminders will soon fade away, and the ordinariness of everyday life will take its place. Our problems will return. There will be bills to pay, promises to keep, people to be cared for. There will be more responsibilities than opportunities, more demands than "gifts" received, more to be asked of every day than any day can give. Our joy will give way. We know it will. And our joy is tempered thereby.

There are other factors that divert us from joy, including a sense that maybe we shouldn't experience it at all. There is the story of a man who had just had his annual physical and was waiting for his doctor's report. After a few minutes the doctor came in with charts in his hand and gave him the news, saying, "There's no reason why you can't live a completely normal life as long as you don't try to enjoy it." Within our culture is the notion that joy is related to those things that we shouldn't be doing. It's all the "fun stuff" that we should avoid.

And yet we know from the scriptures that such a view is not sustained by our understanding of the Christian faith. In the Gospel of John, at what he knew would be his last supper, Jesus said, "These things I have spoken to you, that my joy may be in you, and that your joy may be full" (John 15:11). Apostle Paul was in prison when he wrote these words: "Rejoice in the Lord, always."

Frederick Buechner, a theologian and novelist in his late fifties, recognized this when he spoke on behalf of his own age group, which is often referred to as the "self-denial" generation. He says that there was an attitude

> that I had no right to be happy unless the people I loved—especially my children—were happy too. I have come to believe that that is not true. I believe instead that we, all of us, have not only the right to be happy no matter what but also a kind of sacred commission to be happy—in the sense of being free to breathe and move, in the sense of being able to bless our own lives, even the sad times of our own lives, because through all our times we can learn and grow, and through all our times, if we keep our ears open, God speaks to us his saving word.[1]

I am not a very good handyman. While I have a box of tools and a workbench and have stumbled my way through various household projects, inside and out, I fully recognize that fixing things is not my gift. But I often delay hiring someone to repair things that need repair simply because I prefer not to spend the money to pay for the labor. I consider this good stewardship. My wife considers it cheap.

For a long time I had problems with my garage door opener. When I pulled into the driveway and pressed the remote control button in the car the opener would always kick in and raise the door. But when I got out of the car and prepared to enter the house, pressing the button on the wall inside the garage never seemed to work. I had to go back into the car and lower the door by using the remote control. Clearly, there was something wrong with the button.

I took the button apart and cleaned the contacts. I tightened the screws holding the wires in place and replaced the button on the wall. Still the garage door did not raise or lower by pressing the button. I put up with this problem for far longer than I am willing to admit, not wanting to spend the money to call an electrician to resolve the problem. I decided the button must be defective and needed to be replaced. I went to the hardware store and found a garage door button that looked different but should work. I triumphantly returned home.

I disconnected the old button and attached the new one, tightening the wires and snapping it firmly in place. I pushed the button and waited for the garage door to open. Nothing happened. I punched it again and again. Nothing. Snarling, muttering, I decided that there must be a broken wire leading into the button, so I removed the new device, clipped the wire about six inches above where it had been installed and reconnected the fresh, unbroken wire to the new button. I punched the button. Nothing happened.

I now had a brand-new button connected to newly stripped wire and installed about six inches above its previous location, and six inches above the now mismatched button for the other garage door, which had always worked perfectly. It looked stupid but worse—the button still did not operate the garage door.

I refused to acknowledge this embarrassing dilemma. For months I operated the garage door with the remote control inside the car. Each day I walked past the buttons on the wall, diverting my eyes but always thinking of my own inability to repair a simple defective switch.

And then one day I had to make an adjustment to the tension on the garage door opener. I got a stepladder and climbed up to turn the knobs that made that adjustment. As I was doing so I happened to notice the wire that ran from the button on the far side of the wall up the wall and across the ceiling and connected to the garage door opener. The screw was loose and the wire had disconnected from the terminal. My mouth dropped open. I slipped the wire around the screw, tightened it, climbed down the ladder, and walked over to the button. I punched it. The garage door opened. I punched it again. The garage door closed.

All along I had assumed that the source of the problem was with the button. I had pushed the button and the door had not responded. Clearly this was a defective button. But the whole time the problem was located in a place quite different from where the button was attached to the wall. I had been maintaining, repairing, and replacing the button, when the problem was up the wall, across the ceiling, at a terminal on the garage door opener itself.

Perhaps this story will tell you two things. First, I am not a likely host for public television's *This Old House* or a future lead actor in *Home Improvement*. Second, the problems of life that conspire against joy may have to be diagnosed differently than we thought. Sometimes we try to fix the symptoms that we see, repairing the places that hurt or are visible. But more often than not, the hole is in our soul, and that is what must be healed.

I told that embarrassing story at a conference in the Temple on addictions and codependency. I am the child of an alcoholic, and the grandson of an alcoholic. Sadly, I see in my own life certain behaviors that, while perhaps not as destructive as alcohol or drug dependence, still inhibit my personal growth and my ability to be who and what I could otherwise be. It is at such times that I experience a certain turmoil within, wondering why I cannot align my life with the values and qualities and commitments that I readily affirm, but so often find myself unable to fully achieve. I think many of us are like that, and the joy that should be at the heart of our very lives is temporized and sometimes destroyed as a result.

There is on this earth a profound sense of restlessness. In Western culture at least, there is a loss of focus, depth, and authenticity in so much of life. We see it in obsessive behaviors and in addictions of many kinds and in mindless violence that appears to arise from the ashes of despair and from the absence of meaning. The great malady of the twentieth century, say many observers, is a loss of soul.

And yet, to this often soul-less, hurting world we are called to build communities of joy. The foundation for such a task is sure and firm.

After love, joy is surely the quality most frequently identified as part of the Christian life.

Jonathan Edwards, the eighteenth-century Puritan preacher, said the way to tell true religious experience from that which is false is to look for joy, the dead giveaway that God is present in someone's life.[2] C.S. Lewis described his conversion experience as being "surprised by joy."[3] And Paul Tillich defined joy as the truest expression of ourselves: "Joy is nothing else than the awareness of our being fulfilled in our true being, in our personal center."[4] Clearly, joy is not just a byproduct of a faithful life, but is at the very core of everything we are about.

It is for such reasons that we see depictions of Christian communities joyfully facing an awful fate: standing up to persecution or suffering enormous hardships. Something is resident within them and nothing can serve to diminish the joy that is emblazoned on their inward parts. As Doris Donnelly has written: "Joy... is not the sentiment of people who have lost their marbles and their hold on reality. Nor is it a pious wish, but rather a permanent, all-pervasive character of the Christian, irrepressibly active, filled with inward satisfaction and outgoing benediction."[5]

By the same token, and perhaps because of its very nature, joy is not a solitary emotion but something that requires community to keep vibrant and alive. It is not to say that one cannot be joyful in a private and personal way. But the fullest expression of joy must find itself within the celebration of the Christian community, in which the evocation of that spirit grows out of history, struggle, and being together. To have depth, joy must have story. Just as a good novel has to have the tension of plot, characters at risk, emotions frayed and fragile, outcomes uncertain, so our joy must be grounded in the exigencies of life itself, with all of its complexity and uncertainty and painful, questing struggle.

In our Communities of Joy launches throughout the church, we quoted frequently from Paul Jones's statement that "when the church is a community of joy, evangelism occurs as contagion."[6] The meaning of that statement is that we express a joy that we have discovered within our community, even in its pain and struggles, and have no choice but to share that joyful outpouring to all who will hear. Evangelism becomes the powerful outflowing of what burns within.

All this is to say that congregations of joy have to find ways of expressing those deepest yearnings of the human spirit, that inexorable desire to discover God, that pleading search of the soul. We make a fatal mistake if we believe that joy comes from good projects, effective programs, and popular activities. We are off-base if we think joy is the result of good teaching, powerful preaching, or tasty potlucks. All these things may be present in communities of joy, but they do not create them.

While there may be any number of factors that contribute to the building of communities of joy, let me suggest that attention be given to qualities of **substance**, **openness**, **participation**, **celebration**, and **intimacy**.[7] Each of these elements is a significant contributor to the kindling and tending of joyful congregational life.

1. *Substance.* There is something very wrong with church life as I am experiencing it today, including within our own movement. I am embarrassed to find young people coming to me, asking why it is that they don't hear or understand what the church is all about, that they don't know our history or comprehend the message of the Bible or the other scriptures. Within recent months I have been scored pretty well by senior highs who claim they have never learned the basics of the church and they have friends in other movements who can talk circles around them in terms of their church life.

I recently talked to a fifteen year old who has been raised within the church, although one parent is not a member. He had not yet been baptized because his parents wanted him to make a mature decision between the two faiths represented within his family. He presented to me his complaint that his prebaptismal class did not in any way tell him about the church he was to join, even though his instinct is to become a member of our body.

In our effort to be relevant and contemporary, we have moved too far away from the foundations of scripture, history, and theology on which our community is founded. A community of joy understands its own story and embraces the *substance* of faith, even if it must push against those traditions in order to make that faith relevant. If what we push against is mush, there can be no growing, no stretching, no new insights. Package the substance in new and exciting styles. Freshen it with toe-tapping music and contemporary visuals and engaging pedagogy. But give it *substance*.

2. *Openness.* All too often churches are closed societies. We talk to each other and use our code words and common understandings to communicate in a way that tends to exclude rather than include. It is easy to see why we do it. In a way, it is the benefit of community for us to embrace those things that unite us and to feel a certain pride in our shared values and experiences. But a community of joy must develop a style of life together that opens the circle and invites others in. That has never been more urgent than now.

Churches are losing the spirituality sweepstakes. Our staid forms of worship and congregational life are being replaced by other types of quests, by the smorgasbord of spiritualities that are on the cultural landscape. We must find ways to be a welcoming community, inviting into our midst the unchurched, the seekers, those struggling on the fringes of life. We must be a community of *openness* and acceptance, providing a firm foundation on which to stand, but agreeing to be explorers as well.

3. *Participation.* I suppose this is the current buzz word in the church, emphasizing as we are, especially in our VisionQuest endeavors, the importance of participation at all levels. Make no mistake about it. This is not just a faddish new management concept due to be replaced a couple of years hence by something else. It is a profoundly significant new way of visioning the mission of the church and living our faith. It is a change in culture, not just a revised chapter in the *Congregational Leaders Handbook*. If you are a pastor and are not vastly widening the participation of people in your congregation, you are on the wrong road. Turn back.

What this means is that the global family we call the church has a new job. That job is to share in the task of creating the future and to contribute to decisions about how that task will be accomplished. It means that leaders need new skills of facilitation, team-building, and task design so that the gifts of all can be blended into the process of being the church. This is the call to be a prophetic people, to use all of God's children as the source of insight and understanding.

We Latter Day Saints have been pretty close to a "priesthood of all believers" for a long time. It's good to see the rest of society catching up with the idea that became part of the fabric of the Restoration movement, albeit sadly disabled at times by stifling models of authority that often snuffed out creativity and energy. Communities of joy provide opportunity for all to participate in building the kingdom and engaging in the cause of Zion.

4. *Celebration.* I tend to be a person who admires rationality and eagerly responds to ideas, especially if expressed in elegant prose. In my religious life, I have read widely and thoroughly enjoyed scholarly musings about scripture, history, theology, ministry, and community. I can get excited by ideas that stimulate me to new ways of thinking and that shake the cobwebs out of my sometimes crusted brain.

In recent years I have had to confront unexpected ways of experiencing the church as I have traveled with brothers and sisters in Africa and the South Sea islands and have seen our Haitian, Latin American, and Indian Saints transform the way we worship. From out of the cultural experiences of so many peoples we are finding new ways of expressing our joy. It is just in time, because all the evidence demonstrates that there is a deep yearning for worship that is more expressive, more holistic, more celebratory, and less cerebral. From praise music to the classics, from testimony to liturgy, from scripture to drama, from preacher to soloist, there are so many venues for worshiping God. Communities of joy celebrate the powerful good news that God is with us—we sing and dance and laugh and play because God's love fills us to the brim and it just has to get out. We can't sit anymore. We must move to the rhythm of the celebrating community, praising God not just with our words but with our whole being.

5. *Intimacy.* Great cathedrals have been built as tributes to the awe we feel in the presence of God. Massive structures, replete with incredible artwork, icons, and imagery, all testify to God's power and overarching presence. Our Temple spirals upward to the heavens, eliciting gasps from those who enter the sanctuary for the first time and are struck by the vastness of space gently embraced by the twists and turns of the winding structure.

But the Temple was also designed with an eye to the individual worshiper, providing a sense of intimacy within the immensity of its space. Communities of joy cannot simply stand in awe of God, but must also find a way of touching every heart, of permitting each person to feel he or she is loved, blessed, and worthy. We have too much facelessness, too much lostness, too much casting around for meaning and identity in the midst of an impersonal and overwhelming world. The church is composed of friends in Jesus Christ. When one is friend, one is honored and acknowledged, and never left to feel alone. Communities of joy are bastions of *intimacy*, in which the love of God permeates every heart and touches every needful, searching soul.

Substance, openness, participation, celebration, and intimacy—these are hallmarks of communities of joy that we are called to build in the twenty-first century. It is sobering to contemplate the task, in the midst of such a world as this. But sobriety, like fear and pain and disappointment and uncertainty, is caught up and embraced within the Christian concept of joy. It is real stuff, not giggly stuff, not happy faces, not situation comedies or birthday cakes. Joy resides deeply within, for only something of such power and depth can give rise to the highest aspirations and fervent longings of the human heart. It is the promised community of God, spoken of in Isaiah, and still awaiting fulfillment:

> For now I create a new heaven and a new earth and the past will not be remembered and will come no more to mind. Be glad and rejoice for what I am creating because I now create Jerusalem "Joy" and her people "Gladness." I shall rejoice over Jerusalem and exult in my people. No more will the sound of weeping or the sound of cries be heard in her.... They will build houses and inhabit them, plant vineyards and eat their fruit.... My people shall live as long as trees...the wolf and young lamb will feed together...they will do no hurt, no harm on all my holy mountain.—Isaiah 65:17-25 NJB

In the communities where we serve, we are each called to create a joyful Jerusalem, worthy of those who built before us, and brimming with promise for those yet to come.

Notes

1. Frederick Buechner, *Telling Secrets* (San Francisco: HarperSanFrancisco, 1991), 102.
2. As cited in Doris Donnelly, "Good Tidings of Great Joy," *Weavings* 8, no. 6 (November/December 1993): 7.
3. C. S. Lewis, *Surprised by Joy: The Shape of My Early Life* (New York: Harcourt Brace, 1956).
4. Paul Tillich, "The Meaning of Joy," in *The New Being* (New York: Charles Scribner's Sons, 1955), 146.
5. Donnelly, 10.
6. W. Paul Jones, "Joy and Religious Motivation," *Weavings* 8, no. 6 (November/December 1993): 43.
7. Similar elements are suggested in a book on contemporary worship by Timothy Wright, *A Community of Joy: How to Create Contemporary Worship* (Nashville, Tennessee: Abingdon Press, 1994). I have used his model in a somewhat different way, and broadened and applied it to a different purpose, but acknowledge the kernel of thought that is present in this work.

SHEPHERDS
ABIDING
IN THE FIELD

Chapter 15

Congregations of Hope

Danny A. Belrose

Someone said that despair has four heads: *agnosticism*, which makes one lose courage in the search for knowledge; *pessimism*, which makes one lose courage in the search for progress; *cynicism,* which makes one lose courage in the search for virtue, and "*theological papers,*" which make one simply lose consciousness. As I would not categorize myself a theologian, you will be spared the struggle of wrestling with profundities. (I make *no* guarantee for maintaining your consciousness). Despite the facetiousness of the fourth head of despair, it is nonetheless true that if there is one disease rampant in our time it is cynicism. Cynics have no eternal context or moral frame of reference, and their verdict in every crisis is: "So, what did you expect?"

One of the most crippling things in life is no settled aim, no steady drive, no consistent purpose, and no far-off divine event. Too many of us live unfocused lives—what William James called "double-mindedness." The unfocused life is never able to keep a steady course, like a boat without a rudder, tossed and swirled about by conflicting wind and wave.

But for the person for whom religion is life, daily existence has contacts with horizons beyond here and now. Life becomes an anvil on which character is fashioned and shaped; life is a window through which God's light of truth comes into human existence. This is what Ian MacPherson meant by saying, "When Jesus takes possession of the heart everything else is changed." Jesus, in the apostle Paul's words, becomes our "living hope."

Certainly this is true corporately as well as individually. Christian congregations are communities of Christ called to be alive in the living hope of Jesus. Unfortunately, what is true for individuals is also true for the church. There are congregations that are "double-minded" and unfocused. What, then, are the earmarks of a congregation of hope? Before addressing this question, I want to look briefly at Christian hope.

Don H. Compier has this to say:

> What then is hope? The New Testament includes it in the lists of gifts of the Spirit. Since God offers it as a present, we cannot attain to it by our own effort.... Often we confuse it with optimism, but these are not equivalent terms. As the apocalyptic literature demonstrates, one can be completely pessimistic about the current situation and yet live in hope. Hope has an "in spite of everything" quality. In the suggestive phrase of the Brazilian theologian Vitor Westhelle, hope "overdetermines" human situations.... God has a way of drawing unexpectedly good results from even the worse predicaments. Hope, then, means that one should never give up, that the game isn't lost no matter how lopsided the score may be at present.[1]

Compier makes the important point that hope is an act of grace—a divine gift. It is the gift that "keeps on giving." Hope always expects something new. It looks ahead toward that which is yet. It accepts and risks the unspecified. But Christian hope is not "pie in the sky in the sweet bye-and-bye" wishful thinking.

I remember in my teens purchasing the Royal Canadian Air Force "5BX Plan." It was five basic exercises designed to incrementally achieve physical fitness. On the inside back cover, centered on the page in small bold type, were four words: "Wishing is not enough!" Hope is not devoid of energy and action.

Christian hope may seek to transform reality, but it does not ignore reality. We must flat-out admit the cold reality of *hopelessness*. Some things are hopeless! TV evangelists won't tell you that, but then, they don't live in the same world you and I live in. The fact is, if we try to gift-wrap life in a "Jesus can do it all" Christianity, we are in for shattered dreams and a life of denial. Christianity is not in the business of peddling the impossible dreams of wishful thinking—we are not selling timeshares in the millennium. Hope is not compatible with falsehood. Despite criticism to the contrary, our faith does not impose on us glorious generalities and "unauthentic truths." Christian hope does not live in a Pollyanna fantasy of optimism. Compier states:

> We must fight our tendency to flee to secular optimism, to declare that things aren't really so bad.... True hope cannot coexist with falsehood. Unless we open our eyes to reality with all its horrors we will never begin to see that

186

the triumph of peace will come in spite of the immense suffering spanning history and our globe.[2]

Christian hope, then, is neither denial nor wishful thinking. I would love to have a full head of hair (preferably from the normal hair line position, i.e., above the eyebrows, but at my age I can't grow hair where I need it, only where I don't want it!). I would love to have the energy and dexterity I possessed when I was twenty-five. But my wishing won't make it so. It's utterly hopeless! The track star who refuses to train will not make the team. Students who choose not to study and then at exam time pray for divine intervention, might as well save their breath to blow on their porridge. Wishful thinking is hope without substance. It is void of energy. It is hoping for the impossible without trying to make it possible.

Keith Russell, in his keynote address at the 1996 Congregational Leaders Workshop, summarized the tragedy of the present age when he said: "Many have given up hoping for anything better. We have lost our ability to imagine a new and better future."[1] But we are not without hope—not even "unreasonable hope." The game is not lost. Christian hope "overdetermines." God does draw "unexpectedly good results from the worse predicaments." You see, there is such a thing as *unreasonable* unreasonable hope! Which is to say, there are some unreasonable hopes that are not unreasonable.

A better name for this type of hope is, perhaps, the Great Hope. It is the Great Hope that goes beyond our reason and our efforts, yet is not merely wishful thinking. It is the Great Hope that holiness will be triumphant. It is the hope that with God's help we might yet get it right! That the world can, with effort, commitment and sacrifice, get its ducks in a row. It is this hope that is the lifeblood of hopeful congregations. Okay, enough theory—what are the earmarks of a congregation of hope?

Hopeful congregations are on a journey.

Hope demands a target! Is your congregation on the way to somewhere? Is it on a journey? Or is it just wandering? The issue here is that God is not redundant. God does not intend congregations to be facsimiles. They are not to be "cookie-cutter" congregations having no unique presence or voice as the body of Christ within a specific community. George Barna speaks against such "me-too" congregations with this admonition: "It doesn't matter what we do. God will bless our efforts." This statement is a prescription for half-baked, half-blessed ministry. God does care what we do. If he didn't care, he would not have given dreams and words to prophets.[4]

Hopeful congregations know where they have been, where they are, and where they are going! Let's look at these requirements:

Hopeful congregations know where they have been.

Hopeful congregations have a healthy view of the past. This includes not simply an appreciation for their specific congregational history, but a healthy perspective regarding the evolution of the Christian movement. This requires the ability to view history free from exaggerated claims, distorted perspectives, holy prejudice, and romantic idealism. Canadian theologian Douglas John Hall says, "People are enticed into believing that the way into the future is through a return to some remembered past—usually a past more golden in remembrance than it ever was in reality!"[5] Hall goes on to say:

> There are many dimensions of that past that should be treasured: We knew, most of us, what it meant to belong...we participated. Nobody spoke about "participation" and we would not have understood all that, but we simply did it.... [W]e actually played games, we actually sang the songs (for two or three hours running)—and nobody had to have the words photocopied![6]

Unfortunately, we have sung too many choruses of "Give Me that Old Time Religion": It was good for Paul and Silas and it's good enough for me! Frequently the old-time religion we are singing about isn't old enough, isn't good enough, and not gospel enough. For many, that old-time religion is only as old as Grandma and Grandpa and it is colored with sweet memories that overshadow its shortcomings. This is not to suggest that the past is not helpful, informative, and enriching. It is to say that we need not be enslaved by false perceptions of the way we think things were.

Our view of history is at best an interpretation. Hopeful congregations learn from the past, but live in the present. They are not bound by, "That's the way it was and that's the way it should be!" or "We've done that before and it didn't work!" The question is, Are your congregation's best days behind you or in front of you?

Hopeful congregations know who they are and where they are.

Vital congregations know their environment, their ministerial assets, their gifts and skills, and their competition. In World War II during a regiment boxing match, a pathetic young man jumped into the middle of the ring between rounds and carried a large placard on which he had desperately scribbled the words, "Does anyone know who I am?" A victim of shell shock and amnesia, he saw this as his one chance to find out who he was. Hopeful congregations constantly work at discovering who they are. Here are some of the placards they raise:

- Why do we exist as a congregation?
- How can we be the body of Christ where we are?
- What do we offer? What is our Christian service?
- What skills do we have? What do we do best?
- Do we have concrete missional objectives?
- Are we a program church or a relational church?
- Do we really know each other—do we visit one another?
- Do we get involved beyond ourselves?
- Do we offer small group ministries and support?
- Do we have a streamlined, participative decision-making structure?
- Are our programs competent? Do we have too many programs? Too few?
- Is our church accessible? Are our leaders accessible?
- Do we have visibility in the community? Does anyone know we are here?
- Do we own our facilities or do they own us?
- What are our financial resources for mission?
- What are our realistic limitations?

Hopeful congregations know where they are called to go.

There's no sense in going further, it's the edge of civilization,
So they said, and I believed it—broke my land and saved my crop
Built my barns and strung my fences in the little border station
Tucked away below the foothills where the trails run out and stop.
Til a voice, as bad as conscience, rang interminable change on one everlast-
    ing Whisper, day and night repeated—so;
Something hidden. Go and find it. Go and look behind the ranges
Something lost behind the ranges. Lost and waiting for you.
                                        —From "The Explorer" by Rudyard Kipling

Hopeful congregations hear "the Whisper." They go beyond the ranges even when they are unsure what may be waiting. They are willing to be surprised. Hopeful congregations live the future now!

They do not establish the kingdom but live as though the kingdom were already in our midst. They look into God's promised future and seize a chunk of it which they bring back to the present. They provide a demonstration project, a preview of things to come. They invade principalities and powers of the present age with a foretaste of God's community on earth. They plant the leaven of that community in the doughy lump of society.

They are engaged with God in creating the future. As Barna would say, "The future is not a 'done deal' waiting for response."[7] There is a negative way of looking at the future which is like looking through binoculars at a distant scene and becoming so enamored of it that we miss the beautiful scenery all around us. Many are simply putting up with the present while they wait for the future. They are waiting for something to happen (marriage, promotion, retirement, whatever). They wait for some future season while the present season slips by unnoticed. They are not living the future now, nor are they trying to create future possibilities; they are just waiting for it to arrive.

Hopeful congregations do not wait for the future. They help fashion it from the whisper of possibilities. The future looms before us as options and alternatives. It is when we pin our hopes on preferred alternatives and begin to move in the direction of those alternatives that we make the future now. The student who looks ahead at his or her vocational dream measures the present needs against the future requirements and expectations. If I want to be a medical doctor ten years from now, I will plan out my required courses for next year and the year after that and so on. The future suddenly impacts the present.

Hopeful congregations not only hear the whisper, "Something hidden, go and find it," they focus their present and future activities on that call. They engage in discovering their vision. For "Where there is no vision, the people perish" (Proverbs 19:18). Barna provides us with some clarity about vision:

[V]ision is foresight with insight based on hindsight...vision is "seeing the invisible and making it visible." ...Vision for ministry is a clear mental image of a preferable future imparted by God to His chosen servants and is based upon an accurate understanding of God, self and circumstances....A fuzzy perspective is not vision...vision entails change.... Vision is about stretching reality to extend beyond the existing state.... Vision is not the result of consensus; it should result in consensus.... It is important that people own the vision for ministry, not that they create it.[8]

Again, Keith Russell reminds us of the importance of envisioning the future:

> The early churches had a vision of the future which empowered the present and gave hope to the believer…it could see beyond its time while not abandoning the age in which God had put it….Their understanding of the present was shaped by their vision of the future.[9]

Hopeful congregations have a healthy eschatology, what Don Compier calls an "eschatological vocation." Whatever else we may say about eschatology—the Christian doctrine of the last things—we can say that it assures people that evil and death will not have the last word. We believe in the ultimate victory of the God of life. We may not agree on the details of that victory—the when, the how, the maybes—but Christian hope is riveted in this trust.

Hopeful congregations engage themselves in discovering their specific mission and are prepared to be stretched and challenged beyond their comfort zone. They do not become all things to all people. They seek to discover their particular call to ministry. The temptation is to say "yes" to every opportunity for service and good works. Too often their energies are drained by trying to ride off in all directions, when God is saying "I want you to become skilled in one thing." Don't major in mediocrity. Find God's task for your congregation, refine it, mold it, polish it, and use it to make a difference. A big "YES" takes care of a lot of little decisions. A big "Yes" gives a congregation the power to say no to activities, that in themselves may be beneficial but may become detours on the path to God's "Whisper" or unique call for the congregation.

Hopeful congregations serve without strings attached.

To do the right thing for the wrong reason, this is the greatest treason.
—Thomas à Becket[10]

We do not serve others for the sake of ourselves. Sometimes we give way to the subtle temptation of expecting beneficial bi-products from Christian service. "If our congregation does a good job of helping battered wives, we will become noted for that in our community." That's fine if it witnesses of our Christian vocation and the hope of transformation of community. It's not fine if it overrides the call to do service. Hall summarizes it this way:

191

Service that does not have strings attached. Service which can think clearly about peace and justice and the integrity of creation—without wanting to have its own reward for such altruism, or its "commercial" at the end. In the kingdom of death that our world has become, the mission of the church must be understood as the stewarding of life: not the life of the church, but the life of the world, of creation.[11]

Hall also points out that littleness may be an advantage. Small things can make a big impact.

[W]e shall have to become more convinced than most of us probably are that a theology which finds strength in weakness and significance in littleness and purity in brokenness might have something entirely significant to say to our world.... Surely the biblical story is about the possibilities of littleness...there are things that majorities, precisely because they are majorities, cannot achieve.[12]

Hopeful congregations are not then measured by their size, but by their hopeful vitality that spills out and makes a positive difference to life.

Hopeful congregations take risks.

They put people before programs. They provide freedom to fail. They operate on God's economy. Frequently our penchant for doing business reduces the church to a business. We tend to look to the "bottom line" (and, of course, that is necessary), but sometimes we do so at the detriment of ministry. We do invest time, money, and energy into ministry; accountability is important. In our rush to realize immediate gains we may unwisely and prematurely pull back or abort efforts when the quick results we are expecting aren't realized.

We are not purchasing baptisms. We are not collecting tithing statements or tabulating baby blessings. We are not creating pie charts and bar graphs. We are investing in a divine dream. God's economy measures results differently than we do. God's love leaves arithmetic at home. It is always in the "red."

Hopeful congregations do not accept the unacceptable.

We are not caught in what Japanese theologian Kazoah Kitamor called American Christianity's "monism of love." Hopeful congregations live out the love of Christ. This, however, does not mean uncritically accepting the status quo. Hall helps out here:

Love doesn't just accept everything. If it is love, it cares about the real condition of the beloved; and if the beloved is in fact a distortion of the person that he or she could be, then the only role that true love can assume is one of truth and intention to change. "Jesus loves me" does not mean that Jesus likes me, and makes no great demands upon me. Jesus loves me—therefore I had better be prepared for some embarrassing moments of truth, and some hard work![13]

Hall is telling us here that far from accepting the status quo, God wills to alter what is unacceptable. Hopeful congregations are willing to engage in the effort to transform that which is unacceptable. They do not sit idly by watching lives crumble and communities suffer while singing, "Yes, Jesus loves you!" They get off the bleachers and get onto the playing field. They say, "This is not as it should be!"—and work at making it better. Hopeful congregations are agents of transformation who are also willing to be transformed. Hopeful congregations make a distinction between Christ and culture. In other words, hopeful congregations are called to be a counterculture, an expression of life that at times must swim against the stream of conformity.

Hopeful congregations are embraced by humility.

Such congregations are teachable and flexible. They recognize the need to be open to new possibilities. As new truth emerges they do not merely assimilate it as new information; they are willing to be changed by it. Someone said that "revelation is not complete unless there is a change in thought and action." Learning congregations see the need to become new containers in order to receive new wine. They see the need to continually upgrade their efforts to develop new leaders as well as new followers.

Hopeful congregations provide sanctuary.

Hopeful congregations are "safe places." The church, to be the church, must always provide opportunity for life's pressing issues to be addressed. Its members must be confident that they can express their feelings, viewpoints, hopes, and dreams without fear of ridicule or rejection. This does not mean we must all agree, but it does mean we must at least be willing to disagree in love. To be a Christian is to confront life in a new way. It is to be able to see the sacred in the most secular of things. Hopeful congregations create an atmosphere of trust where joys, defeats, victories, loss, grief, tears, and laughter can be shared in mutual respect.

Hopeful congregations are holy congregations.

A root meaning of the word "holy" means to be "separate." I am not suggesting that we set ourselves up as being separate from life—a peculiar people with peculiar habits, beliefs, and practices. We are not called to be a peculiar people. We are called to be like Jesus, and in so doing if that makes us peculiar, so be it.

There is a hunger for the holy. Hopeful congregations provide interface with the Divine. Hopeful congregations must have worship that is celebrative, forgiving, empowering, and transforming. Hopeful congregations make the most out of prime-time Sunday. They plan worship that facilitates divine encounter not just entertainment. They do not confuse availability with ability (for example, "It's Brother Jones's turn to preach. Grant us courage for the facing of this hour!"; some worship services are not measured by joy of the Spirit, but by sheer endurance). Hopeful congregations sing, pray, preach, testify, and dance with enthusiasm. If you have to tell visitors you are a joyful, hopeful congregation—then you are not!

Finally, hopeful congregations dream dreams worth dreaming and pursue passions worth pursuing. Hopeful congregations are joyful congregations—and it's obvious. They celebrate their hopefulness in enjoying the task of ministry. Ministry is not a burden but a blessing—and it's obvious. They are loving congregations—and it's obvious. They are forgiving congregations—and it's obvious. They are going somewhere—and it's obvious. They demand more. They promise more. They deliver more—and, it's obvious. They know that "wishing is not enough." It's obvious!

Notes

1. Don H. Compier, "Proclaiming the Gospel of Peace," unpublished paper in possession of author, 12.
2. Ibid., 13.
3. Keith A. Russell, "New Testament Images of the Church: Implications for Today," an unpublished paper given to the 1996 Congregational Leaders Workshop, 1.
4. George Barna, *The Power of Vision: How You Can Capture and Apply God's Vision for Your Ministry* (Ventura, California: Regal Books, 1992), 127.
5. Douglas John Hall, *The Future of the Church: Where Are We Headed?* (Toronto: The United Church of Canada Publishing House, 1989), 2.
6. Ibid, 10-11.
7. George Barna, *The Power of Vision*, 48.
8. Ibid., 28-29, 45.

9. Keith A. Russell, "New Testament Images of the Church," 3.
10. As quoted in "Murder in the Cathedral," Part 1, in *The Complete Poems and Plays* (New York: Harcourt, Brace and Company, 1930), 196.
11. Douglas John Hall, *The Future of the Church*, 41.
12. Ibid., 34-35.
13. Douglas John Hall, "We Would See Jesus," in *The Living Pulpit* (January-March 1994).

SHEPHERDS
ABIDING
IN THE FIELD

Chapter 16

Becoming a Community of Love

David R. Brock

I grew up on dreams about a community of joy, hope, love, and peace: no more tears, swords into plowshares, peaceful coexistence in the animal kingdom, and people gathered in harmony from the four corners of the globe to live out the prayer "...on earth as it is in heaven." "In Zion, if one person has a car, everyone has a car, and if one person is without a car, no one has a car!" was the way I remember my Sunday school teacher, Mandy Ferris, describing the justice and equality of that city there on the horizon of our dreams.

On virtually every Sunday morning in the mid-fifties we left a ranch near Dodge City to drive seventy miles for fellowship with a small congregation of Reorganized Latter Day Saints in a well-worn remodeled house in Liberal, Kansas. I'm not sure I understood why we traveled that distance, why we were so strongly tied to that group of people above all others, but I sensed even then the longing in my dad and mom to become something more because of that faith community. I began to understand something about the benefits as well as the costs and obligations of belonging. I knew my identity and destiny were somehow wrapped up in those people and their "seek first the kingdom" perspective which, if not always fully demonstrated in daily living, was the standard against which we knew we were to measure ourselves. Looking back, I can echo Abraham Joshua Heschel's expression of gratitude and reverence for his forebears: "I was very fortunate," he told an interviewer, "in having lived as a child and as a young boy in an environment where there were many people I could revere, people concerned with problems of inner life, of spirituality, and integrity. People who have shown great compassion and understanding for other people."[1]

The years of innocence necessarily evolved into confrontation with the shadow side of myself, my community, and my all too self-centered dreams of a better world. Despite the sometimes harsh realities encountered on the path of adolescence and young adulthood (no Santa Claus; hoeing corn under the humidity and heat of Missouri's August sun; losing in the bottom of the ninth; dealing with a cousin's death; seeing acrimony and ragged conflict in the heart of my congregation; struggling with unanswered prayer and empty, dark silence when a word of hope or a ray of light was desperately sought; having the original dreams of the eschaton and the "center place" ripped away as I learned of "The Other America," as Michael Harrington described it) I was held and shaped throughout by a community, imperfect and not-yet-faithful, but nonetheless abundantly graced by God's love. And I am grateful.

I was baptized, declared beloved, and patiently Junior Churched, Boy Scouted, and piano lessoned in Atherton, Missouri. I was Zion's Leagued and youth camped among those I still call friend and family in Boise, Idaho. Whole new worlds of knowledge and insight opened as I attended Graceland College and served in the Older Youth Service Corps in the inner cities of Chicago and Portland, Oregon. My life has been indelibly marked by the people and places of this particular community.

As is so often the case the experience of community arrives in glimpses, hints, fleeting moments, and impressions: a *kairos* moment of divine encounter during a Communion service on the Graceland campus in June 1970; a pastoral moment with the Saints in Kinshasa, Zaire, who spontaneously surrounded, touched, held, and prayed for a young sister who collapsed on the floor of the church upon learning of the death of her husband; a bold reconciliatory move by Sunday Charlie Akpan to calm an angry crowd and possibly save the life of a woman caught stealing in a Nigerian village; eighty-three confirmations and twenty-five baby blessings among Turkana nomads all on a Sunday morning in the east African desert; a moment of awe as a church family tenderly holds and joyfully tends a severely handicapped child during the celebratory dedication of a newly completed building in the mining town of Las Vegas, Honduras.

More hints and impressions from closer to home: notes of concern and support received; prayers offered with a drop of oil and hands gently laid, or longings of the heart silently and anonymously lifted up from continents away; a multigenerational worship in a crowded home in Houston; an ongoing pancake outreach breakfast in Austin; a meeting of young RLDS professionals to discuss faith and work in the executive dining room at Mutual of Omaha headquarters and at a campground in the Wisconsin woodlands.

And where have you experienced moments of Christian community in your life? Sometimes they are only fleeting moments. "They tantalize and then, perhaps because we are in a hurry to attend to other matters, they disappear. Nevertheless they arise as brief upwellings that proclaim, 'Christ is here and together we are in him!'"[2] I testify that we are becoming a community of love.

New Testament Images for Today's Mission

Through his insightful book, *In Search of the Church*, Keith Russell gifts today's communities of faith with a creative reexamination of New Testament images. He draws insights from the Synoptic Gospels, Pauline and pastoral letters, and John's Apocalypse. I wondered as I grappled with this theme (with possibly as much or more focus on "community" as on the concept of "love"), if the Acts of the Apostles might also offer helpful images in our search. I begin with a familiar passage near the end of chapter 2:

> So those who welcomed his message were baptized, and that day about three thousand persons were added. They devoted themselves to the apostles' teaching and fellowship, to the breaking of bread and the prayers. Awe came upon everyone, because many wonders and signs were being done by the apostles. All who believed were together and had all things in common; they would sell their possessions and goods and distribute the proceeds to all, as any had need. Day by day, as they spent much time together in the temple, they broke bread at home and ate their food with glad and generous hearts, praising God and having the goodwill of all the people. And day by day the Lord added to their number those who were being saved. —Acts 2:41-47

How do I find a link between that community and my own? Baptisms are now counted in ones and tens, rather than thousands. Signs and wonders are more often attributed to cyberspace wizards and shuttling diplomats than to ministers and disciples. Not nearly as much attention is paid to the teachings of the apostles as was apparently the case in those days—believe me! Economic relationships are far more private and distant. Worship time in the temple has dropped dramatically. Bread is broken more often at local restaurants than at home, and we can only hope that sandwiched into power-lunch table talk is some praise of God by hearts made glad and generous. Where is the connection? What images and insights call to us, warn us, encourage us across the centuries?

This past spring I traveled to Albuquerque for five days of visiting with the Saints of New Mexico. How, I wondered, is a community of love forged and sustained among RLDS members scattered in small congregations across the expanses of the desert Southwest? On Friday evening Dan, Nadine, and Lauren picked me up at the airport. As we made our way past the minor league baseball stadium, the annual Native American festival, and other city landmarks, we quickly began to reestablish the ties that bind us together: a West Texas/New Mexico reunion at Sacramento Mountain Retreat in 1979; occasional conversations through succeeding years about common interests in sports, professional development, and things theological. A bundle of African experiences were unwrapped as we shared about Nadine's dad, Ken; memories of a friendship forged forever by five years of side-by-side ministry across that amazing continent. And oh the stories we could tell: a torch-lit journey on a dark meandering jungle path in Liberia; a near riot in the crowded lobby of the Airport Hotel in Lagos, Nigeria; the melodic march of a whole congregation to baptism at a stream in Akwa Ibom State. But those are not the focus here and must be recounted another day.

The next morning we arose early to pick up other Albuquerquians for a four-and-a-half-hour trip to the campgrounds. As we traveled I listened and at times entered into a broad-ranging conversation between people of different generations, opposing political persuasions, a breadth of professional experience and interests, diverse theological views and missional priorities, yet people who obviously were bound to each other by fellowship and mutual support through years of congregational and district life together.

Once on the campgrounds community ties were widened as we shared a meal and cleaned and repaired the chapel with brothers and sisters from west Texas. New Mexico District members then gathered for an afternoon conference of reports, confirming testimonies about priesthood calls, and financial considerations. Connections continued with a Sunday afternoon picnic in Las Cruces (after worship and World Conference review) and a Monday meal at an Albuquerque restaurant to recount a journey of faith. Later, at a house church gathering in Santa Fe we heard the story of a man troubled by a childhood on inner-city streets, young adult years in Vietnam, and a search for adulthood in a variety of professions, people, and places until finding a sense of balance and spiritual at-homeness in this small congregation. The next evening, in an open discussion among thirty-some members crowded around a square of tables at the Penn Street Church, brothers and sisters spoke from the heart about the vision and purpose of the church, whether or not our children will have faith, and how we have expressed our Christian witness in the workplace.

The spirit of New Testament Christianity was apparent in conversations shared during long New Mexico highway journeys between homes and congregations. Dilemmas in the life of the community were raised during a two-hour discussion of a family's efforts to embrace and support a homosexual son. We considered questions about the if, how, and when of sharing their story with the congregation. Another day's travel brought an amazing view into a silent, misunderstood, and relatively unknown culture as I heard a mother express her understanding, yet simultaneous incomprehension, of the pain and blessing of her deaf son's world. Hours of discussion with a long-time district leader revealed a life story of baptisms and blessings, building programs and financial commitments, transformed and redirected lives, the tragic death of a son, mistakes and disappointments inside the church, yet all of it held together by God's grace-filled blessing within a community of love.

When we belong to each other in such a community, ties are strong enough to allow the recounting of suffering and failures as well as moments of triumph and grace. The One who is our common source of compassion binds us together through the language of shared story and prayer.

In one of the most poignant passages of Acts (chapter 20:17–38), Paul, on his way to Jerusalem, stops in the seaport of Miletus and sends a message inland asking the elders in his beloved Ephesus to come meet him. Knowing he likely will not see them again, he openly expresses his love and concern, speaks words of warning and encouragement, commends them to God and each other, and says good-bye in a spontaneous prayer appropriate to such a moment.

> When he had finished speaking, he knelt down with them all and prayed. There was much weeping among them all; they embraced Paul and kissed him, grieving especially because of what he had said, that they would not see him again. Then they brought him to the ship.

On a cool mid-July evening in Mexico City, several church leaders gathered on the second floor of the Iglesia Restaurada de Jesucristo in Colonia Roma Sur. As we considered the challenge and opportunity of establishing mission communities in one of the world's largest metropolitan areas, Elder Abigail Santos led us to the heart of the matter. She expressed through tears of guilt and sadness how hopeless she felt at times. She questioned her ability to provide effective ministry. She struggled for answers and direction. She talked of the countless times she and her family had traveled across town to the church for services with no one but themselves in attendance. She wondered out loud about whether she could hope for a different future.

As the folly of our all-too-ready advice gave way to a wiser period of careful listening, Seventy Don Ivans asked permission of the group to pray. Consent willingly granted, he rose, walked across the circle, knelt, took Abi's hand, and prayed in halting Spanish for God's blessing on her, her family, and the mission of the church in Mexico City. In that moment our gathering was transformed into a circle of hope and healing. We were becoming a community of love. And as Don prayed, the youth choir, unaware of our actions, began to practice a hymn in the sanctuary below:

Cristo es la peña de Horeb, que está brotando,
Agua de vida saludable para ti.
Ven a tomarla que es más dulce que la miel;
Refresca el alma, refresca todo tu ser.[3]

Christ is the spring of Horeb that is flowing
With healthy waters of life for you.
Come and drink, for it is sweeter than honey;
It refreshes your soul, refreshes your whole being.

We are not the church of Acts 2, brothers and sisters. Our reality is different in so many ways. "Those who strive to be New Testament churches," says Leith Anderson, "must seek to live its principles and absolutes, not reproduce the details. We don't know many of the details, and if we reproduced the ones we do know, we would end up with synagogues, speaking Greek, and the divisive sins of the Corinthians."[4]

I believe, however, that the same Spirit that bound those first saints together continues to form and shape us into the body of Christ in today's world. Like them, we are experiencing life together. We are sharing in something. We are a fellowship, a companionship, a partnership of faith and service. We live, suffer, die, inherit, and reign with Christ. We share potlucks and Communion meals. We share our material wealth. We share in development and commissioning of leaders. We share prayers and acts of healing ministry. We are *koinonia*.[5] We are becoming a community of love.

Don Compier expressed our identity and calling well in a paper presented at a Council of Twelve-sponsored seminar in January 1996:

> As I have learned more about the various ecclesial organizations, I must humbly yet honestly say that few can equal and none can surpass the communal emphasis which has typified Latter Day Saints at their best. As we know the earliest adherents of our movement did not accept the reigning doctrines of rugged individualism. While they would make their accommodations with general society later, that initial commitment to counter culture continued to bear fruit for many generations, and it still does. Latter Day Saints eat together and go to camps together and just generally hang out and shoot the bull more than most of their coreligionists. Perhaps when all is said and done we proclaim peace best by inviting neighbors to share such community with us. Reigning doctrines of individualism and privatism have left millions hungry for meaningful human companionship. I believe that many will respond to the persistently outstretched hands of friendship, even if our name or our history really seem odd at first. Whatever else we may accomplish, may our theology and our programs never do less than encourage people to come together and talk and share and recognize their common humanity as Godward beings. Jesus, Paul, and Peter all agreed that love fulfills the whole law. Theology's deepest reflections into the divine mystery time and again come to a standstill before the realization that love is the beginning and end of all. Love is the goal, and love is the road there. Beloved, let us love one another as God has loved us. Amen.[6]

The Societal Context

Current reality in my life and in the society in which I live indicates all too clearly, however, that you and I do not want to pay the costs of discipleship, the requirements of life together in a community of love. To paraphrase Paul Edwards, "We don't really want peace. We want to have, to get ahead, to be comfortable, to be number one."

Becoming a community of love is about conversion. It is about a conscious relationship with Jesus Christ that brings one into a conscious relationship with other people. It is about a long journey from individualism to being a "corporate" person. Individualism is so strong in us, says Gordon Cosby, that we have to be converted step by step. "Becoming a corporate person has to happen step by step because community is very, very frightening and extremely difficult. It is much more difficult than that new person realizes."[7]

In a now widely reviewed 1995 article, Robert Putnam of Harvard (referencing Alexis de Tocqueville) makes sobering observations about the decline of the "intellectual and moral associations" in today's America. An unorthodox image makes the point:

> More Americans are bowling today than ever before, but bowling in organized leagues has plummeted in the last decade or so. Between 1980 and 1993 the total number of bowlers in America increased by 10 percent, while league bowling decreased by 40 percent. (Lest this be thought a wholly trivial example, I should note that nearly 80 million Americans went bowling at least once during 1993, *nearly a third more than voted in the 1994 congressional elections* and roughly the same number as claim to attend church regularly....) Whether or not bowling beats balloting in the eyes of most Americans, bowling teams illustrate yet another vanishing form of social capital.[8]

The "Bowling Alone" illustration symbolizes the notable decline in the vibrancy of American civil society over the past several decades. There has been an erosion of community life that has brought personal being into crisis.[9] There is fear that, individually and collectively, we are losing control of the forces that govern our lives. There is a sense that in our families, neighborhoods, and nation, the moral fabric of community is unraveling around us.[10]

It is possible that the analysts may overstate the crisis of the loss of community and civic responsibility. They may be missing emerging signs of civic engagement as an old order gives way to the new. We can only hope! But I believe we must join in their concern about the quality of community in our nation today. And I believe we must have a sense of the larger context in which the church is expressed in our world or we cannot become the community of love that is so needed.

That is our context. We are called to community in the midst of those societal conditions. We are often swimming upstream. But we can be faithful to our tradition, faithful to the call to establish the cause of Zion in the midst of the pervasive individualism that is a frightening mark on our society. "The hour calls for moral grandeur and spiritual audacity," said Abraham Joshua Heschel at the close of a June 16, 1963, letter to President John F. Kennedy on civil rights issues. This hour demands no less.

The Criteria for Communities of Love

I can affirm that we are becoming a community of love. But we are not there yet. How do we love the same people week after week? How do we put genuine love ahead of bitter disagreements about faith and doctrine? What about love and politics, love in the midst of wide socioeconomic differences in a congregation? How do we love members whose spiritual compass is the opposite of our own? How, for example, does the pietist tolerate the activist? How do we talk about becoming a community of love in a congregation that has shrunk to the merge or close stage? How do we learn to acknowledge and face the hatred within all of us, rather than deny or cover it up? How do we demonstrate love for and in the broader community of which we are a part? How do we deal in love with a heinous destructive act in the body?

The inward journey: A few weeks ago I had a disturbing conversation with a brother in the church. He was displeased with the actions of fellow ministers, disappointed about actions that had not been completed, disturbed about changes that had been made. I found myself growing defensive and angry as the conversation progressed and finally chose to express my own sentiments. My somewhat martyristic response was not helpful. He was hurt by my reaction. A barrier was erected between us. I didn't sleep very well that night as I ruminated about my actions and his.

The next morning I read the following from Elizabeth O'Connor: "The mission of the church is just loving people. And our confession? *What is our confession? It is that we do not know how to love.* Until we have made the confession, there is nothing to be learned."[12] I read further.

> For truth to be deep in us, we need to meditate upon it.
>
> One evening [an educated and cultured man] stayed with two colleagues at his laboratory to work on a project.... When they had finished late that night, he invited them to his home for coffee. The conversation moved from their work at the lab to art, and he fell to sharing with them his interest in Greek architecture. Remembering a new volume that he had on the subject, he took it down from the shelf and handed it to his more advantaged coworker, who quickly glanced at the pages and returned it to him. He was already putting the book back on the shelf when he glimpsed from the corner of his eye the hand of the other man extended to receive the book. The picture hardly registered. He did not come to terms with what had happened until later when he was in bed, and then he saw again the hand of the other man reaching to receive the book he had never offered. Unconsciously he had made the judgment that this man, being self-tutored, would not be interested in art. In an automatic way he had excluded him.
>
> The "considerate" host had not thought himself capable of treating another fellow human like this, but he had enough understanding to know that this was not an isolated incident in his life.... He left his bed and spent the rest of the night sitting in his study reflecting on what had happened. He wanted

the picture of it burned in his mind and heart so that it would keep him alert and help him avoid the possibility of his going through life ignoring the outstretched hands of his friends. Martin Buber defines sin as our failure to grant to others their pleas for community. Certainly this was the sin that was dealt with that long night....

Instead of deploring our reactions, we need to reflect deeply on them and on those situations that evoke them....We might begin the practice of meditation by learning to hold before us each night a fragment of our day, looking at it without judgment, turning it this way and that way, until our understanding of it deepens, and we can see and hear and turn to be healed.[13]

After reading these words, I could do no other than on that same day meet with my brother, ask forgiveness, and invite our continued journey together. The small but essential steps toward love in community are often created in moments of quiet reflection.

Likewise, it is in the looking back, the reflecting, the giving thanks in moments of quiet that we fully receive the gift of community in Christ. Quietness lets one enter more fully the fleeting moments of community. If we hurry by under clouds of preoccupation we will perceive only the vague shadow of a good moment rather than its infinite depth.[14]

Service to humankind: Commitment to becoming a community of love must issue in some relief of the suffering of humankind—locally or around the world—because God is calling us to connect with the suffering. At some point we've got to suffer to relieve it, to bring about liberation and to bring about freedom. That will become very specific for every community.

Deeply spiritual [people] experience the suffering in the world as their own suffering. The world is not something apart from them. Their skin is not a dividing membrane that separates them from the world, but a permeable membrane, through which events of the world and events of their inner life flow into one another.[15]

The measure, however, is not how much one suffers, but is simply the amount of love bestowed in the life of another person, and how open we have been to receive.

Have I perhaps bestowed too little love upon this other person, that he has become so cold and empty? Have I perhaps caused him to become what perhaps he really has become? The other person, whom God has joined to me, is never what he is apart from me. He is not only bone of my bone; he is also boredom of my boredom and lovelessness of my lovelessness.[16]

And it is exactly the same with our relation to God. If a person is

206

steeped in emptiness and boredom and is tired of life, the reason for it is that he has not allowed himself to be loved by God and has not put himself in his hands. One who does not love makes the other person wither and dry up. And one who does not allow himself to be loved dries up, too. For love is a creative thing.[17]

My wife keeps reminding me that the central transforming truth of Jesus' ministry lay in his ethic of love. Christ's message is a pivotal point in history because it marks a turning from salvation based on external behaviors and rules of conduct, from human efforts to coerce ourselves into being kind, decent people that God can love. Instead Jesus proclaimed the good news that real change requires us to become receivers of undeserved love in our inward parts. Jesus named love as the power that tames the hungers of our ego, releases burdens of fear and guilt, exorcises the demons of shame that move us to loveless response to the stresses and threats of everyday life. If we are to become a community of love we must take upon us the central passion of Jesus of Nazareth: to heal and restore people, life, and creation through the power of divine love.

As Elizabeth O'Connor explains,

> while everything is asked of us and we must do everything, the very change that we seek and yearn for and cannot live without is not in our power to effect. While we must do everything, there is nothing that we can do. Something has to come from beyond us. There then remains but one thing to do: to take our confession on our lips and throw ourselves upon the mercy of our Lord. Perhaps then water will flow around us and we will hear a voice saying, "with thee I am well pleased."[18]

The journey outward in mission is also the journey inward.

Stewardship of our material wealth: Gordon Cosby feels that one of the most important disciplines for anybody coming into a community is a discipline of money. Money, and what it represents, is an idol for almost all of us. To think that one is going to have genuine community without giving up money is an illusion. Oftentimes, he says,

> that's been a more healthy discipline for us than prayer, because you can fudge on prayer and make everybody think you are doing it. If you have a money discipline, it's clear whether you are or are not following it. We've had more people who have not come into this community because they couldn't deal with the money discipline than because of any other discipline.[19]

That is a touchy subject in our society and within the church. It is a private matter, we say. But cut out all the references in the teachings of Jesus that have to do with material wealth and the impact on relationships both human and divine and see how much is left. Keith Russell reminds us that money has such an impact on who each one of us is and what we are becoming that we cannot possibly leave the question of stewardship to the individual. Becoming a community of love requires that we think through priorities, establish values, and make decisions that are an alternative to the dominant cultural value system. He asks us to imagine belonging to a congregation where we could get help with our thinking about money; where we could begin to understand our feelings about the rich and the poor; where brothers and sisters in the church could help us resist the pressure in our society to measure who we are by what we own or what we can buy; where we could talk about debt and what to do about it.[20]

Giftedness: The body of Christ operates around the gifts of the Holy Spirit which have been identified and which are being exercised. And where you exercise a gift, there is authority. That sort of movement of the Spirit within the life of the church is what we've got to depend on. It is my firm conviction that our gift and therefore our authority and identity as a movement are expressed in our efforts to become a community of joy, hope, love, and peace in Christ. That is our heritage. I believe Bob Mesle expressed it well a few years ago when he wrote:

> The best thing about the history of Zion is that it affirms our historical commitment to quality human communities. If we do take "The Cause of Zion" as our theme for the 1990s, I recommend that we do so by specializing in community. Just as one speaks of the Quakers as a "peace church," we might hope to become known as the "community church"....
>
> This is a realistic proposal. Concretely, we are already doing many of the things such a program would involve. We already encourage neighborhood councils, sponsor Boy Scout and Girl Scout troops, support Outreach International, encourage civic participation by our members, work with community development in the Philippines, and teach pastoral care classes. Building on these programs and our historical emphasis on Zionic community, our Christian education and pastoral care offices could work toward helping our members to learn more about conflict resolution, pastoral counseling, a basic grasp of effective citizenship, how to organize volunteers, what specific relief agencies are most effective, and what individual and local groups can do, practically, to nurture progress toward global community....
>
> Community is a good choice of missions because it meets the first criterion of a good theology: it addresses issues of fundamental human experience and concern. Community gives us a way to talk about families and famines. All persons everywhere, whatever their theologies, begin their lives in a

community. For this reason, it would also seem likely that community would be a theme with tremendous power to bridge cultural boundaries. Certainly African, Japanese, and American people will take different approaches to community, but it is an important concern for us all.[21]

Becoming a Community of Love

At the closing worship service of a youth camp in Saltillo, Mexico, Evangelist Humberto Salas read the well-known scripture about a towel and a basin, took four bowls of water to the center of the room, set out a roll of paper towels, and after washing his son's hands and sharing words of support and love, invited the circle of worshipers to wash each other's hands while offering words of love and encouragement. We began slowly, with timidity, a sense of uncomfortable vulnerability, and some embarrassment, but in a short time we were waiting for one of the four bowls to be available so we could wash another pair of hands. I have seldom experienced the spontaneous outpouring of such a genuine, mature expression of support and affection for fellow humans that I sensed in those moments of worship.

The true test of love, of course, is not given in such moments. But for just a moment, possibly such as on the day of Pentecost so long ago, there was an unbidden, undeserved outpouring of unconditional love and acceptance within the gathered community that offered us a heretofore unseen glimpse of what life in a community of joy, hope, love, and peace could be.

> For it is love that can and will put us back together again. It is love that can heal us and make us whole. It is love that enables us to discover that which is fore-given—a love that expresses its power in forgiveness, a love that can reconcile our estrangements, re-unite our separations, re-member our dismemberment and heal the faults and fractures of our adolescence.[22]

Questions for Consideration

1. Where have you actually seen Christian community this past week?

2. What claim is it making on you and on all of us touched by its life?

3. How have you experienced *koinonia* in the church?

4. What do we need to do to more fully experience *koinonia* in our congregations?

Notes

1. Susannah Heschel, "Bringing Heaven Down to Earth," *Tikkun* (March/April 1996): 49.

2. Steven V. Doughty, "A Fresh and Formative Gift," *Weavings* (September/October 1996): 41.

3. "Cristo es la peña de Horeb," *Himnos de Vida y Luz* (Independence, Missouri: Herald House, 1990), 172.

4. Quoted from Leith Anderson, *A Church for the 21st Century*, in Charles Trueheart, "Welcome to the Next Church," *The Atlantic Monthly* (August 1996): 44.

5. Gerhard Kittel and Gerhard Friedrich, eds., *Theological Dictionary of the New Testament*, abridged and translated by Geoffrey W. Bromiley (Grand Rapids, Michigan: Eerdmans, 1985), 449.

6. Don H. Compier, "Proclaiming the Gospel of Peace," unpublished paper presented at a seminar sponsored by the Council of Twelve (Independence, Missouri: January 15-17, 1996).

7. N. Gordon Cosby, "The Call to Community: Depending on God's Grace," *Sojourners* (July 1986): 37.

8. Robert Putnam, "Bowling Alone: America's Declining Social Capital," *Journal of Democracy* (January 1995): 70.

9. Gibson Winter, "America in Search of Its Soul," *Theology Today* (January 1996): 471.

10. Michael J. Sandel, "America's Search for a New Public Philosophy," *The Atlantic Monthly* (March 1996): 57-58.

11. This section is based on principles lifted up by Gordon Cosby in an interview with Jim Wallis in "The Call to Community: Depending on God's Grace," *Sojourners* (July 1986): 39.

12. Elizabeth O'Connor, *Search for Silence* (San Diego, California: LuraMedia, 1986), 29.

13. Ibid., 46-47.

14. Doughty, 42-43.

15. Quote from Patricia Mische, in Tom Hampson and Loreta Whalen, *Tales of the Heart: Affective Approaches to Global Education* (New York: Friendship Press, 1991), 130.

16. Helmut Thielicke quoted in O'Connor, *Search for Silence*, 53.

17. Ibid.

18. Ibid., 50.

19. N. Gordon Cosby, "The Call to Community," 37.

20. Keith Russell, *In Search of the Church: New Testament Images for Tomorrow's Congregations* (Bethesda, Maryland: Alban Institute, 1994), 49-50.

21. C. Robert Mesle, "Zion and the Future of the RLDS Church," *Restoration Studies IV* (Independence, Missouri: Herald House, 1988), 37-38.

22. L. Robert Keck, *Sacred Eyes*, 4th ed. (Boulder, Colorado: Synergy Associates, 1995), 160.

SHEPHERDS
ABIDING
IN THE FIELD

Chapter 17
A Time of True Shalom

Barbara M. Higdon

A Star Trek convention took place recently in Des Moines. "Trekkies" gather frequently in many places, but Iowa is an especially appropriate venue. After all, Captain Kirk was a native of Ottumwa. I am not a "Trekkie," and I did not attend, but the local news gave the Des Moines event a lot of coverage. Some people had dressed as their favorite character for the occasion. Pointy-eared Vulcans were there as were Klingons who reported that it took upwards of four hours to create the likeness. Most of the people, however, looked like you and me. A reporter stopped one woman to ask why she was there and, with a catch in her voice, she said, "Star Trek gives me hope for peace in our world."

Her statement has stayed with me. Could it be that the artists among us have once again created an imaginary world that articulates our deepest yearnings and shows us some ways to realize them? Take the Klingons, for example. In the first generation a warlike race—in the second, the guards who have adopted the values of the Federation but who recently seem to be struggling with their commitment to peace; or the Star Fleet Command which contacts new civilizations not to conquer but to dialogue when they discover alien practices that ignore basic decencies; or the eternal struggle between Spock and "Bones"—between logic and emotion, head and heart—the outcome of which often balances the best of each; or the fierce Romulan general who sacrifices his career to work for peace in opposition to his own warlike kind; or the celebration of diversity in the makeup of the crew of the Enterprise and of the spin-off Voyager; or the willingness of the space explorers to learn from the most unlikely teachers.

Not bad lessons, those, for a time when a worldwide hunger for peace at every level of human experience is stronger than at any other time in human history. Many recent events, large and small, predict the possibility of an alternative future for humankind. They grow out of the realization that we simply cannot afford to continue doing the business of living together as usual. They grow out of the realization by more and more people that the strong proclamations for peace within the faith traditions of the world's great religions are meant to be taken seriously (this despite the distortions of the fundamentalist sects). For us of the Judeo-Christian tradition, even that most bloody collection of books, the Old Testament, proclaims a better vision—of spears into plowshares, of wolves and lambs and children in harmony, and of human beings transformed:

> If you do away with the yoke, the clenched fist, the wicked word, if you give your bread to the hungry and relief to the oppressed.... [God] will always guide you, giving you relief in desert places. [God] will give strength to your bones and you shall be like a watered garden, like a spring of water whose waters never run dry.—Isaiah 58:9-11 JB

Expressions of these yearnings share a remarkable similarity. Richard Falk describes it as a "transformative vision" of the future:

> SOLIDARITY—the sense of vital concern about the human species as a focus of emergent loyalty; UNITY—the shared and unified destiny of the planet; SPACE—the non-territorial circumference of human concerns; TIME—the extension of human concerns in time to the ancient past and to the most distant future; NATURE—the experience of nature as encompassing, inspiring, and sustaining; PEACE—the renunciation of violence as the collective basis of security and innovation; PROGRESS—the gradual realization of human potentialities for joy and creativity in all dimensions of individual and collective existence; HUMILITY—the awareness of limits applicable to human endeavor...SPIRITUALITY—the understanding that awe and mystery are as integral to human experience as bread and reason.[1]

I could illustrate each of these elements specifically from recent events and public statements by world leaders. But I would rather turn to two questions: How does the World Church create a community of peace? and How do we, in the places where we serve, create communities of peace?

Will you consider three prerequisites? Whether we are talking about the World Church or your congregation, it seems to me that solidarity, moral deliberation, and resistance must be present before genuine communities of peace can be established. A community of peace must first be a community of solidarity. It must employ within itself what Scott Peck calls the technology of peacemaking. Pseudocommunity is made up of all of us who keep our masks tightly in place. When we allow our masks to slip, the pseudocommunity descends into chaos which produces emptiness resulting from the loss of the old, false community. And finally when true community is achieved, it must continue to renew itself, and it must regard peacemaking, not as an add-on, but as an integral part of its identity. Peck reminds us that this is hard work and that too often we have opted for the easy and lazy way out.

Second, a community of peace must be a community of moral deliberation that thrusts the church into the arena of public affairs. We must bury forever the old notion that it is inappropriate for the church to get involved in "politics." Isn't the great lesson of the Holocaust that churches cannot remain silent in the presence of sinful public policy? Most social problems are complex (if they were not they would be solved without public debate). Our involvement, to be effective amidst this complexity, must discover strategies for doing social ethics through dialogue: getting the facts, understanding competing interests, and measuring solutions against Christian principles. Out of that discussion public positions can be developed that incorporate a variety of perspectives. The World Church or the congregation can then speak to the important issues of the larger community with an authentic voice.

The third prerequisite is the presence of a community of resistance. How can we claim to be Christians when we not only fail to name the sins of our culture but also willingly participate in that sin?

The World Church as a Community of Peace

We did not invent the pursuit of peace as a primary mission for Christian denominations. In fact, after Martin Marty participated in the first Peace Colloquy, he wrote in *Christian Century*: "To my knowledge, no one before 1984 would have thought of the Reorganized Church as belonging anywhere near the peace-church tradition." That we are not the first or the only Christian denomination to emphasize peace should not diminish in any way the importance of the call to peace in Section 156. Thank God we no longer believe we have exclusive claim on the inspiration of the Holy Spirit. Thank God we can acknowledge that the Holy Spirit ever goes before us. What we can claim and celebrate is the knowledge that God's call to us to pursue peace is not generic but specific to who we are as a faith community.

213

Martin Marty is right that we do not have a strong, specific peace tradition. Peace and justice have not been totally ignored in our past, but, I submit, they have been only peripheral until recently. Two of the strongest strands of that emphasis have been the social gospel articulated by Frederick M. Smith during his tenure as president and the humanitarian work that has accompanied our recent mission thrusts abroad.

We are fortunate to have our church seal, but we can't claim too much from its existence. Adopted in 1874, it uses the word and depicts the peace described in Isaiah 11. We have not discovered why it was chosen, but the symbols were in common use during the nineteenth century. Almost every gallery of primitive American art has its peaceable kingdom canvas, more than fifty of which were painted by the Quaker Edward Hicks who lived from 1780 to 1840. His pieces, by far the most famous then as now, also depicted in the far distance William Penn signing a peace treaty with the Indians, suggesting perhaps a convergence, however dim, of the kingdom of God with the kingdom of this earth. But to keep us humble, Jack Garnier's cartoon comes to mind: a smug lion with a toothpick dangling from his mouth standing beside the skeletal remains of a lamb.

Our challenge is to create for peace a theological and operational reality from our particular confessional identity. That identity is inseparably connected to the Temple, which inspires our peace witness and is, in turn, inspired by our peace witness. I have seen this reciprocal inspiration happen since 1991.

I want to make a personal confession. I experienced a real crisis of faith at the 1968 World Conference. You may remember that Section 149 instructed us to get busy on the Temple. I had been so sure that my church had put the more bizarre elements of its past, of which I considered the Nauvoo Temple and its practices to be the most bizarre, behind it. But here enshrined in revelation in 1968 was a reaffirmation of what I simply could not accept. The very word "temple" invoked for me the patriarchal tradition of the Old Testament, which was so oppressive to women, not to mention the early Restoration additions of baptism for the dead, sealings, and other esoterica. And what about the cost? What kind of stewardship would it be to spend millions of dollars on another building when there was so much need in the world?

Another blow was the reaction of good friends, people I thought I knew well. They were ecstatic. Had we all these years not belonged

214

to the same church? I felt trapped and alone, and I thought seriously about leaving the church. It was not a good time. I don't know whether I stayed because I didn't have the courage to abandon a life-long habit, or whether the "Hound of Heaven" caught me, but I comforted myself with the thought that the Temple would not happen in my lifetime so I could just forget about it and get on with my stewardship of teaching at Graceland. I certainly got that all wrong.

One of my life's great ironies is that in 1991 I found myself as the volunteer director of the Temple Peace Center. For me the dedication of the Temple to the pursuit of peace and the creativity and transformation that the building and its programs have inspired have been reconversion experiences. I want to describe some of those.

The Temple Peace Center, created in 1991, gave focus to the challenge to pursue peace for the World Church. Its mission statement attempts to articulate theologically and practically that objective: "The Temple Peace Center responds to God by helping people envision and create a more just, compassionate, and peaceful world." As you know, it has, along with the Abundant Life Center whose mission is very close to its own, conducted a number of workshops on peace issues and is networking with local, national, and international organizations that share similar missions. Three activities—the Children's Peace Pavilion, the Young Peacemakers Clubs, and the Peace Colloquy—are attempting to reflect a witness that is our own.

In the process of building the Children's Peace Pavilion we visited and studied a number of other children's museums across the country. We have yet to find one that is similar to what we have created at the Temple. The pavilion divides peace into four units: peace for me; peace for us; peace for everyone; peace for the planet. My testimony to you is that God's Spirit blessed the pavilion's creators abundantly as they accomplished something for which they were not trained and for which they had no useable models to follow. God's Spirit also blessed the effort to secure outside funds to support the activity and provided volunteers who spent thousands of hours doing the skilled work of designing, building, wiring, painting.

The response of people to the pavilion has been more enthusiastic than we could have hoped. We thought it would take a long time to persuade the public schools that it was not thinly disguised proselytizing. But from its opening day public school children have come literally by the thousands. And they come back with their parents. We thought many of the exhibits and activities would not work and that we would have to redo much of it. But with very few changes from the initial concepts, its vision of peace ministers powerfully to all ages. Its influence is spreading. The Omaha-Council Bluffs Stake is preparing a traveling pavilion, and Sheryl Holstein reports that one in Atlanta will be ready to go shortly.

The Young Peacemakers Clubs took the pavilion concept on the road. Using the same divisions of peace, it presents a series of easily produced activities that model and teach peace. It has proliferated all over the church and has been introduced in the public schools in several communities. It has attracted outside funds and has great promise for replication in other countries.

The Peace Colloquy has provided an opportunity for the church to endorse the peacemaking work of outstanding people and to further that work by in-depth exploration of its nature and strategies for its replication. The colloquy has witnessed to the world our concern for practical peacemaking and our eagerness to join our efforts with others.

I don't mean to imply by omission that the activities of the Peace and Abundant Life Centers are the only initiatives that are building a World Church community of peace. The uses of the Oblation Fund, VisionQuest, Outreach International, World Conference actions, to name only a few, also reflect the determination to pursue peace and reveal the ongoing but slow process of making the pursuit of peace organic to our movement.

Our second question is more directly useful: What can we do, in the places where we serve, to create communities of peace? In a fine paper discussing the core values of our church, Tony Chvala-Smith identified one of those values as the expectation of new things. Is that another way to describe Zion? What is your expectation of new peace initiatives in your congregation?

Imagine what new things could take place in your congregation that would make it more nearly a community of peace. Don't let limitations of personnel or finances, or any of the other usual constraints influence your imagination. You might find it helpful to follow a three-step process: first envision a range of possibilities. Do this in silence and then share your list with a partner. Second, choose one possibility, your favorite, from that list. Visualize it in its completed form and describe it to your partner. Third, model your choice verbally, describing a more specific design along with the skills and resources you would need to bring it about. Not allowed are the words "It can't be done" or their equivalent.

Silently test the outcome of this little exercise against four principles: Does your vision have the capacity to strengthen your existing congregational community and its relationships? Does your vision provide an opportunity to achieve a holistic approach to peace? Will your vision create meaning for those who participate? And finally will your vision empower the members of your congregation in new ways?

What outcomes can we expect from the hard work of building communities of peace? The first is a negative one. We demonstrate to the world that we are not a cult when we open our doors and our minds to the most effective work for peace the world has to offer and when we grapple intelligently and compassionately with the moral dilemmas of society. Second, we strengthen our Christian witness as we proclaim Christ as the Prince of Peace, and we join others in leading the way in the transformation of society. Finally, our peace witness is a new basis for invitation to participate for member and nonmember alike.

I do not accept Martin Marty's assumption that the only way to be a peace church is to emulate the tradition of the Mennonites, Quakers, and Brethren, as admirable as they are. They are not who we are, and we have the opportunity to find our own way and add our unique contribution to humankind's pursuit of peace.

My friends, we have an enormous and wonderful challenge before us. Our Christian witness compels us to speak peace, justice, and compassion to a world in desperate need. Our scriptures do not provide us with even a definition or a set of specific instructions. What we do have is the story of how one person and his followers pursued peace in their day and time, a time so unlike our own that only the principles are relevant for us and our world. The message to small, scattered congregations found in Ephesians 2:14-18 summarizes these principles:

> For Christ himself has brought us peace by making all the peoples of the world one people. With his own body he broke down the wall that separated them and kept them enemies...in order to create out of the races of the world one new people in union with himself, in this way making peace. By his death on the cross Christ destroyed their enmity; by means of the cross he united all races into one body and brought them back to God. So Christ came and preached the Good News of Peace to all—to those who were far away from God, and to those who were near to Him. It is through Christ that all of us are able to come in one Spirit into the presence of the Creator.

217

What we must seek is the living word of God for today, which in our best moments the RLDS Church has always done, which word will have the power to move, change, and inspire us. The task is enormous and we are a small church, but we do not act alone. People of spiritual goodwill all over the world are responding to the imperative for peace in unprecedented numbers and in unprecedented ways. Their efforts are beginning to make a difference.

Most important, we do not act alone because the Spirit of God precedes us and shows us the way if we have eyes to see. Do we dare believe that it is the pursuit of peace that can have the unifying power to bring together people of good will, wherever they dwell, whatever language they speak, and whatever or whomever they call God? May we resolve to do the work of peace in those places where we serve, and in the words of Captain Kirk, "to boldly go where no [one] has gone before."

Notes

1. Richard Falk, "Satisfying Human Need in a World of Sovereign States," in *World Faiths and the New World Order*, eds. Gremillion and Ryan (Washington, D.C.: Interreligious Peace Colloquim, 1978), 135-136.

About the Authors

Danny A. Belrose is a member of the Council of Twelve Apostles responsible for the Southeast Apostolic Field, which includes the southeastern United States, Haiti, and the Caribbean. A World Church appointee for fifteen years, he has been missionary coordinator, presiding elder, district president, president of Seventy, and regional administrator. He holds a master of theology degree from St. Stephen's College.

John N. Billings has been an appointee for twelve years, now assigned as East Central States Region administrator. John was pastor of both urban and rural congregations and was instrumental in developing the Urban Ministries Temple Satellite Center in Chicago. Involved in many peace and justice ministries, he serves on the Cabinet for Interfaith Partnership of Metropolitan St. Louis, the Missouri Impact Board of Directors, and the steering committee for the Missouri Christian Leadership Forum.

Linda L. Booth is assistant director of communications for the World Church. She is a counselor to the president of the Quorum of High Priests and has served for several years as a congregational pastor. She was one of the primary developers of material for the Communities of Joy emphasis.

Carolyn K. Brock is a nurse and author with a broad range of interests. Her experiences in health care and cross-cultural mission have led to a vocation of promoting wholeness and spirituality ministries in church and community. She currently assists as a consultant to the Abundant Life Center at the Temple in Independence. She authored *Asante Africa* and co-authored *The Gift of Peace*, with her husband Dave.

David R. Brock is a member of the Council of Twelve Apostles, responsible for the Latin America/Southwest USA Field. Previously he was a president of Seventy and served the church in Latin America, Africa, and several parts of the United States.

Anthony Chvala-Smith is a native of Michigan. He and his wife, Charmaine, have served the church in many capacities. Tony studied theology at Princeton Seminary, the Toronto School of Theology, and Marquette University (Milwaukee), where he received his doctoral degree. He currently is theologian in residence at church headquarters and an instructor at Graceland College.

Mary Jacks Dynes is president of the Fifth Quorum of Seventy and has been an appointee to the Pacific Northwest Region for three years. Mary has served in various congregational, district, and regional capacities throughout her life. She has a master's degree in counseling, psychology, and theology, and currently is pursuing a doctorate in evangelism. Her interests are in relational ministry, missionary outreach, and liturgy with an emphasis on the sacraments.

Paul M. Edwards is director of the Temple School Center and dean of the Park College Graduate School of Religion. A historian and philosopher, he is the author of several books, the most recent being *F. Henry Edwards: Articulator for the Church*. Paul is also the president of the Quorum of High Priests.

Barbara M. Higdon is president emerita of Graceland College in Lamoni, Iowa, retiring in 1994 after a distinguished career in higher education. She is a past president of the Iowa Peace Forum and has served as the director of the Temple Peace Center. She authored the book *Committed to Peace* in 1994.

Barbara P. Howard retired from Herald House in 1995 after more than twenty-five years as an editor. She had edited the news section of the *Saints Herald, Restoration Witness, Daily Bread, Stepping Stones*, and *Zion's Hope*. She authored several books including *The Scriptures Speak to Women Today, Be Swift to Love, Journey of Forgiveness*, and *Journey of Joy*. Her articles have been published in the church's periodicals as well as *Christian Century*, and she has also authored hymns for *Hymns of the Saints* and *Sing for Peace*.

Kenneth L. McLaughlin is a member of the Council of Twelve Apostles, currently responsible for the Pacific Field and as advocate for children and youth outreach ministries. Since 1969 he has served in most congregational leadership and teaching roles, including pastor; as a staff executive in the Legal Services Division; and as an appointee in the Upper Ohio Valley Region. His religious studies have been at Park College and Trinity Lutheran Seminary.

W. Grant McMurray is president of the RLDS Church, ordained to this responsibility in 1996. Before that he served as counselor in the First Presidency, World Church secretary, and assistant church historian. Grant holds a master of divinity degree from Saint Paul School of Theology in Kansas City, Missouri.

David D. Schaal is a World Church appointee, currently serving as president of the Michigan Region. He has also been a stake president, missionary, and pastor of both small and large congregations. David has written sections of the *Congregational Leaders Handbook* and is a leader in congregational consulting services.

Joe A. Serig has been a member of the Council of Twelve Apostles since 1982, serving in Europe, the British Isles, Africa, the southwest United States, Hawaii, and in Native American ministries. His assignment since 1984 has been the Central Field USA. He has been a pastor, stake high council member in two stakes, and stake evangelism director. He has been Christian education director, Pastoral Services commissioner, Program Services director, and Program Planning director for the church.

Stephen M. Veazey has been a member of the Council of Twelve Apostles since 1992, now assigned to the Africa/East Central USA Fields. Steve previously served as a president of Seventy, a field missionary, and helped establish the World Church Missionary Office. He has written numerous materials on missionary ministry.

Leonard M. Young is director of field resources at church headquarters. He has authored and edited books on congregational life including *Communities of Joy: New Experiences in Congregational Living.* An appointee for fifteen years, he previously pastored congregations ranging in size from fifteen to 350 members.